Praise for *Powers*

'As India and China stand at a crossroads, *Powershift* goes a long way to explain how we got here and where we might go. This is a book that will long be consulted and read for the way in which it deals with fundamental issues of India's foreign and security policy'

Shivshankar Menon, former National Security Advisor

'*Powershift* should be on the shelves of every China-watcher in India and should be read carefully'

Vikram Sood, former Chief of R&AW

'As one of India's leading foreign policy analysts, Zorawar Daulet Singh has a knack for illuminating the unobserved crucial stands of Chinese policy in relation to India and the Asia-Pacific region. His new book comes at an opportune moment given the multiple powershifts underway or being attempted in the neighbourhood and this region'

Arun Singh, former Minister of State for Defence

'*Powershift* offers a comprehensive, up-to-date survey of the border issue, an analysis of the impact of changes in the global order on India-China relations ... a timely, important and cogently argued contribution to the current policy debate'

Chandrashekhar Dasgupta, *India Today*

'There is depth and detail in this book, making it a ready reckoner for any scholar or researcher wanting to understand the dynamics at play between dragon and elephant, whether military, geopolitical or economic ... a very engrossing read'

Rekha Dixit, *Week*

'An insightful and timely re-examination of the increasingly volatile relationship between India and China. Zorawar Daulet Singh asks some important questions about India's interests and capabilities in relation to China, and makes some sensible suggestions for de-escalation'

Amitav Ghosh, *Wire*

'Nuanced, insightful and objective ... The book draws a comprehensive picture of the global scenario from an enlightened Indian standpoint which takes a lucid and unbiased view of China's ambitions, compulsions, concerns and interests'

Come Carpentier De Gourdon, *Sunday Guardian*

'Zorawar Daulet Singh ... a prolific commentator and author ... has presented policy prescriptions that are realistic and hard-headed and backed his arguments with a rigour and detail which are often missing in the current Indian policy discourse on China'

Manoj Joshi, *Tribune*

'*Powershift* makes an excellent case for a hard, unsentimental look at how to reset the relationship between India and China ... [A] wise and well-argued approach'

Rana Mitter, *Telegraph*

POWER SHIFT

Zorawar Daulet Singh is a historian and strategist based in New Delhi. A founder of Northcap University, a private university located in Gurugram, Haryana, he is also associated with the Institute of Chinese Studies, New Delhi. Daulet Singh was previously a fellow at the Centre for Policy Research, New Delhi. For the past decade, he has been a regular commentator and columnist on India's foreign policy. He holds a PhD in international relations from King's College London and an MA in international relations from the School of Advanced International Studies, Johns Hopkins University. His previous books include *Power and Diplomacy: India's Foreign Policies during the Cold War*, *India–China Relations: The Border Issue and Beyond* and *Chasing the Dragon: Will India Catch up with China?* In 2021, *Powershift* won the Kalinga Literary Festival Diplomacy/ Strategic Affairs Book of the Year Award.

POWER SHIFT

INDIA-CHINA RELATIONS IN A MULTIPOLAR WORLD

Zorawar Daulet Singh

PAN

First published 2020 by Macmillan
First published in paperback 2022 by Pan
an imprint of Pan Macmillan Publishing India Private Limited
707 Kailash Building
26 K. G. Marg, New Delhi – 110001
www.panmacmillan.co.in

Pan Macmillan, The Smithson, 6 Briset St, Farringdon, London EC1M 5NR
Associated companies throughout the world
www.panmacmillan.com

ISBN 978-93-90742-88-2

3 5 7 9 8 6 4 2

Typeset in Bembo Std by Manmohan Kumar
Printed and bound in India by Replika Press Private Ltd.

CONTENTS

PREFACE

The year 1988 can be seen as the opening chapter of a second era of an India-China détente, the first attempt having collapsed spectacularly in 1959. Three decades of engagement has not only transformed India-China relations at the bilateral level – it is no longer only about a long undefined and undemarcated border – but the relationship is intersecting with and being impacted by complex changes in Asia and the world. The balance sheet of this phase has drawn a range of verdicts and even fierce disagreements. For many observers, it has not gone far enough in solving old problems and disputes, nor has it precluded new differences from cropping up. Indeed, the recent crisis in eastern Ladakh and the lapse into medieval violence on the night of June 15, 2020 shook the foundations of the era of engagement. For others, it has attained something that most large neighbours have historically found difficult to achieve – a degree of stability and a modicum of economic interdependence. Most, however, agree that the past casts a long shadow and the emerging world order has brought the relationship to a crossroad where choices being made today will set in course events that could profoundly impact India's economy, security and the regional order. It is imperative that India's policymakers get this right.

My foray into the India-China relationship began in 2007. It soon led to two co-authored books in 2009, which were received positively by the foreign office, strategic community, and, to my delight, professional 'China watchers'. I have approached this fascinating interstate relationship primarily from a geopolitical and historical perspective, rather than as a Sinologist. Approaching this subject from a policy-relevant and historical vantage point has allowed me to address questions and themes that might not evoke the attention of most area studies scholars. My broader interest in diplomatic history and strategic studies have also shaped how I perceive the interactions between these two large countries. It has also made me sensitive to the big picture as well as the international and geopolitical setting for the bilateral relationship.

The book is based on my work on various aspects of India-China relations over the past decade. It hopes to provide an informative and nuanced glimpse into the key issues that shape India-China relations, the motivations and interests of both sides, and how they are learning to cope with each other's rise on the world stage. What distinguishes this book from most work on India-China relations is its quest to engage with a broad gamut of foreign policy themes. Whether it is the complicated history and the intricacies of the border dispute including the recent tensions on the Himalayan frontier, the changing US-China relationship, the geopolitics of Greater Eurasia and the Indo-Pacific, China's growing connectivity footprint in the region, BRICS (Brazil, Russia, India, China, South Africa) and a changing world order, or the conundrum of formulating a far-sighted China policy, the book casts a wide net in unpacking India-China relations. But perhaps the key reason for bringing this work to a larger audience is its policy relevant character. Each chapter responds to debates in the strategic community – conversations that have remained largely confined to an elite community of scholars, analysts, journalists, and former officials. This book has been planned to bring those themes to the public square.

If there is one overriding message in this book it is that India and China are poised to intersect on several fronts and issues. This is not a relationship that is likely to be eclipsed despite the many distractions and domestic priorities that will occupy Indian and Chinese leaders for the foreseeable future. And, while they may not become friends, India and China can learn to sensibly manage their complex relationship and evolve their existing modus vivendi to incorporate a framework where a gentler rivalry or competition is handled maturely and at the same time does not inhibit the pursuit of their common or overlapping interests.

The book has been divided into three, hopefully coherent, sections; a structure that enables readers to choose topics that most piques their interests. The opening section dives into the past to understand the roots of the India-China territorial dispute and the reasons and context for their armed clash in 1962. That phase of our history has never been seriously debated by Indians and our inherited convictions about the Himalayan frontiers have often come in the way of an honest appraisal of the past. Until we do so, it would be difficult to learn the correct lessons or imagine a settled frontier with China. The section also looks at the negotiating postures over the decades and reveals why a seemingly straightforward settlement continues to elude both Delhi and Beijing. Finally, I trace the origins of the recent crisis in eastern Ladakh and the challenge of restoring peace and tranquility to the Himalayan frontiers.

The second section explores the intersection of the India-China relationship with dizzying changes in the international order. It engages with themes such as the rocky transition towards a multipolar world, the nature of competition between US and China, the resurgence of Eurasia, China's geopolitical re-orientation after 2013, and the role of BRICS in promoting non-western approaches to globalization and development. It is important for the reader to get a pulse of these broader themes since India's China policy will continue to evolve in a changing and turbulent international environment. Keeping an eye on the questions of world order is, thus, crucial for crafting sound policy as well as engaging in effective debates on India-China relations.

The final section engages with the broader debates in India by weighing in on high policy and strategy including debates over military doctrines that are most relevant for managing regional security. This theme is also closely linked to the type of roles that India wants to play in the emerging world order. Although many insist India can no longer afford to straddle different regions in a competitive world order, its geopolitical and civilizational identity as an Asian, Indian Ocean and a Eurasian power implies Delhi will look in multiple directions as it adapts itself to a multipolar world. It not only examines the recent ideas and plans of connectivity that have emerged as new faultlines but also possible opportunities for innovative cooperation between India and China in the future. Finally, the section delves into the challenges, opportunities, and risks confronting India's policymakers as they look at various options in crafting a new equilibrium with a rising China.

JUST LIKE SEVEN decades ago when the dramatic re-emergence of India and China, after their prolonged and traumatic encounter with colonialism, would transform this region's geopolitical landscape, the India-China equation is once again poised to influence the course of Asia. And the fate of this relationship is far from preordained. There are forces that are bringing both countries to craft a tenuous co-existence and stabilise a fragmenting world order. There are also circumstances that are bringing new frictions and differences to the fore as India and China pursue their regional interests and ambitions, often oblivious and insensitive to each other. Many believe the relationship is destined to sour. So far, both leaderships have chosen to delicately manage this competition-cooperation see-saw, although recurring border crises in the past decade have repeatedly questioned whether Delhi and Beijing can maintain such a balancing act for much longer.

Yet, a military conflict or even a Cold War would serve neither sides' interests, a lesson learnt the hard way from Sino-Indian history of the late 1950s and 1960s. But avoiding conflict cannot be an enduring pillar for India and China to navigate the future. When situated against the broader picture of an emerging multipolarity, uncertainty on the future of globalization and interdependence, and, the still long journey towards socio-economic and high-tech rejuvenation of their countries, there is a strong logic for managing the rivalry and lessening regional tension. Indeed, Asia's rejuvenation and the global transition to a reformed multipolar order are difficult to achieve without a stable and mature India-China relationship.

Collectively, these impulses – to avoid the fate of the European powers a century ago and resist the trend towards national egoism – can sustain a relationship of competitive but peaceful co-existence. For two large neighbours and proud civilizations, that would be an outcome worth striving for.

Zorawar Daulet Singh
September 2020

A COMPLEX RELATIONSHIP: AN INTRODUCTION

When Narendra Modi and Xi Jinping met in October 2019, the site chosen for their meeting was Mahabalipuram, on the outskirts of the south Indian city of Chennai. Modi told Xi that the site was 'an outstanding example of India's cultural heritage and architecture, and witnessed India-China's civilizational exchanges and historical connections for more than a dozen centuries.' Xi is reported to have extolled 'Tamil Nadu, a maritime transit hub for cargoes in the ancient Silk Road,' for its 'long history of exchanges with China and close connections with China on maritime trade since ancient times.'[1]

The symbolic use of civilizational connections to present an alternative image for India-China relations is, of course, not new. A century ago, pan-Asian thinkers were the first to revive the memory of a longer history in India-China interactions. Welcoming Rabindranath Tagore during his famous tour of China in April 1924, Liang Qichao, a renowned intellectual of that era, spoke of:

> a great and cultured country, India. Both in character and geography, India and China are like twin brothers. Before most of the civilized races became active, we two brothers had already begun to study the great problems which concern the whole of mankind. India was ahead of us and we, the little brother, followed behind...Indian thought has been entirely assimilated into our own world of experience and has become an inalienable part of our consciousness. It has helped us develop our faculties and has enabled us to achieve notable results in various fields of literary and artistic endeavour.[2]

As our understanding on the pre-colonial period has grown, we have come to appreciate the depth of connections that actually existed over nearly two millennia between Asia's two oldest civilizations. We now know that India and China interacted at multiple levels – culture, ideas, people-to-people, trade – exchanges that were probably so broad, extensive, and multi-directional that we have yet to fully revive all those connections despite all the technologies and communication tools at our disposal today. People-to-people exchanges were the most important part of these connections – traders, missionaries, pilgrims, diplomats, soldiers, refugees, migrants and tourists – of the two countries over a millennium of interactions. Prior to the 10th–11th centuries, it was Buddhist connections that predominated between India and China and, thereafter merchants and commercial interactions became important as maritime technologies and trading networks grew while the continental silk routes faded away.[3]

In the year 399 AD, a Chinese monk named Faxian began his journey to India on the first successful recorded visit of a traveller from China to major Buddhist sites across the subcontinent. Faxian's detailed account of his extraordinary journey provided information about the customs and geography of several towns across India, and described the key maritime and overland routes from China to India. Faxian's complex journey to the subcontinent itself attests to the advanced state of geographic knowledge of that time among traders and pilgrims. He entered India through an overland route by crossing the Pamir mountains in Central Asia and eventually reaching the banks of the Indus river. But he returned to China using the maritime route, from Tamralipta, a port in present-day West Bengal, then through the Bay of Bengal to Sri Lanka and onward through Java to China.

This seminal travelogue brought India into Chinese consciousness, as intellectuals of the time sought to understand and study the subcontinent. Over the following centuries, a vast amount of knowledge of the subcontinent's geography entered China and grew with further visits by Chinese explorers.[4] Often though, it was through third parties – Arabs, Persians, Southeast Asians – interacting with India or indirect linkages that defining technologies and ideas were transmitted. For example, Chinese paper and gun-making technologies reached the subcontinent through Arab and Persian intermediaries in the second millennium. Indian knowledge of astronomy may have entered China through Central Asia. The 7th century saw the first transfer of Indian know-how of manufacturing sugar from sugarcane, a process that would be used in Chinese cuisine. The Chinese were also aware and interested in 'the existence of several different traditions of healing and longevity in South Asia.' There is also evidence of technological knowledge sharing such as Indian steel-making and Chinese ship-building techniques flowing between the two regions.[5]

All this occurred in a context of broader interdependence that existed between various parts of Asia and Eurasia, again, not dissimilar to our time even if the transport and communication technologies that enabled those connections were rudimentary compared to today. The level of grand political direction guiding the evolution of those networks was less evident than our time when central political authorities are far more engaged in shaping geoeconomic connections than they were 1,000 years ago. However, let us also not forget the famous Zheng He expeditions across the Indian Ocean when for three decades in the early 15th century, China was the most formidable naval and commercial power in the regional maritime space – often described as the 'Indo-Pacific' today – until it suddenly retreated from the scene. The influence of Chinese ship-building techniques also spread during this time to southern Indian coastal towns.

The purpose of this brief introduction to the pre-modern interactions is to convey to readers that India and China did have connections before their traumatic colonial encounters severed the old organic social, cultural, and commercial networks and re-connected these two regions under a more exploitative global political economy system. As some of the chapters will argue, the new connectivity visions and plans in Delhi and Beijing do not have to be antithetical to each other. There is room to formulate realpolitik policies that secure strategic interests without closing the door to constructive cooperation and interdependence. This is particularly important for South Asia – one of the least integrated regions in the world – that has so far been on the margins of a dynamic geoeconomic revolution in the rest of East Asia.

The Cold War Era and the Border Dispute

It is only in the late 1940s that India and China began the process of coming to terms with each other as contiguous neighbours and as sovereign entities. For a brief period, both countries were able to adjust to the new post-war order and handle their differences reasonably well. However, inherited suspicions and unresolved territorial differences from the colonial era were to re-surface at the turn of the 1950s, a process that became more complicated in the backdrop of the Cold War that was simultaneously generating a culture of ideological and geopolitical antagonism across Asia. The relationship underwent a dramatic shift towards tension and conflict including a major military confrontation in 1962.

The year 1962 is embedded in India's national consciousness. For several decades, it was impossible to dispassionately introspect on the war or reflect on the deeper issues underlying the India-China dispute. I too began studying the border dispute in the backdrop of all the images and perceptions that have animated the popular narrative of this dispute. And, few loomed larger than Neville Maxwell's account of the 1962 war.

It is now well known that Maxwell's account insofar as it relates to the events preceding October 1962 is fairly accurate since it was based on the Henderson Brooks Report (HBR), an officially sanctioned operational review of the military's performance during the war. The report remains declassified except for a section that was leaked to the public by Maxwell in 2014. But since the HBR's mandate was never to scrutinize the political handling of the conflict or the civil-military interactions preceding the war, it is highly improbable that it would contain much that would indict the political leadership of the time, although much can be inferred by bringing together the pieces to create the bigger picture of that era.

My principal interest in the subject, however, is broader than scrutinizing battlefield mistakes or evaluating Delhi's conduct of the war. That is a theme best left for military historians. Although without access to the relevant archival documents, including the higher direction of the war, even this task becomes a formidable one. To some extent this absence of historical reflection has been alleviated by a 1992 Indian Ministry of Defence study titled, *History of the Conflict with China* that has been available in the public domain for the past two decades. This competent study has validated the tactical inefficiencies of the Indian side in the conduct of the war.

My interest lies in understanding the geopolitical dynamics in India-China interactions and how each side perceived its frontiers and expressed this through a series of policy choices that we now know in retrospect had extraordinary and enduring consequences. Much of our history has suggested India was weak and insecure in the lead up to 1962. But the picture was far more complex. Policymakers actually perceived that India's overall bargaining position was better than China's and that it compensated for India's military disadvantages on the frontier. This belief shaped Indian choices and posture right upto October 1962.

The events of 1962 were an extreme manifestation of their impasse but not the cause of the India-China dispute. A more useful way to offer an alternative to the Maxwell thesis – which erroneously conflates India's mistakes and posture prior to the war with the structural cause of the entire dispute itself – would be to broaden the discussion and treat the war as a sort of 'punctuated equilibrium' that never entirely altered the way both sides viewed their frontiers or indeed each other. Therefore, the first few chapters step back and dwell on the wider question, that is, how both sides arrived at completely different positions on their inherited frontiers before proceeding to examine the more proximate causes of the military conflict.

Another way to transcend the Maxwell thesis is to extend the time frame upto the present day. The day formal negotiations began, Maxwell's image of a stubborn and unyielding India unwilling to negotiate a mutually beneficial settlement had given way to a more pragmatic reality. Formal talks commenced in the early 1980s when both sides committed themselves to a structured and peaceful dialogue process. It is worth pointing out here that unlike most other disputes like the India-Pakistan or Arab-Israeli entanglements or the many disputes in the South and East China seas, the situation on the India-China border is not one where either side truly covets territory held by the other side. The vital territorial interests of each side are already satisfied by the present status quo. What we have are political claims and counter-claims but neither side actually believes it can ever receive anything close to its official claims in a future settlement.

So, this naturally leads to the question: why is the border issue not solved when the status quo is the most logical border alignment and neither side has seriously entertained a recovery of its expansive territorial claims? There is still no consensus among scholars and former policymakers on how we should study and interpret the India-China border dispute! Should we focus on the colonial history of frontier-making and decisions taken much before independent India and the People's Republic of China (henceforth, PRC) came into being? What role does Tibet play in this story? Is the dispute shaped by mutual mistrust and insecurity about the other side's geopolitical intentions and according to which the border issue comes alive whenever anxieties are heightened? Or does China attempt to coerce India and keep it off balance, a strategy some claim is part of China's strategic cultural DNA and general approach towards its periphery? Also, how much importance should we assign to India's domestic politics and how no leadership has been able to hold onto a pragmatic and historically sound position on the dispute and seriously attempt a boundary settlement? And finally, what role do third parties, the United States (henceforth, US) in particular, play in shaping the attitudes and perceptions of these two large neighbours? Section I of the book will engage with some of these questions.

Returning to their negotiating journey, for several years these bilateral conversations were in essence talks about talks: sort of a strange pre-bargaining ritual that has very gradually evolved into more concrete understandings. One notable outcome is a 2005 agreement, the 'Political Parameters and Guiding Principles for the Settlement of the India-China Boundary Question', which was the apogee of the conflict resolution process so far.[6] The April 2005 agreement indicated that both India and China had substantially converged their positions on the overarching principles that would guide subsequent negotiations. The agreement declared that a 'package settlement' – implied to mean that India's claim to Aksai Chin would be swapped for China's claim to Arunachal Pradesh – as the only way forward along with a mutual recognition that this would involve only minor territorial adjustments and would not upset settled populations on either side. Yet, the exercise got suspended in politics soon after and both sides have been unable to engage in meaningful negotiations for the past decade. When they do decide to move ahead seriously, Delhi and Beijing would do well to look back at history, for, the status quo has always been the key to a legitimate and dignified settlement.

Today, the border question is no longer solely an issue of domestic politics in India, which many believe had obstructed a 'swap deal' upto the early 1980s. For over a decade, broader geopolitical factors such as the triangular dynamic between US, China and India, the uncertain relationship between India and China in the subcontinent, and, China's political insecurity over Tibet have been affecting the incentives and calculus on both sides to pursue a final settlement. How these geopolitical factors play out in the coming years will feed into the boundary question. Indeed, as I show, geopolitics has always been historically relevant, particularly in influencing Chinese enthusiasm for an early settlement.

As we look at military preparations and postures post the Ladakh standoff, it is impossible to predict whether the conjuncture of world events would hasten or stifle a mutually acceptable settlement to this longstanding Himalayan stalemate. But it is difficult to envisage an endgame that involves anything more than a token exchange of territory by these two large Himalayan powers.

Normalization

After their 1962 war, both sides would take several decades to re-establish some kind of a normal relationship. The rapprochement began in the mid-1970s, with India's ambassador arriving in Beijing in 1976 just as the Chinese people were mourning the passing of Mao Zedong. In 1979, India's then Foreign Minister Atal Bihari Vajpayee held an important meeting with Deng Xiaoping who had just initiated China's 'reform and opening up' policy. Although a golden opportunity to solve the territorial dispute may have been lost at this stage, both sides did agree on some of the basic principles that would accompany a normalization of the relationship. This understanding eventually culminated in an important leadership summit in 1988 that produced the overarching framework that has guided the relations ever since. The understanding was built on three pillars – while differences and long-standing disputes exist, both sides agreed these would be addressed peacefully. That is, through diplomatic or political means rather than through coercion or military force. And as both sides keep moving towards a resolution of their differences and disputes, they agreed on a parallel approach whereby they would simultaneously pursue common interests wherever they exist or become apparent. In essence, it was a dual-track approach where dispute resolution would be attempted while each side took incremental steps towards engagement. The idea being that confidence and interdependence built on other fronts might create a conducive environment to reach a fair settlement. Of course, that has not happened so far, and today many question whether the 1988 framework should not be discarded all together.

Nevertheless, having decided that the border dispute would no longer hold back cooperation in other spheres, trade grew by 300 per cent between 1988 and 1993, although in absolute terms this would pale in comparison to the explosion in bilateral trade after 2003. In 1993, China even agreed to supply nuclear fuel for India's strategically important Tarapur reactor after the US and France refused. Both sides also attempted to stabilize the line of actual control (LAC) and articulate norms for border management. In 1993, they agreed to delink a settlement of the boundary 'from the maintenance of peace on the border' with both sides also formally renouncing 'the use of force to settle the issue.'[7] Of course, a major factor for the broader stabilization of India-China relations was the sudden emergence of a unipolar world with the collapse of the Soviet Union. Shared anxieties about this new and unpredictable world order along with a common need for a quiet periphery to focus their attention on domestic concerns – security, political stability, and the economy – would bring Delhi and Beijing to complete their normalization.

While the India-China modus vivendi is admittedly a parsimonious one, it kept the peace on the frontier for four decades and enabled both countries to tap new areas of cooperation. The Ladakh crisis and the eruption of violent clashes in the summer of 2020 broke this uninterrupted peace and has called into question the efficacy of previous border agreements. It is equally true that this framework has not addressed their main geopolitical differences, which in some instances have expanded. Neither has it solved Asia's oldest territorial dispute. So, in this sense, the Sino-Indian rapprochement is different from typical grand bargains or settlements that emerge after a period of major power conflict – such as the 1979 Sino-American normalization or the 1989 Sino-Soviet rapprochement and the subsequent settlement of the Russia-China territorial dispute in 2004. In the India-China case, both neighbours were attempting to move ahead without actually solving their problems, a formula that was exposed in 2020.

Nevertheless, the net result of the 1988 understanding was the broadening of the relationship, which today encompasses a very diverse range of issues and extends to nearly every major issue or region in Asia. In short, India and China can explore new avenues that they could not delve into during the Cold War phase where the frontier question dominated everything else.

India–China Relations Today

My preferred framework for understanding the relationship is that it has competitive aspects pertaining to the region, one unresolved boundary dispute, cooperative features particularly on many aspects of world order and multilateral institutions, differences and incompatible ideas on regional geopolitics, and areas where overlapping interests exist but have yet to manifest in concrete policies and collaboration. Sections II and III will explore these diverse aspects that together reveal the complexity of India-China relations. Section III will engage with some of the key themes in India's policy debates on China.

What has led to the tailspin in India-China relations in recent years? We will not find the clues in some valley or a narrow stretch of road in the upper Himalayas. Rather, the main reason has been a systematic buildup of negative images of how each side viewed the other's foreign policies along with a collapse in geopolitical trust. For India, China's attempt to raise its economic and political profile in the subcontinent was seen as an encroachment on, and an affront to, Indian authority in the neighbourhood. For China, India's pursuit of deeper military engagement with the former's main strategic rivals – the US and Japan – was viewed as a serious challenge to its future security. Convinced that only an assertive policy would work, since 2015 both Delhi and Beijing began exploiting leverages and pressure points to keep the other side off balance. India tilted closer to the US, China towards Pakistan, and on a scale not witnessed even during the Cold War years.

Yet, neither side has been able to extract any concessions or improve the terms of their bilateral interactions. On a range of issues – the Nuclear Suppliers Group (NSG) membership, Pakistan-sponsored terror and hydrological cooperation being the most prominent – India failed to receive any positive contribution from China. With India's boycott of the BRI (Belt and Road Initiative), China too found itself confronting not only the only major holdout against its flagship international initiative but also its most suspicious and non-cooperative neighbour in Asia. Beijing also noticed that New Delhi was beginning to openly involve external powers to collaborate with it in an anti-China strategy in South Asia and the Indian Ocean. Worse still must have been the spectacle of India brandishing its Tibet card. Such unbridled competition has raised the costs for both India and China.

The April 2018 Wuhan summit between Narendra Modi and Xi Jinping was an attempt at course correction and defining some norms that could serve as a renewed set of guidelines to policymakers and bureaucracies in both countries. It was built on five pillars. The 'simultaneous emergence of India and China', two major powers with independent foreign policies is a reality. The relationship has regained importance and become 'a positive factor for stability' in the global power flux. Both sides recognise the 'importance of respecting each other's sensitivities, concerns and aspirations'. Both leaderships would provide 'strategic guidance to their respective militaries' to manage the border peacefully. And finally, both sides would strive for 'greater consultation on all matters of common interest', which includes building a real 'developmental partnership'.

These short, if feeble episodes, to reach a new equilibrium through the informal summits in Wuhan (2018) and Chennai (2019) have obviously not been enough to reach a new modus vivendi. The crisis in eastern Ladakh for most of 2020 has shown just how intense threat perceptions and suspicions are on both sides of the Himalayas. This book argues for a new equilibrum to mitigate the recurring cycles of intense competition in recent years.

THE IMPORTANCE OF India-China relations in India's overall foreign policy today cannot be overstated. Not only is China's rise changing Asia's geopolitical landscape, and, to only a slightly lesser extent, the global balance of power, its involvement in South Asia in recent years has extended its previous position as India's largest neighbour to one of an engaged great power across the subcontinent. Unlike in the Cold War era, when a backward China had been confined to a limited role in South Asia's security and economy, four decades of reform and opening up to the world has provided China with the financial wealth, industrial strength, and military capacities to pursue a more ambitious role in South Asia.

India's China policy is, thus, a profoundly consequential process for the Indian government, and it entails opportunities as well as risks with implications across a gamut of issues: to India's global status and effectiveness in international institutions, geopolitical security, and economic transformation. The persistence of an unresolved border dispute in this context only reinforces the importance of crafting a sensible and effective China policy. What should be the key features of such a policy?

India's China policy should aim to responsibly compete with its largest neighbour in the subcontinent, albeit asymmetrically but effectively. This should not preclude creatively leveraging China's economic power to transform the region, a pragmatic strategy that smaller South Asian states have been pursuing to their advantage. Policymakers should also recognize the wider ramifications of China's rise in world politics and remain acutely sensitive to when and to what extent India's other strategic partners respond to and support Indian interests and concerns. The creativity lies in leveraging geopolitical opportunities where they exist without succumbing to a 'ganging up' game that leaves India vulnerable to pressure from China, while India's friends, who have their own stakes with China, look on. It is a fine balancing act, and historically Indian strategists have got it more right than wrong. It is also worth remembering that there has been a similar belief in both countries – that competition beyond a certain threshold only benefits other powers. Finally, competition must not negate the quest to proactively cooperate on issues where common interests are evident such as on shaping the future of globalization in Asia and order-building in the international system. The mantra for the political leadership should be to *manage* this complex relationship rather than fall prey to binary choices that stifle India's own rise.

Finally, a China-obsessed discourse for India's foreign policy has often distracted and led policymakers astray from the bigger picture and central geopolitical and developmental tasks before India. Many in India's strategic community have declared that China is the number one challenge for India and advocate a geostrategy and foreign policy built around China. This is a reactive approach. It is also an utterly narrow perspective. India's China policy should instead be guided by three grand strategic goals: an inclusive security architecture in Asia that facilitates a non-violent transition to multipolarity without radically disrupting economic interdependence; an open and reformed international order to better reflect the developmental interests of India and the Global South; and, geopolitical stability and sustainable economic development in the subcontinent. And since China is important to the successful pursuit of each of these strategic goals, the challenge before Indian policymakers is to envisage and execute a policy framework that allows for progress on these three ends. China policy, therefore, must be part of a bigger foreign policy and world order vision for India, not the other way around.

I

BORDER DISPUTE

This section dives into the past to understand the roots of the India–China territorial dispute and the reasons and context for their armed clash in 1962. That phase of our history has never been seriously debated by Indians and our inherited convictions about the Himalayan frontiers have often come in the way of an honest appraisal of the past. Until we do so it would be difficult to learn the correct lessons or imagine a settled frontier with China. The section also looks at the changing geopolitics that have shaped negotiating postures over the past six decades and reveals why a seemingly straightforward settlement continues to elude both Delhi and Beijing. Finally, I trace the structural origins of the recent crisis in eastern Ladakh and the challenge of restoring peace and tranquility to the Himalayan frontiers.

1

HIMALAYAN STALEMATE: A SHORT HISTORY OF THE INDIA–CHINA DISPUTE

It was once observed, 'perhaps nowhere else in the world has such a long frontier been unmistakably delineated by nature itself'. How then, did India and China defy topographical odds and lock themselves into an impasse that was ultimately tested on the battlefield in October 1962, and has been simmering below the surface ever since? This chapter dwells on this question, and, attempts to get to the heart of this dispute without resorting to the polemics that often animate this issue.

In 1976, after a long post-war hiatus, India and China resumed their diplomatic interactions. This chapter retraces the trajectory of India-China border diplomacy that resumed in the late 1970s, and, sheds some new light on the negotiating postures of the two countries. This helps us evaluate the efforts over the past three decades in resolving the boundary question. The orthodox view of this phase of diplomatic normalization during the 1970s and 1980s portrays India as a relatively intransigent actor still clinging to the past (pre-1962) and unwilling to truly explore a solution to the dispute. India is also painted as an unimaginative interlocutor, unable to offer proposals or counter-proposals; it is China that is shown to have steered India toward a common position. Here we offer a corrective view by taking into account India's efforts to resolve the dispute. India was not the only unyielding actor in this dyad; China too, despite its oft-expressed intent for a comprehensive settlement, has been less than enthusiastic in translating its principles toward concrete proposals, particularly since the mid-1980s. Nevertheless, a modicum of progress has been attained, which is reflected in important bilateral agreements in the 1990s and 2000s. The chapter gets to the essence of the dispute and attempts to interpret the contemporary negotiating postures of both countries and conjectures why progress might have stalled since the mid-2000s.

Finally, we take into account the dispute in an evolving geopolitical context and analyse some of the broader issues that have begun to impinge on how Indian and Chinese policymakers think about a dispute resolution process.

A Truncated India Meets a Unified China

In retrospect, certain fundamental factors can be identified that framed the context of interactions between the two young nation-states in the 1950s. Despite having attained a bloody independence in 1947, a truncated India still viewed itself as the inheritor of the legacy of British India's frontiers. While the new Indian leadership was acutely aware of the changed context, its perception of the northern frontiers was naturally based on the institutional memory of a century of frontier-making by British strategists and policymakers.

It is now accepted that the frontier politics of British India had failed to produce a single integrated and well-defined northern boundary separating the Indian subcontinent from Xinjiang and Tibet. The legacy, however, was more nuanced across different sectors of the border. In the eastern sector, the British had largely attained an ethnically and strategically viable alignment via the 1914 Simla conference of British India, China and Tibet, even though the Chinese repudiated the agreement itself. The 1914 Conference was essentially concerned with China-Tibet issues and 'the opportunity was also taken to negotiate the frontier to be established between Tibet and northeast India'.[1] The underlying rationale for the British at the time was to carve a buffer around an autonomous 'Outer Tibet' that would eventually fall under its sway. 'Inner Tibet' was intended to stay within China's fold. While this attempted zonal division of Tibet never materialized because of Chinese resistance to the idea, the fortuitous by-product of this episode was the delimiting of a border alignment between India and Tibet that mirrors almost the de facto position today.

It is instructive that China's principal concern a century ago was not the precise boundary between Tibet and India but the borders and the political relationship between Tibet and China. 'Every single Chinese document objecting to that (1914) convention confined the objections only to the border between Inner and Outer Tibet. Not once was the Indo-Tibetan border mentioned'.[2] This was natural as the Chinese, utterly weak after the collapse of the Qing dynasty, were primarily concerned about the British extending their sway over much of Tibet. Anyhow, the McMahon Line became the border between India and Tibet.

A brief segway here on British-Indian policy during the 1940s over the question of Tibet would be useful for the reader because it provides an often-neglected historical context to the policy framework inherited by India after 1947.[3]

The 1914 Simla conference between British India, Tibet and China had outlined the basic contours of the India-Tibet border as well as the autonomy of Tibet within some sort of sphere of influence of Mainland China. In fact, India's northern frontiers were not even on the original agenda of that conference, but, in order to delineate the borders between inner and outer Tibet, the process also inevitably required circumscribing the territorial limits of outer Tibet that lay contiguous to India's frontiers. So the India-Tibet border in the form of the McMahon Line emerged as an afterthought of the core aim, which was to carve out a portion of Tibet where the British could play a significant role in direct contact with the Tibetans as the Chinese got embroiled in their domestic turmoil after the collapse of the Qing dynasty.

Until the 1940s, the situation had not acquired the sense of urgency for the British to make good on their commitments. Neither had British India extended their full administration to the northern frontiers, nor had they come to terms with the scenario of what they would do if China regained her domestic strength & unity and sought to re-absorb Tibet. By 1944, these questions were being intensely debated between officials in London and Delhi. These debates were precipitated by signals from mainland China that suggested growing attention towards Tibet. A January 1944 Chinese broadcast intended for America stated that Tibet would again be drawn into the Chinese state and that the Chinese government proposed to build a railway into the heart of Tibet. 'The Tibetan reaction to this (Chinese) campaign has been apathetic', noted British officials in India. By August 1944, the Chinese had dispatched a representative to Lhasa.

Three key themes stand out from these debates. While the British continued to prefer some form of Tibetan autonomy and expressed the 'importance of the maintenance of the Tibetan buffer in the post-war period' they were unwilling to expend the costs of enforcing it and were reluctant to face the prospect of what would occur if the Chinese moved into Tibet. So, we can notice a deep contradiction in these debates: the British want the Tibetans to stand up for themselves yet be careful not to provoke the Chinese; neither was any serious military assistance envisaged and British frontier officials were categorically instructed to avoid making any statement to the Tibetans that could be construed as a 'wide commitment' or military guarantee of last resort. As one cable noted, 'the Tibetan Govt. must realize how difficult it would be for the British Govt. to give any such guarantee in a matter affecting a country with whom they are allied in world struggle.' So the only support envisaged was diplomatic support. By March 1947, those Tibetans who were keen on independence were 'talking about loss of British support in maintenance of their autonomy' and did not expect much from the forthcoming Indian government. On the whole, the records reveal a British ambivalence throughout this period.

Second, the British valued their equation and link with mainland China and were deeply reluctant to jeopardize the broader advantages and commercial interests that came with a stable relationship with China.

Third, the British were keen to formalize the McMahon Line alignment. However, even here, the British were willing to make concessions to appease the Tibetans. For example, on the question of Tawang, they were prepared to cede that area as a quid pro quo for explicit acknowledgement by the Tibetans on the rest of the McMahon Line. Let me quote the pertinent part of the instructions from London in November 1944: 'You should show willingness to be accommodating over details of McMahon settlement and should continue offer of friendly adjustment in Tawang area.'

Between 1947 and 1950, as the Chinese civil war enters its climax, it leads to a brief but fascinating phase where all the three parties attempt to pursue their interests.

The Tibetans, while they appear to be somewhat divided, are suddenly entertaining thoughts of independent statehood, or at least something more than the 'autonomy under Chinese suzerainty' framework that the 1914 conference had established. Tibetan delegates to the Asian relations conference hosted in Delhi in March 1947 even privately brought up the notion of historical British Indian annexation of Tibetan territories and sought a return of among other areas, Bhutan, Sikkim, Darjeeling and parts of Ladakh. Tibetans, it appears from Indian assessments, believed that a federation of Tibetan-speaking countries including Sikkim and Bhutan was in the realm of the possible. As one Indian official at the time noted, 'We are suffering the results of delay in vindicating the McMahon Line…'. In July 1947, the Tibetans formally asked India for a return of the territories including Bhutan, Sikkim, Darjeeling and parts of Ladakh.

The Chinese meanwhile were, ironically, also seeking to de-legitimise the 1914 conference and all their correspondence with India during this period are aimed at projecting their sovereignty over Tibet, repudiating any special Indian rights in Tibet drawn from previous treaties, and, probing for India's future intentions and extent of political commitment to Tibet. The Chinese also suggested a fresh treaty that would provide for negotiations towards an agreement on the 'delineation of frontiers between China and India.'

Having inherited the British position and perceptions on Tibet along with all the inner contradictions and ambiguities that came with it, Indian policymakers proceeded with the intention of diplomatically supporting Tibetan autonomy along with encouraging the right of Tibet to conduct its foreign relations without Chinese intervention. India also sought to gain formal acknowledgement of the McMahon Line alignment from the Tibetans. The generous January 1946 British offer of ceding Tawang in lieu of Tibetan agreement to the 1914 Line is reiterated by India in July 1948 as part of an effort to make good on the 1914 agreement.

The last policy review of April 8, 1947, before India formally assumed power from the British Indian regime is interesting:

> To prejudice her relations with so important a power as China by aggressive support of unqualified Tibetan independence...is a policy with few attractions. It follows that while the Government of India are glad to recognise and wish to see Tibetan autonomy maintained, they are not prepared to do more than encourage this in a friendly manner and are certainly not disposed to take any initiative which might bring India into conflict with China on this issue... In regard to the Indo-Tibetan boundary, the Government of India stand by the McMahon Line and will not tolerate incursions...

Notwithstanding the above, India did provide military aid to the Tibetans even as the Chinese Communists were on the verge of forming a new regime in late 1949. India supplied 2.1 million rounds of ammunition between August and November 1949, though the Tibetans had asked for larger quantities of weapons and modern arms. Indian officials in Lhasa and Sikkim reported that Tibetans would try and resist an invasion. Other officials seemed to argue for the futility of protecting Tibet from the PLA (People's Liberation Army) unless India was prepared for a direct military conflict with China.

Still, there seemed to be a consensus in Delhi on providing Tibet with some military aid because on December 29, 1949, literally one day before India officially recognized Mao's China, Indian military officials and diplomats were laying out the policy of supplying weapons and training to the Tibetan military. On December 30, Nehru himself remarked in a meeting with senior officials that on the question of arms and ammunition to Tibet, India should 'consider this in accordance with understandings with Tibet, and perhaps give the Tibetans a little more than has been customary.' He also wanted this support to remain discreet so the Chinese would not get the impression that India was 'actively encouraging the Tibetans to fight the Chinese.'

In any event, the Chinese would move first and decisively. In the fall of 1950, India was presented with a fait accompli when the PLA moved into Lhasa. In May 1951, China would go on to sign a fresh agreement with the Tibetans upholding Chinese sovereignty along with a special status for Tibet within the new PRC. Finally, it is also worth recalling that both the UK and the US governments completely rebuffed Tibetan overtures for assistance and political legitimacy in the United Nations (UN). In January 1950, the US reached out to Delhi to categorically convey to Tibetans that 'the US government would not in any event be in a position in the present situation to lend effective aid to Tibet.'

The unwinding of British India's Tibet policy and its sudden re-emergence in the late 1950s, when India-China relations turned sour, is central to understanding the India-China border conflict.

THE 'WESTERN SECTOR' between Xinjiang and Tibet and Jammu and Kashmir, which was to become the crux of the boundary dispute with China in the late 1950s, was never formally delineated nor successfully resolved by British India. The fluid British frontier approach in this sector was shaped by the geopolitical and geoeconomic goals of its empire and was never designed to meet the basic requirements of a sovereign nation-state. The 'expansion of British interests and thus the frontier was not a progression of a boundary line slowly being shifted farther and farther out. The British were concerned not with a border but with access – routes, passes, ease of transport, and availability of fodder for transport animals. The frontier was not a territorial unit with a defined border: routes defined the colonial frontier'.[4] For the most part, the British were interested in preserving their exclusive colonial privileges in the subcontinent from the great powers in Eurasia, the most formidable of which was the Russian empire.

There were almost a dozen attempts by the British to arrive at exactly where the boundaries should lie. Most, however, were exploratory surveys by British frontier agents reflecting British expansion in the north-west frontiers rather than a concerted attempt to establish an international border. And, they varied with the prevailing geopolitical objectives of British foreign policy, vis-à-vis the perceived threat of Russian expansion. For instance, when Russia was seen as expanding its influence in Xinjiang, some British strategists advocated an extreme northern Kashmiri border. At other moments, opinion tended to favour a relatively moderate border, with reliance even being placed on Chinese control of Xinjiang as a buffer against Russia.

The conventional views in writings, which overplay the Anglo-Russian rivalry and its actual influence on British-Indian frontier policies, have been challenged. Malcolm Yapp, for instance, suggests that, 'the most important element in the debate about the defence of India, although it was disguised by the character of the debate, was not the external enemy (Russia) but the internal threat (maintaining British control over the Indian polity)'. He has also argued that, 'The external enemy, which served to rationalize or legitimize British actions in the north-western regions was primarily a device by which the British and British-Indian systems could be linked, through which they could discuss the allocation of resources from a common pool to meet a common danger, but a device which in reality concealed quite different purposes'.[5] Nevertheless, regardless of its motives, the consequences of the British actions were profound: the Indian frontier was defined as an arena to wage a great game – whose victim, the colonized Indian subcontinent, would inherit not just the policy attitudes but also a frontier that was, in some significant parts, undefined or ambiguous.

In the western Karakoram range, in contrast, British boundary-making was more purposeful. The Anglo-Afghan Agreement of 1893 delimited the Durand Line across the Hindu Kush Mountains. The Anglo-Russian Agreement of 1895 extended the border of Afghanistan north and eastward to include the Wakhan Corridor as a buffer between Russian and British spheres of influence.[6] The only serious, albeit futile, attempts by the British to map the northern border with China were in 1899 and 1905.[7] The Chinese never responded to the British proposals.

At the time of the transfer of power, no definite boundary line to the east of the Karakoram Pass existed. In the official 1950 India map, Kashmir's boundary to the east of the Karakoram Pass was expressed as 'still undefined', while the 1914 McMahon Line was clearly shown as the boundary in the eastern sector.

The only two points accepted by India and China were that the Karakoram Pass and Demchok, the western and eastern extremities of this sector, were in Indian Territory. Opinion differed on how the line traversed between the two points. In effect, an independent India and China were faced with a 'no man's land' in eastern Ladakh, where the contentious plateau of Aksai Chin lay. This situation would have sufficed had Chinese power remained weak or relatively ambivalent to its southern periphery, as it had been during most of the British colonial presence in India.

But across the Himalayas, the restoration of Chinese power in 1949, and its entry into Tibet in 1951, demonstrated that China's new rule led by Mao Zedong sought a more robust approach to restoring China's authority over its southern borders. Indeed, the new Chinese government had given every indication that it would pursue the old objective of uniting Tibet with China. To be sure, the Chinese communists were merely continuing the approach of the Republican regime they had just defeated in the civil war. In November 1932, when the Dalai Lama had suggested to Chiang Kai-shek that the solution to Sino-Tibetan relations lay in the 1914 Simla Convention, Chiang's reply was: 'Keeping in mind the friendly and brotherly relations between Tibet and China every perplexity…and all matters should be settled between ourselves without the intervention of an outsider. Therefore, to agree to the request for the treaty, with the British government as an intermediary power, to be resumed and concluded would be absolutely impossible as it would be like agreeing to one's own body being dismembered.'[8]

It is evident that India's leadership found it difficult to adjust to the new power equilibrium. Institutional memory of previous British-Indian policies vis-à-vis the frontiers and its attendant impulse for a forward presence had to be reconciled with the structural reality of a rejuvenated China, which after 1951 became India's de facto neighbour. The main dilemma for the Indian side was to somehow reconcile the colonial legacies of British policies that had produced the foundations for a northern boundary, albeit imperfect, as well as special ties with the smaller Himalayan kingdoms adjoining those areas, with the postcolonial reality that obliged India to discard the symbols of the very policies that had bequeathed to India these territorial and geopolitical privileges, and yet, in substance rely on that British inheritance. An element of hypocrisy was unavoidable if an independent but weaker India was going to secure herself against an expanded and stronger China.

The essence of the Indian response was an uneasy combination of realism and accommodation. And in the absence of military modernization constrained by economic and institutional resources, diplomacy via an attempt to leverage the superpower rivalry assumed the major burden of advancing India's diplomatic position and preventing conflict. Relatively less effort was expended on developing India's frontier areas and the military-industrial capacity to support India's claims in the post-1947 phase.

Further, the spillover effects of the Cold War were being felt in South Asia. As the result of an American decision in the early 1950s to buttress Pakistan as a client and regional military power, India's options of external balancing were reduced. The choice before India to submit itself as a client to US international goals – in essence, return to the role played by British India – were unappealing to the foreign policy consensus among the founding generation of Indian elites who sought to preserve India's strategic independence. The US-Pakistan alliance was formalized in a mutual security agreement in May 1954 with the commitment of US military assistance. This was soon followed by Pakistan joining the Southeast Asia Treaty Organization (SEATO) and the US-sponsored Baghdad Pact in 1955, thereby making Pakistan America's 'most allied ally.'[9] This dramatic development further reinforced the logic of engaging China, in order to remain neutral during the Cold War, as India's nationalist consensus eschewed the option of joining the western alliance system. Prime Minister Jawaharlal Nehru responded at the time, 'the United States imagine that by this policy they have completely outflanked India's so-called neutralism and will thus bring India to her knees. Whatever the future may hold, this is not going to happen'.[10] This backdrop explains much of the Nehru government's early efforts to forge an accommodation with China and the 1954 agreement over Tibet should also be viewed in such a context.[11]

The 1954 Sino-Indian agreement over Tibet was essentially a Chinese fait accompli that extracted a de jure Indian endorsement of China's sovereignty over Tibet and India relinquished its special British-era privileges of having a say in the matter of Tibet. The agreement had a validity of 8 years, and after relations turned sour, the Chinese would have to wait another five decades to receive a de jure reiteration of the 1954 Indian position. This finally came in a joint declaration in June 2003 in Beijing. Even though there was no reason to adopt such a position, the Indian leadership had viewed the 1954 agreement as an implicit trade-off that resolved the dispute over the Himalayan borders. On 1 July 1954, shortly after the April agreement, Nehru stated to his senior officials that, 'All our old maps dealing with the frontier should be carefully examined, and where necessary, withdrawn. New maps should be printed showing our northern and northeastern frontier without any reference to any "line". These new maps should also not state there is any undemarcated territory… Both as flowing from our policy and as a consequence of our Agreement with China, this frontier should be considered a firm and definite one which is not open to discussion with anybody'.[12]

This was an extraordinary decision and flew in the face of the declared position of the Chinese side. Chinese premier and foreign minister Zhou Enlai had explicitly clarified to Indian negotiators that only those 'outstanding questions between us which are ripe for settlement' would be addressed by the 1954 agreement. Zhou Enlai made it abundantly clear to Indian negotiators that the larger frontier question was not under the purview of the 1954 agreement and this was repeated again when the Tibet agreement was finalized a few months later.[13] Nehru, however, chose to ignore Chinese statements and continued to believe through the 1950s that the frontiers were more-or-less a settled matter. The available evidence suggests that Nehru's unwillingness to unilaterally raise the boundary issue at the time was based on a notion that China might respond by offering to negotiate a fresh boundary, which would have been disadvantageous to India. Nehru instructed his negotiators that if the Chinese raised the boundary issue 'we should express our surprise and point out that this is a settled issue'.[14] In retrospect, not explicitly linking China's ownership over Tibet with a reciprocal and wider dialogue and understanding on the frontiers was an extraordinary error of judgment, and India continues to bear the consequences of this policy.

For China, the 1954 agreement was principally to ensure its security interests and sovereignty over its southwestern provinces and not to solve boundary questions. Thus, for China, it was all about Tibet.[15] As the PLA commanders at the time noted, 'Tibet is located in China's south-west border area, neighboring India, Nepal, and Bhutan and serving as China's strategic gate in the south-west direction...Both the British and the US imperialists have long cast greedy eyes on Tibet, so Tibet's position in [China's] national defense is extremely important'.[16]

India on the other hand, gave no expression to its revised cartographic policy, that is, new maps of 1954 showing a settled northern frontier and never tried to get formal recognition for the boundary. Had 'India given practical, and rapid expression to such a new policy between 1947 and 1950, by the setting up of military posts along the new border and creating suitable infrastructure for their logistical support, it would not have been possible for the PRC in the early 1950s to construct its own line of communication between Xinjiang and Tibet...without at the very least, attracting attention in Delhi '.[17] And even though the historical record did not support India's claims in Aksai Chin, the Chinese by virtue of their expanded presence in Tibet would henceforth view Aksai Chin as a strategically-located area to maintain access to Tibet. That Delhi knew little of these remote eastern parts of Ladakh was evident in the subsequent course of events such as the discovery of the newly constructed Xinjiang-Tibet highway after it was reported in the Chinese media in 1957. The neglect on the Indian part becomes more apparent when we consider that China had decided to construct the road through Aksai Chin in early 1952 to improve its lines of communication into Tibet.

India's actions in the more easily accessible sub-Himalayan region were more purposeful. The PLA's march into Tibet in 1950–51 brought the security of the northern frontiers of India into the spotlight, which hitherto had been given little attention. This lent urgency to the Indian government's efforts to extend administrative jurisdiction into the North-East Frontier Agency (now Arunachal Pradesh). This also included extending jurisdiction over Tawang, after Major Bob Khathing's expedition to successfully bring Tawang into Indian territories in February 1951. Until then Tawang, though south of the 1914 Line, was considered to be under the de facto control of Tibet, which appointed the head Lama of the Tawang monastery. This extension of Indian administrative authority was *not* contested by China at the time. As a result, the Himalayan states of Bhutan, Sikkim and Nepal assumed even greater importance from the Indian security perspective than British India had ever attributed to these 'buffer' states. By October 1950, when the PLA began its advance to Lhasa, they were to become the frontline states and India acting swiftly, concluded a treaty with Bhutan in August 1949. In December 1950, a treaty was also worked out with Sikkim, whereby it became an Indian protectorate. Nepal remained a close ally.

Thus, by the mid-1950s both sides seemed to have come to a tacit arrangement – India had made a virtue out of a necessity and accepted Chinese sovereignty over Tibet, and China had accepted India's dominant influence in the sub-Himalayan space. While the legality of the borders was yet to be established, as in Zhou Enlai's words 'once the conditions are ripe', this situation by itself was not unstable. What then reheated the frontiers by late 1950s and led to a gradual but sustained path towards acrimony and even military confrontation?

Superimposed on these boundary questions were two significant geopolitical developments. First, China's inability to manage events in Tibet by the mid-to-late 1950s; and second, the tumult of the Cold War, which spilled over into South Asia manifesting via the Sino-Soviet split compounded by perceived Chinese threats from the US and Taiwan on its coastal borders. The Soviet Union after Stalin's death beginning to undertake its own rapprochement and an opening to the West to stabilize ties with the Western block, a process that leads to acrimony with China, that reacts by an ideological backlash at home with a return of Maoism and a shift towards a more hardline approach to domestic affairs and foreign policy.

It was the instability in Tibet that finally unravelled India-China relations. The failure of China's Tibet policies and its explosion in 1959 led to a chain of events and re-altered the prism through which either side would henceforth perceive the intentions of the other.[18] The evolution of India's Tibet policy played a part in influencing Chinese perceptions vis-à-vis Indian intentions and was thus directly relevant to the Chinese calculus prior to the armed conflict in 1962. After the 1954 agreement, Nehru reportedly hoped that 'with the last vestiges of Chinese suspicion against India removed, China might adopt a reasonable attitude and Tibetan autonomy could yet be saved in substance and India's own interests safeguarded'. It has been suggested that India's tacit acquiescence of or limited covert support to the US policy to arm Tibetan rebels amplified Chinese threat perceptions, especially after the internal rebellion in Tibet exploded in 1959 and the Dalai Lama was given refuge in India.[19]

By 'early 1959, with many Tibetans increasingly determined to use force to defend what they saw as their basic values and way of life, and with Mao equally determined to resort to force to pursue a definitive resolution of the Tibet issue, the stage had been set for the emergence of a major crisis in Tibet. Even a small spark could ignite a wider conflict.' But by late March 1959, the Dalai Lama and his followers had fled to India and 'the PLA had effectively and almost completely eliminated the armed resistance in Lhasa...several PLA units moved into southern Tibet, approaching the borders with India'. Thus, 'in 1959, when the PLA's suppression of the Tibetan rebels allowed Beijing to extend its military and political control to Tibet's entire territory, the combination of this issue and the border disputes led to a severe crisis in Sino-Indian relations.'[20]

John Garver notes, 'India became the main object of Chinese projection of responsibility for the difficulties that Chinese rule encountered, and in fact Chinese themselves created, in Tibet'.[21]

Nevertheless, there is now evidence that India played a major part in extricating the Dalai Lama in March 1959 and providing him political asylum in India. In retrospect, India's own nuanced stance vis-à-vis Tibet, where, while it accepted China's control of the region in the 1954 agreement, yet continued to foster Tibetan autonomy, albeit through peaceful methods, where Indian dealings with the anti-Chinese Tibetans were supposed to be a 'low-cost, low-priority hedge', not meant to interfere with the more important Indian effort to improve ties with China, was too ambitious and reinforced Chinese misperceptions.[22] Indeed, as former National Security Advisor (NSA) Shivshankar Menon has observed, 'To the Chinese, the timing of India's rejection of their (1960) offer, soon after India had given asylum to the Dalai Lama in March 1959, seemed to confirm their belief that India had designs on Tibet, which was in full-fledged revolt against Beijing's rule…The Chinese were convinced that the guerilla war in Tibet from the mid-1950s to the early 1970s was aided and made possible by the CIA and Indian agencies.'[23]

Even though it was at a tactical level, the Indian forward policy initiated in November 1961 has been attributed as an immediate driver of the conflict in 1962. The official Indian history of the war published by the Ministry of Defence in 1992 offers a candid reflection on the events leading upto 1962.[24] Insofar as the Western sector, arguably the *causis belli* of the conflict, is concerned, the authors point out that India's 'forward policy', while not entirely without logic 'went too far, got too reckless, and lost its balance in its later stages'.[25] It was not without logic since 'a wide corridor of empty space separated the forward Chinese posts from the Indian positions in eastern Ladakh', both sides pushed forward in an effort to show that the remaining area was not empty. The basic assumption behind this forward policy was the belief, especially of the Intelligence bureau, that the Chinese 'were not likely to use force against any of our posts, even if they were in a position to do so'.[26]

Nonetheless, the authors note that 'In the implementation of the 'forward policy' the army headquarters had a direct hand and even issues normally dealt with at the battalion level (move of sections or patrols) were being dictated from Delhi, based on maps of dubious accuracy.'[27]

> The Aksai Chin highway connected Gartok in Tibet with Yarkand in Xinjiang Province of China. This route was a two-way road capable of taking even the heavier Army vehicles. The total distance was around 1,200 kilometres. This road passed through an extremely hostile terrain, rising from 1,500 metres in Xinjiang to about 5,000 metres in the Aksai Chin area. For the Chinese, the Ladakh region formed part of Xinjiang military region, with one Army (possibly the 3rd Army) deployed there. In addition, in order to pacify and "Hanize" the region, in the early 1950s itself the Chinese had disbanded two armies and settled them on collective farms in Xinjiang that had a predominantly Muslim population with ethnic affinity with the Muslim republics in the Soviet Union. Out of this army, probably one division was earmarked for Ladakh... By July 1962, the Chinese had inducted a complete division in Ladakh.[28]

Clearly, China too had its own forward policy; but it had a well-defined objective. The policy comprised securing the strategic road through Aksai Chin to maintain all-weather access to Tibet and garrisoning all adjacent areas for protection of that road.

Delhi's absurd reading of Chinese threat perceptions in that they would not respond to Indian forward policies, was based on both, a lack of appreciation of Chinese interests in eastern Ladakh and, more importantly, a complete misreading of the international situation. Senior officials in the Indian security establishment had become convinced that a combination of the Sino-Soviet split that had come out into the open in 1959,[29] and, that China's predominant security concerns on its eastern front with the US and Taiwan, would dissuade Beijing from the use of force. As one observer later remarked, 'the possibility of the Chinese launching a very carefully controlled limited operation, with very limited objectives, appears to have been overlooked altogether'. Again, this was due to a belief that in the prevailing nuclear bipolar order, a Himalayan war would automatically escalate to a global conflict and would, thus, deter the Chinese from contemplating any use of force.

On 23 June 1962, the Chinese Ambassador in Warsaw received an assurance from the US Ambassador that Washington would not support a Nationalist invasion of the mainland. This was publicly confirmed by President Kennedy on June 27 at a press meet. On October 14, China's Ambassador in Moscow secured guarantees from Khrushchev that in the event of a Sino-Indian war, the Soviet Union would 'stand together with China'. The Chinese attributed this Soviet support, a reversal of its earlier policy of neutrality in the Sino-Indian dispute, to a Soviet desire for Chinese support in the event of war with the US, given the impending Cuban missile crisis in last week of October 1962. Presumably, Moscow had revealed to Beijing that it was planning to make public the deployment of missiles to Cuba.[30] These two developments had untied China's hands to initiate a punitive strike on India.

Retracing the final months before the October war, Klaus Pringsheim notes, 'China appears to have baited an elaborate trap, enabling her to prove later that it was India which had refused to negotiate, Nehru who had announced the order to oust the Chinese, the Indian press which had bragged of an impending offensive, and Indian troops which had first attacked'.[31]

In retrospect, why did India not agree to an east-west trade-off – Arunachal Pradesh for Aksai Chin – based on the status-quo position of Indian and Chinese forces?

In 1956, when Zhou Enlai first raised the matter of the eastern sector with Nehru in Delhi, he said that while China never recognized the McMahon Line, 'it is an accomplished fact, we should accept it…So, although the question is still undecided and it is unfair to us, still we feel that there is no better way than to recognise this Line'. In a January 23, 1959 letter, Zhou while rejecting the legality of the McMahon Line, had offered 'to take a more or less realistic attitude' towards it. In April 1960, on his last visit to Delhi, Zhou had stated, 'As China was prepared to accommodate the Indian point of view in the eastern sector, India should accommodate China in the western sector… We hope, that the Indian Government will take towards the western sector an attitude similar to that which the Chinese Government had taken towards the eastern sector…an attitude of mutual accommodation'.[32]

By the time, in the late 1950s, Nehru and the Ministry of External Affairs were prepared to contemplate concessions on Aksai Chin where, in Nehru's famous words, 'not a blade of grass grows', contradictions with China had spiralled out of control and public opinion constrained any effort at yielding ground to the Chinese. For instance, on six occasions between August-September 1959, Nehru admitted that Aksai Chin was disputed territory. Clashes on the frontiers, however, further vitiated the atmosphere and would thereafter shape the strategic interactions between the two sides. The first armed clash with China occurred in the eastern sector at Longju on 25 August 1959. On 21 October 1959, at the Kongka Pass in southern Ladakh, Chinese guards killed nine members of an Indian patrol team and took 10 prisoners.

The favourable posture of the superpowers towards India on the boundary question also reduced the incentives for India to make concessions after 1959. Chinese efforts to alter the Indian misperception – that China was too isolated and internally weak to respond via limited military and diplomatic signals – failed to attain the desired goal and only reinforced the Indian view that China would bark but not bite.

But the main underlying reason that prevented a swap deal was that the Indian side could never get itself to equate the two disputes: the eastern sector, in the Indian perception was a settled frontier. And, while, minor adjustments were possible in different sectors, India found it difficult to accept that the eastern sector was legally as disputed as Aksai Chin, the latter having been surreptitiously acquired by the Chinese in the 1950s.[33] The 'Indian government was determined not to grant legitimacy to the concept of a Chinese "line of control" in Ladakh'.[34] The inflexibility of this position was sustained by a presumption, based on fear, that accepting the entire frontier as disputed would open it up for arbitrary Chinese claims across sectors. Further, by early 1960, Nehru had been persuaded that India's case on Aksai Chin was stronger than had previously been acknowledged. This position only reinforced the earlier perception that all sectors could not be viewed as equally disputed. During the April 1960 talks between Zhou Enlai and Nehru in Delhi, in what was perhaps the last opportunity for a negotiated settlement, Nehru's response to Zhou's suggestion of both sides renouncing all territorial claims snuffed out any such possibility: 'Our accepting things as they are would mean that basically there is no dispute and the question ends there; that we are unable to do'.[35]

Finally, one could also speculatively attribute an additional variable on the calculus behind India's stand on Aksai Chin. It can be conjectured that the concurrent dispute with Pakistan on Kashmir, may have played a role in shaping early Indian thinking. Perhaps, the Indian government felt that legally accepting Chinese claims on Aksai Chin would have complicated India's ideologically more potent dispute in the sub-Himalayan space with Pakistan over Kashmir? However, until the relevant archives are opened up we cannot test this argument.

Border Diplomacy Since the 1970s

The 1962 war froze both positions on the border and it would take a hiatus of 15 years for diplomatic relations to be re-established. In 1976, Prime Minister Indira Gandhi decided to exchange ambassadors.

In February 1979, on India's initiative, Foreign Minister Atal Bihari Vajpayee visited China. This was the first high level bilateral visit since Zhou Enlai's visit to India in April 1960. Initially planned for October 1978, it was perhaps fortunate that the visit eventually took place in February 1979, after the 3rd plenum of the 11th Central Committee of the Chinese Communist Party (CCP) had taken its epochal decisions on reforms and the opening up of China. After a period of fluctuating fortunes, Deng Xiaoping was firmly in command.[36]

From India's perspective, the visit was largely exploratory. Meaningful progress on the boundary question was not expected nor were concrete suggestions to this end possible. For India, the main objective was to ensure that the boundary remained a priority and to resist the Chinese view that it could simply be frozen as an intractable problem 'leftover from history'.

The only idea proposed by the Indian side was the option of a partial settlement of the boundary in segments where there was no dispute. This too was put forward fleetingly as a sort of trial balloon. It was quickly abandoned, oddly leaving behind a legacy of confusion regarding the so-called sector-by-sector approach.[37] There had been no exploratory talks on it through diplomatic channels, either in Delhi or in Beijing. On arrival, at India's request, a meeting was arranged between the Indian foreign secretary and a Chinese vice foreign minister. The proposal advanced included the possibility of arriving at a partial settlement, particularly in the 'Middle Sector'[38] where there was, in the Indian view, negligible divergence between the two sides. It was, however, quickly dismissed by the Chinese Minister implying that an initiative was in the works on their side and the Indian delegation should patiently wait for the meetings scheduled with their leaders. The conversation was outside the main proceedings of the visit and its agenda, akin to an informal exchange of views.

The Package Proposal

The proposal was an official one made to Vajpayee without any prior diplomatic feelers. Deng Xiaoping reiterated his package deal to a visiting Indian journalist in June 1980. Nearly all published accounts of this phase of border diplomacy seem to have ignored the fact that Deng's offer was an official one made to an Indian foreign minister in 1979. While retaining the usual rhetoric about long term amity, Deng summarily boiled the boundary question down to a dispute over two areas of unequal importance, in which India actually gained as it was in possession of territory (present day Arunachal Pradesh) that was larger, inhabited and endowed in comparison with what China had in the western sector (Aksai Chin). A comprehensive settlement on the basis of the exchange of claimed territories in the two sectors would settle matters for good, subject to what he described as adjustments 'here and there' as necessary through detailed discussions in follow-up action, once the broad sweep of the principle was settled.

Since the Indian side had no prior knowledge of Deng's package offer, Vajpayee was compelled to improvise in his reply. He said that Deng's formula was similar to Zhou Enlai's offer in 1960, it entailed obvious difficulties as the situation on each sector of the long boundary had its own peculiar characteristics, that it should be possible to deal with areas of little or no difference first and then move on to others where there was greater divergence between the two sides and, therefore, a sector-by-sector approach could be adopted. Deng ruled out a piecemeal approach, then using the expression 'package solution', to describe his proposal, one that would settle the entirety of the boundary in one go.

Foreign Minster Huang Hua in his memoirs later revealed that the package offer was again repeated to India's Foreign Minister Narasimha Rao in June 1981. According to Sharada Prasad, Indira Gandhi's press advisor, Deng repeated the 'package deal' to Indira Gandhi's close advisor Gopalaswami Parthasarathy in September 1982. Again, India was unable to even accept the swap principle let alone endorse it as the basis for a settlement.

In retrospect, it could be conjectured that an opportunity for establishing a principle, if not the essence of a solution, was lost. The 'package solution' could have been retained by the Indian side, thereby forming the basis for further negotiations.

For instance, India could have left open a channel for further communication claiming Deng's idea needed further study, that it would need to be fleshed out and could be supplemented in due course by rival or parallel ideas. This could have been a valuable baseline reference, given the waning of the strength of the package idea, in ensuing Chinese rhetoric, especially, in recent years. However, the surprise of the offer initially and then an acute sensitivity to domestic politics circumscribed the Indian response.

During the 1979 visit, Vajpayee also held talks with Chinese Foreign Minister Huang Hua. On the boundary question, Huang proposed, and the Indian side accepted, the following formula or 3-point agreement:

(1) Recognizing its importance, the two sides would undertake the efforts necessary for early solution of the dispute.
(2) While the process was underway, both sides would ensure that peace and tranquility was maintained in the border areas.
(3) There should be no impediment to the development of bilateral relations in various fields.

Subsequent diplomacy has developed under the aegis of this formula. Even the important agreements reached in the 1990s and the 2000s can be seen to have emanated from the principles derived from the 3-point agreement of 1979. Later, the 1988 summit between Rajiv Gandhi and Deng Xiaoping enshrined this modus vivendi. The formulation was one within which it was possible to stress the primacy of a solution to the boundary problem without necessarily making it a precondition or obstacle with regard to the broader development of relations: thus reconciling the strongly held views of both sides.

After the visit of Vajpayee in 1979, Huang Hua's return visit to Delhi, the first by a Chinese Foreign Minister to India, occurred in June 1981. On India's initiative, an annual dialogue at the level of vice ministers was established.[39]

When the first round of talks commenced in Beijing in December 1981, both sides faced the awkward task of defining a procedure and a methodology. The Indian delegation put forward three alternatives:

(1) Review of historical evidence, technical matters and geographical features of the boundary regions.
(2) Implementation of the Colombo Proposals of 1962 as a starting point for full territorial review, the contribution of impartial third parties providing a dependable and neutral formula. The Colombo Proposals was an effort by six Afro-Asian countries led by Sri Lanka who met in December 1962 to seek a compromise on the border conflict that could bring the two Asian powers to the negotiating table. The essence of the proposal was that 'there must not be any territorial gain on account of military operations'. It called for China to pull back to its pre-war position on the border, while allowing for India to maintain its position in the forward areas).[40]
(3) An exercise to locate and define the alignment of the Line of Actual Control (LAC).

The aforementioned potential framework can be characterized as proceeding from a maximalist position – that is, Chinese withdrawal from Aksai Chin as a precondition to negotiations – to the pre-October 1962 LAC reversing Chinese territorial profits during the war, to identifying the actual status quo positions on the ground at the time.

While the first option had been India's pre-1962 posture, and thus outdated, the other two were reasonable and demonstrated a flexible Indian position. The Chinese, however, rejected all three, casting doubt on their seriousness to pursue a solution.

This is because options 2 and 3 provided the Chinese an easy and logical passage to a package settlement. The proposal to locate the LAC, even with the rider that this would be without prejudice to the formal claims of the two sides, was an unusually bold one for the Indians to advance, as it would have inevitably led to settlement along the status quo. By reviving the Colombo Proposals, India was actually paring down its territorial claims.[41]

It is worth noting here that the conventional viewpoint on this phase of talks has generally attributed India's unyielding position as the principal obstacle in arriving at a mutually acceptable framework. The record, however, is more nuanced. The Chinese, despite their oft-repeated preference for a package framework, were unwilling to extend their principles to its logical conclusions as demonstrated in the example above. That the dominant narrative from India has failed to reflect the substance of the Chinese position can be attributed to China's better handling of public diplomacy, unlike India's that chose discretion over management of domestic and international public opinion.

Eight rounds of talks were held between 1981 and 1988. In the first round, in December 1981, India unwilling to accept China's 'package' framework, proposed a sector-wise examination of the dispute. In the fourth round of border talks, in October 1983, China accepted India's insistence to discuss the dispute on a sectoral basis. A Chinese official at the time stated, 'it is in favour of a comprehensive settlement, but does not oppose separate discussions on the east, middle and west sectors of the boundary if this may lead to overall settlement'.[42]

India's approach was based on the logic of addressing the dispute in a sequential manner: flowing from easier areas to more disputed ones, ironically, a famous Chinese diplomatic principle. India assumed that since the eastern sector was relatively solvable, it could be addressed first. This would then create a positive atmosphere for discussions on the western sector.[43] However, it should not be presumed that India was seeking a partial settlement of select sectors of the boundary.

The Chinese side probably rejected this principle of sequencing as it would have implied that the eastern sector is easier to solve than the western sector, thus undermining their bargaining position.

Indeed, in the sixth round in November 1985, Chinese negotiators pressed claims in the eastern sector south of the McMahon Line. In an interview to Indian journalists in June 1986, China's Vice Foreign Minister, Liu Shuqing, said that 'the eastern sector is the biggest dispute and key to the overall situation'.[44] The official Chinese statement after the seventh round in July 1986 stated, 'The Indian side noted a hardening of the Chinese stand, the Chinese pointed out that India was demanding only one side to make concessions'.[45] Tensions in the eastern sector during 1986–87 overshadowed the final rounds of talks. Meanwhile, India extended full statehood to Arunachal Pradesh in December 1986. In 1988, Vice-Premier Wu Xueqian's comments to Indian journalists elaborated on Zhou Enlai's line and Deng Xiaoping's offer, but this time clearly signalling the requirement for India to make concessions in the eastern sector.

It would appear that the Chinese strategy had shifted from its stance in the early 1980s (and its stand from April 1960 when Zhou Enlai stated in Delhi that 'there exists a relatively bigger dispute' on the western sector) as Beijing began to emphasize the eastern sector as the larger part of the boundary dispute.

There might have been several reasons that prompted China to shift its position. For one, it may have been that since Delhi rejected the Chinese offer of an east-west swap twice before,

Beijing was compelled to harden its position in the eastern sector to persuade Delhi to commence negotiations, as well as to ensure Beijing bargains on an equal footing. Second, it has been suggested that from Beijing's perspective, given India's historical reluctance for a 'package settlement', bargaining logic dictated that if concessions in one sector were not to be linked to gains in another, then it made sense to simply push for the maximum claims in all sectors.[46] Third, it has been argued that the emergence of a favourable global situation, after Soviet leader Mikhail Gorbachev's statements in Delhi in December 1986 when he took a neutral stance on the India-China dispute and indicated a new Soviet policy in general to normalize its relations with China, reduced China's incentives to make concessions vis-à-vis India.

Clearly, there was a perceptual gap between India and China on the essence of an east-west swap. The popular Indian position may be stated as follows: it is argued by accepting a swap, India would be making a major concession by 'the legal surrender' of a part of Aksai Chin, which it believes, rightfully belongs to it. China, on the other hand, would gain de jure recognition of territory under its control in the western sector, which includes territory acquired through use of force in 1962, while giving up nothing, except an unjustifiable claim to Arunachal Pradesh. The underlying reason for this Indian position is that the eastern sector has already been delimited in the 1914 Agreement even if its formal demarcation has yet to occur through an agreed bilateral process with China. The western sector, on the other hand, was *never* defined in a treaty with China, and therefore is technically more disputed.

It may suffice to say that it is imperative for Indian opinion to appreciate that Chinese bargaining strategy precludes it from explicitly acknowledging Indian claims to Arunachal Pradesh prior to a comprehensive settlement. Seeking to prematurely do so would be futile, and perhaps only encourage Beijing to reassert its fundamental position to ensure its claims are taken seriously in Delhi.

At the same time, India needs to maintain a negotiating position to preclude China from making the eastern sector the heart of the dispute. Since China's claims on the eastern sector lack any legal basis, the entire strategy to buttress its own position is based on a negative strategy of undermining the Indian case. This underscores the logic for India to avoid getting trapped in a narrative that legitimizes China's efforts to break the McMahon Line. By maintaining its cartographic claims in the western sector, including areas west of the Karakoram Pass, ceded to China by Pakistan and on Chinese territorial profits from the 1962 war in Ladakh, India's bargaining posture would match China's consistent positions on the dispute. Interestingly, India recently asked Beijing to 'cease' activities in Pakistan-occupied Kashmir (PoK). In 2009, the Ministry of External Affairs stated, 'The Chinese side is fully aware of India's position and our concerns about Chinese activities in PoK. We hope that the Chinese side will take a long-term view of the India-China relations, and cease such activities in areas illegally occupied by Pakistan'.[47] This position became more vocal once the China-Pakistan Economic Corridor was announced in 2015, with India reaffirming its sovereignty over areas west of the Karakoram Pass.

Tentative Progress

Rajiv Gandhi's 1988 visit was an important milestone in the path toward diplomatic normalization because India's position converged with the Chinese approach that the border dispute should not obstruct normal inter-state interactions.

From 1988 to 2003, an additional 14 Joint Working Group (JWG) meetings were held, which ended up being largely a bureaucratic exercise. The JWGs did, however, lay the groundwork for two significant confidence-building agreements (CBMs) in 1993 and 1996, which created an array of devices to maintain peace and security along the LAC, and thus, contributed to the stabilization of the status quo. A strong focus on the LAC emerged from these two agreements. Though a caveat preserving the formal positions of both sides is maintained, for instance in Article VI of the 1993 treaty, the line of control becomes paramount. The 1996 treaty on confidence building measures goes further to sanctify the line of control and elaborates on the concept of zones adjacent to it for the purpose of reducing forces.[48]

Over the past decade, as both militaries improved their infrastructure and logistics in the post-2000 period, the military balance began to evolve necessitating new communication mechanisms and norms to maintain the status quo. These have come into being over the past decade, particularly the Border Defence Cooperation Agreement of 2013 that provides for more responsible ways for both sides to patrol their frontiers and actively avoid unnecessary incidents and crisis. A series of standoffs since 2013 with the 2020 Ladakh crisis as the most serious of the lot has called into question the existing body of CBMs as well as the need to define a new approach to conflict management. We will return to this post-2013 phase in subsequent chapters.

Perhaps, the most decisive phase commenced in June 2003 when both countries decided to appoint Special Representatives to lead the border discussions to identify an agreed framework. (21 rounds of Special Representative-meetings have been held as of end 2019.) This decision marked a shift on the Indian side, as from 2003 onward the Prime Minister's Office took direct charge of a political exploration of the boundary settlement. India also reiterated China's sovereignty over Tibet, a reassurance that China values since the original 1954 agreement only had a validity of 8 years (it had lapsed in June 1962). India received a de facto acceptance of Sikkim as an integral part of India.

The negotiating process evolved further, and in April 2005 the 'Political Parameters and Guiding Principles' agreement was signed with both nations envisaging a 'political settlement' and not a 'technical solution'. This was a landmark agreement that substantially bridged and accommodated the positions of both sides. According to *Article III* of the guiding principles, both states agreed to 'mutually acceptable adjustments to their respective positions on the boundary issue, so as to arrive at a package settlement to the boundary question. *The boundary settlement must be final, covering all sectors of the India-China boundary*' (emphasis added). And importantly, from the Indian perspective, *Article VII* reads, 'In reaching a boundary settlement, the two sides shall safeguard due interests of their settled populations in the border areas'. Since the eastern sector (Arunachal Pradesh) is clearly the more populous section of the frontier, by inference the aforementioned clause suggests that a settlement cannot deviate too far from the status quo.

As a Chinese analyst remarked, 'Until now both sides have been holding their cards close to their chests. To arrive at the framework they will have to show their hand. So this is the most difficult phase and we are thus unlikely to see a breakthrough soon.'[49] Yet, the fact is that the Chinese have been reluctant to convert the 2005 understanding to something more concrete on the negotiating table. In 2017, Dai Bingguo, former state counselor and negotiator for a decade, described China's position on the dispute, 'If the Indian side takes care of China's concerns in the eastern sector of their border, the Chinese side will respond accordingly and address India's concerns elsewhere.' Previously, in his memoirs *Strategic Dialogues*, Dai disclosed that by 2012 both sides had agreed that they 'have no intention to solve the boundary question talis qualis (as is)' and 'will make meaningful and mutually acceptable adjustments' in both sectors. Privately, of course, Indian negotiators are familiar with this basic position. Essentially, China seeks Tawang, or at least a substantial portion of it, and is prepared to make similar concessions in the western sector. Because of Tawang's strategic importance, however, India finds it difficult to part with the area in question.

A distinction may be made between the terms 'frontiers' and 'boundary'. A boundary is a clear separation between two sovereign states that can be marked as a line on a map. A frontier is a tract of territory – a zone – separating two sovereign states. In the case of India and China, their frontiers have been defined, for the most part, by nature itself – the Himalayan range. The dispute between India and China is over where their boundary line should run through this Himalayan frontier zone. Yet, because this frontier zone consists of several thousands of square miles of territory, a boundary dispute has become a dispute over territory as well.

It is pertinent here to make a point on the 1914 McMahon Line. The distinction between to 'delimit' and to 'demarcate' is crucial to appreciate the dispute. It was spelt out by Henry McMahon himself in 1935: '"Delimitation" I have taken to comprise the determination of a boundary line by treaty or otherwise, and its definition in written, verbal terms; "Demarcation", to comprise the actual laying down of a boundary line on the ground, and its definition by boundary pillars or other physical means.'[50] Thus, the former signified roughly a region, while the latter is a positive and precise statement of the limits of sovereignty. Since the 1914 Line has not been officially demarcated, the implication is that there could be legitimate pockets of dispute, albeit minor, even along the McMahon Line when it is transposed on the ground, thus, creating a sort of, 'a dispute within a dispute'. Indeed, the practical implications of this are well understood. A former Indian National Security Advisor notes, 'In the McMahon Line itself, because of modern cartography innovations and what not, there will be changes in it. There may be certain amount of changes with regard to the agreement that we may reach. It is possible that there may be some amount of changes in territory.'[51]

The so-called intrusions by either side have thus been primarily the result of conflicting interpretations of the McMahon Line alignment on the ground. On the 'clarification and confirmation' of the LAC, each side has so far only clarified via an exchange of maps its line in the middle sector. For the remaining two sectors there is no mutually agreed upon LAC. At an operational level, this means there is no mutual agreement on where Indian and Chinese troops have a legal right to be positioned along the length of the border. This lack of an agreed 'line' produces what have come to be known as 'transgressions'.

Each side has, occasionally, attempted to lay claims to certain portions of the LAC by the most innocuous means, officially described as telltale signs, leaving behind scattered evidence like wrappers of cigarettes, biscuits or piles of stones to signal and legitimize its presence. As one Indian defence minister has remarked: 'They have their own perceptions, we have our own perceptions. Sometimes their troops are patrolling in areas that we feel are ours and at times our troops are patrolling in areas they feel are theirs...This is the main problem.'[52] Other senior officials have also clarified that India is no pushover when it comes to patrolling disputed pockets or what are known as 'grey zones'. After India's decision to expand road infrastructure and logistical networks in 2007, India's patrolling policy and assertion of presence has improved significantly. India's defence minister told Parliament in 2012, 'Indian security forces patrol up to all areas that fall within the Indian perception of the LAC.' Indeed, as former NSA Shivshankar Menon has noted, 'In almost all the contested areas, India's forces are more frequent visitors than the PLA.'[53] And yet, fortunately, in the 12–16 areas where there is a difference in perception of the LAC 'both sides have generally refrained from establishing a permanent presence or changing the status quo significantly'.[54] The 2020 Ladakh crisis has altered this trend, as both militaries find themselves in a major military faceoff where parts of the grey zones have come under the occupation of the PLA.

It is ironic that just as an elite consensus on a package framework was being forged in India, evolving patterns of interactions in the international system intervened to re-alter the trajectory of the boundary question.

Geopolitics Intervenes

There is a general consensus within the Indian security establishment and China watchers that since late 2006, China has decelerated the negotiation process. Evidence cited is a relative diplomatic hardening of the Chinese stance on the eastern sector – that has alternated between asserting the formal Chinese line on Arunachal Pradesh and stressing only on Tawang – accompanied by tactless remarks by Chinese officials, more vigorous Chinese patrolling and higher frequency of recorded intrusions across the LAC, and, protest of high-level Indian visits to the eastern sector. While many of these incidents could be rationalized as merely reflecting the technical Chinese bargaining position, they probably served a signalling purpose indicative of a change in posture, thus meriting further attention.

The most important geopolitical development has been India's evolving relationship with the US. The famous July 2005 US-India joint statement legitimizing India's nuclear status, and ensuing developments in Indian foreign policy to forge a cooperative agenda with Washington, re-altered Indian incentives and made engagement with Washington an important component of Delhi's foreign policy. It has also shaped Beijing's India policy. Chinese threat perceptions vis-à-vis medium and long-term re-alignments on its southern periphery have influenced its approach to the boundary question. Was Beijing signalling its dissatisfaction at a potential trajectory in US-India relations by decelerating the negotiations from 2006?

According to one perceptive interpretation, the Chinese are probing to 'discern whether or not Delhi is serious about being an autonomous centre of power and following its own course. Or is Delhi drifting into an anti-China alliance structure, however loosely and informally, with the US and Japan? At the same time, the probe could be a device to measure very carefully the US and Japanese reactions to Chinese provocations and stances'.[55]

Future of the Dispute: Triangular dynamics and bilateral imperatives

The context and intensity of bargaining on the dispute is unlikely to be dictated exclusively by bilateral equations. Broader geopolitical variables, especially Beijing's and Delhi's evolving ties with Washington, are impacting the timing and incentives for both sides to move forward. Zhu Feng, a scholar at Beijing University, observed, 'For Beijing, what's the leading strategic pressure? It is always US. It is always [US] alliance politics [involving] Japan or Australia or South Korea. That's why Chinese experts feel so frustrated [as to] why India [has] now taken a lead in the effort to assume that China is a threat...How to resolve it? China should take a look at India more seriously.'[56] This is sensible advice.

Nevertheless, triangular dynamics will remain important in shaping the setting of the relationship. Whether Beijing and Delhi both choose to reassure each other or remain ambivalent or even seek to buttress their bargaining positions by leveraging their ties with Washington and other states will shape how the dispute is viewed by both sides. For most of the 2000s, Washington held the most favourable position in this triangle: The US-China and US-India dyads were far more robust than the relatively weak dyad of India-China. In more recent years, however, as China's rise has prompted the US to redefine and adjust its China policy, that relationship has acquired a more competitive dimension. If India plays its cards prudently, the advantage might accrue to Delhi who now can leverage the changing balance of power to advance its interests across a range of issues. As later chapters will explore, this process is not as simple as India strategists have imagined it to be. There are risks as well as opportunities in the game of power politics.

As Indians, we must learn to appreciate that the US-China-India triangle produces divergent effects at the regional and global levels. At the global level, the India-China dyad might find opportunities for issue-based coordination, such as recently demonstrated over the climate change issue or over reforms of the international financial system, to produce outcomes that constrain adverse US initiatives. As a former India policymaker noted, 'The global trend towards multi-polarity and a more even distribution of power has been accelerated by the recent global economic crisis…Both the trend towards multi-polarity and the financial crisis have actually increased the opportunity and need for India and China to work together on global issues'.[57] Their overlapping interests on transitioning world order towards a stable and interdependent multipolar world has continued to keep India and China on the same page, even if they do not always admit it.

At the regional level, however, Indian strategists would find exploiting the triangle a more difficult proposition, given the apparent convergence between US and China on Pakistan, and on India's place in the South Asian sub-system. This holds true even as US and China have introduced more competition into their relationship elsewhere.

First, US strategic re-involvement in South Asia after its military intervention in Afghanistan, and Washington's increased cooperation with Islamabad helped Beijing's South Asia policy in that the latter was able to share the burden of supporting Pakistan with the US and therefore found some space to increase its engagement with India (particularly until 2015), in many ways mirroring US's policy of de-hyphenation in South Asia. Second, US's historic acquiescence of Chinese nuclear and missile transfers to Pakistan suggests a tacit convergence between Washington and Beijing on Pakistan.[58] After the Obama-Hu joint statement in November 2009 that referred to South Asia as a theatre of common interest, its first institutional manifestation was the 'US-China sub-dialogue on South Asia', which was held in Beijing in May 2010.[59] The US's tumultuous relationship with Pakistan and its more recent public spats have not prompted Beijing to compete or profit from American woes in Afghanistan and Pakistan. It is true that China offers Pakistan an additional lifeline and supports it when Washington looks less eager to invest in Pakistan's economy or certain aspects of military modernization. The China-Pakistan Economic Corridor, with its large investment promises, is a case in point. Yet, there is little evidence of Chinese policymakers looking to become Pakistan's sole benefactor and push out the US from the area. Indeed, there is plenty of evidence to notice that US policymakers too, despite their diplomatic slights against the BRI, are not interested in a squabble with the Chinese in Pakistan.

Similarly, it is fair to surmise that US policy too is not inclined in waging a zero-sum contest with China in South Asia and the rationale in opening a dialogue with Beijing on the subcontinent is to reassure China of US intentions and seek collaboration for US objectives in Pakistan and Afghanistan. Simultaneously, Washington has reassured India that a G-2 style relationship with China will not reappear in South Asia. A decade ago, Robert Blake, US diplomat for South Asia, had observed after his bilateral interactions with his Chinese interlocutors, 'We understand that, the Chinese understand that India can be a very important force for good and for stability in this part of the region. So it is important for all of us to work with India.'[60] The US and India too, held their first strategic dialogue at the level of Foreign Ministers in June 2010. After 2015, India-US strategic relationship received a further fillip as the Narendra Modi government sought to deepen ties across a range of themes. This trend, however, has not disrupted the basic setting in South Asia. US and China still find reasons to avoid open competition in the subcontinent, making it necessary for India to craft a more sophisticated foreign policy that is built on maintaining stability with China, while deepening engagement with the US.

Finally, questions that deserve our attention today are – do the Chinese view the unresolved border as a latent hedge to be preserved until Delhi's posture and worldview becomes more apparent? Will Delhi view a resolution of the dispute as a confidence-building moment to pursue an autonomous path in the security sphere or as a means to break free and pursue a harder alignment with the US? Will the US choose to exploit the contradictions in the India-China equation or maintain a de-hyphenated posture by managing ties with both countries? These themes have retained their significance in a changing international environment.

One of the key insights from previous historical phases including the ongoing phase is that Indian strategists and policymakers need to think more carefully about how the balance of power is being leveraged and how effective that process is for India to confidently and maturely deal with a rising China. Historically, it is true that positive and strong ties with the great powers make the Chinese think far more seriously about their India and South Asia policy. But history also shows the limits of what leveraging that balance of power can do for India, and, that India-US and India-Soviet ties worked to stabilize the India-China relationship when India remained firmly grounded in recognizing and pursuing its own interests rather than bloc or group interests. The next chapter will show how India got it disastrously wrong in the late 1950s. The pragmatism from the Indira Gandhi period of 1970s is quite instructive and relevant for us today. For example, when the Soviets tried to get India to sign onto an anti-China Asian security concept in the late 1960s, India refused to endorse that approach. And yet, India was able to leverage the balance of power and gain significant economic and defense capabilities during those years because of its common interests with Moscow. This is a lesson for policymakers today – when we are being pulled in different directions and encouraged to assume a sort of frontline role. If there is one insight and policy lesson from the 2020 Ladakh crisis it is that India's continental challenges with respect to securing the frontier with China are distinct from maritime geopolitics that predominate US policy priorities.

On the whole, there is strong evidence to claim that only when two conditions simultaneously held, was India able to shape a cooperative posture from China on the frontiers: shrewdly leveraging the international environment and maintaining a robust policy of engagement with China. Whenever the second leg of this approach was weak or not cleverly handled, it increased anxieties and threat perceptions on the other side and the countervailing responses by China led to outcomes where both sides were made worse-off through their competition. This cycle of balancing and counter-balancing has been in full play for the past decade. For India, the policy challenge is to try and de-link or insulate the impact of third parties – particularly when it has a negative impact – and view the China relationship from a longer-term perspective. Naturally, the same mantra would apply to the Chinese too.

Territorial End Game: A de jure settlement around a de facto position

It has been observed that 'nowhere else in the world has such a long frontier been unmistakably delineated by nature itself. The Himalayan crest is the clearest possible determinable dividing line. However, it is equally obvious that the crest line must be established jointly by agreed processes'.[61] Thus, the natural defensive line of northern India, the Himalayan range, has always defined the limits of a solution. And this defensive line is embodied by the 1914 alignment, India's non-negotiable interest. Therefore, from an Indian perspective, it can never be conceived that its boundary with China is ever formalized on the

Brahmaputra plains. Further, the 1914 alignment, aside from its strategic sanctity, also upholds the ethnic and linguistic affinities to peoples south of it, who are distinct from the homogeneous Tibetan or Han people. Tawang is then as much a symbol of India's defensive position (as Lamb writes 'thrusting right to the edge of the Brahmaputra valley') as a vital tactical point that holds the key to the defense of the entire sub-Himalayan space.[62] Similarly, from China's perspective, it too is in possession of its non-negotiable interest – the Aksai Chin plateau. Therein lies the essence of an east-west swapping of claims.

The boundary question, however, has now been subsumed in a larger geopolitical dynamic where relative power shifts are impelling both sides to refine their national interests. The 2020 Ladakh crisis, although its precise local causes are unclear, is linked with a changing international environment where geopolitical uncertainty and major power discord between the US and China has spilled over onto the India-China relationship. In such a global flux, it would only be prudent for India to keep its powder dry even as it endeavours to craft a more expansive bilateral equation with China. And nothing would perhaps alter China's approach more than a purposeful, stable, and prosperous India.

2

HIMALAYAN CLASH: LOOKING BACK AT 1962

The interest in the 1962 clash and its relevance in the geopolitics of India and China have remained alive over the past five decades.[1] However, enquiries into the 1962 conflict have been captivated by the month-long war itself. Typically, the focus has been on operational matters and how the Indian Army held up in the conduct of war fighting. The famous Henderson-Brooks Report (HBR), the outcome of an official inquiry and still held in India's Ministry of Defence archives, is the most authoritative account on this subject. The most salient sections of this report have been documented in *India's China War*, because its author Neville Maxwell got access to a significant portion of the report in the 1960s. With the end of the Cold War and a thaw in India-China ties, the Government of India published an official *History of the Conflict with China*, by the Ministry of Defence in 1992.[2] This study is largely an abridged and redacted version of the HBR. In March 2014, Neville Maxwell released a partial copy of the HBR in the public domain.[3]

A narrow focus on military history or civil-military relations while important, has obscured attention from bigger questions around the 1962 crisis, particularly the causes of and lead up to the conflict. Historians are still not clear on why India and China could not manage their dispute more maturely and prevent a war. In this chapter, I look into the buildup of the India-China crisis in the late 1950s and highlight some of the reasons why both sides pursued the policies that they did, policies that led to a grave miscalculation and ultimately a bloody conflict.

Origins of the Dispute

Both countries inherited frontiers that in parts were either undefined such as in the western sector Aksai Chin region, where the British had neither produced a treaty line nor extended permanent administrative control to eastern Ladakh, or, were delimited but not demarcated such as the 1914 McMahon Line in the eastern sector. By itself, this was not necessarily a situation that was bound to lead to an irreconcilable disagreement and conflict.

What complicated and shaped the context of each side's approach to their inherited borders was China's entry into Tibet in 1950. But even this major geopolitical development, reversing a retreat from the area since the collapse of Qing dynasty in 1911, was accepted by India. The 1954 India-China agreement over Tibet should have settled matters at least from China's side, as it had now attained national unification over all its outlying regions. From India's perspective, even though the territorial status quo lacked legal sanctity there was no reason for further conflict. In fact, the extension of Indian administration over Tawang in 1951, an operation scarcely noticed in Beijing, and reaffirmation of special ties with Bhutan, Nepal, and Sikkim suggested a reasonable geopolitical position for India in the sub-Himalayan region.

Yet, the turn of the 1950s, especially after the rebellion in Tibet in 1959 and the flight of the Dalai Lama, saw a complete breakdown in bilateral relations between India and China. The main factor being China's failure to ensure stability and integration of Tibet with the PRC. The flight of the Dalai Lama in March 1959, as part of what we can now surmise was probably a deliberate Indian intelligence operation, was a turning point. Most historians now agree that it became extremely difficult thereafter for both sides to arrive at any durable accommodation.[4] 'India became the main object of Chinese projection of responsibility' for problems China encountered in subduing the Tibetans, aptly captures the context after March 1959.[5] The ferocity and hostility of the anti-Indian Chinese campaign had surprised most foreign diplomats in Beijing. India's ambassador had reported that the Dalai Lama's presence in India was seen as an affront to the Chinese.[6] It is worth emphasizing here that there was a general belief in India's strategic establishment that Delhi held a Tibet card, which could pressure the Chinese into accepting India's position on the border. Although there might have been differences in emphasis within the Indian government, the idea that China had an Achilles heel that could be exploited was clearly recognized by policymakers.

Most published histories on India's approach to the evolving dispute and conflict with China have not provided a comprehensive context and insight into the perceptions and beliefs held by policymakers about India's position in the world during these years. The available evidence suggests that five inter-related factors shaped how the Indian leadership viewed the emerging challenge and the policy choices that were made.

Contested Worldviews

To begin with, it is important to appreciate the context that framed India's perception and choices since this directly influenced the type of China policy that was adopted. Let us recall Vallabhbhai Patel's famous letter of November 7, 1950, where the deputy prime minister described how China had 'tried to delude us by professions of peaceful intention' and the 'disappearance of Tibet, as we knew it, and the expansion of China almost up to our gates' had created a new challenge for India. In essence, Patel had expressed concern on a future Chinese threat and advocated major countermeasures including suggesting a radical re-orientation of India's foreign policy. The line was, however, disputed by Prime Minister Jawaharlal Nehru at the time:

> The fact remains that our major possible enemy is Pakistan. This has compelled us to think of our defence mainly in terms of Pakistan's aggression. If we begin to think of, and prepare for, China's aggression in the same way, we would weaken considerably on the Pakistan side. We might well be got in a pincer moment.[7]

The entry of Pakistan into the Western alliance system in 1954 only reinforced this outlook where Pakistan backed by US military assistance was deemed as the primary threat or front. Indeed, as I have discussed elsewhere, India's engagement of China and the 1954 agreement on Tibet emanated from India's unwillingness to open a second front.[8] Even when seen in hindsight, Nehru's assessment at the time was a prudent course of action. To pursue a foreign policy course that brought Pakistan and China closer into an anti-Indian axis would have been a strategic blunder and worsened India's security environment. Yet, a basic clash of worldviews with respect to China would not disappear from India's strategic discourse.

By the late 1950s, India's foreign policy debates had become polarized. One group led by Prime Minister Nehru favoured non-alignment, resisting Pakistan and avoiding conflict with China, and, another group from the Congress right and the opposition called for an entente with the West, a common defence pact with Pakistan and a more robust policy vis-à-vis China. Indeed, in November 1959, Nehru remarked that the border issue was being linked to 'an organized, combined attack by our very rightist and reactionary forces… to change our internal as well as our external policy. They will not succeed in doing either…'.[9] If the idea of domestic disagreements and a collapse of the authority and consensus that Nehru's foreign policy had enjoyed through the 1950s is plausible, it would explain the erratic pattern of Nehru's policies and posture that ensued after 1959. In trying to keep the Congress right and broader political opposition at bay, Nehru made a shift in policy and adopted a posture of 'no negotiations' and demonstrated resolve through the 1961 'forward policy'. So even though this approach was primarily intended to defuse criticism from the government's domestic rivals and did not intend to get into a conflict with China, it inevitably led to the confrontation. Therein lay Nehru's real failure – letting himself fall prey to political survival rather than responsibly steer the country away from an impending crisis. But then Nehru's calculations were also shaped by a belief that India held a strong hand on the global stage. This is often missed in most histories on India's China policy.

Balance of Power

Growing confidence that the global balance of power was tilting in India's favour became the general belief in Delhi by the second half of the 1950s. India-US and India-Soviet relations were developing as rapidly as China's ties with the superpowers were deteriorating. After 1956, there had been an important US policy shift towards South Asia and an attempt to engage India by supplying large economic assistance to support India's Second Five Year Plan. In December 1959, Dwight D. Eisenhower encouraged Nehru to take a firm stance with China by assuring him that the US would not let Pakistan take advantage while India was dealing with its northern frontiers. The Soviets too had chosen to reveal their differences with China when they began taking a neutral position on the India-China dispute while privately berating the Chinese for their reckless conduct in Tibet and the PLA's skirmishes in 1959.

After 1959, the Indian government began to perceive both the superpowers' tilt in favour of India on the dispute as some sort of restraint on Chinese behaviour. For example, in September 1959 the Defence Minister V.K. Krishna Menon felt that the Chinese were moderating their rhetoric after 'Soviet advice to be conciliatory.'[10] One could view it as 'soft' external balancing, not dissimilar to how India leverages third parties to quietly weigh in on geopolitical issues today. In 1959, India made requests to the Soviets to moderate Chinese behaviour. Soviet support was expressed in a famous Tass statement of 9 September 1959, which by taking a neutral position on the dispute with India broke ranks with the Chinese. It was a dramatic international development as Sino-Soviet differences were out in the open.

Nehru sensed Moscow's disapproval of China's aggressive attitude with regard to India and the Soviet 'middle attitude' of neutrality was a major development and 'an indirect criticism of the Chinese position.' Nehru felt Nikita Khrushchev's upcoming visit to Beijing would probably bring up the 'question of the India-China border.'[11] In fact, during their contentious October 1959 meeting, Khrushchev had admonished Mao Zedong and other Chinese leaders for escalating the border crisis with India. Mao had felt enough heat to have assured the Soviet leadership: 'You will see for yourselves later that the McMahon line with India will be maintained, and the border conflict with India will end...The border issue with India will be decided through negotiations.'[12] Almost immediately, Indian officials felt this change in attitude as senior Chinese leaders including Mao showed 'in many ways that they want to be friendly and have discussions with us in the near future.' The Chinese wanted to '"step down" as we want to do it without loss of face.'[13]

For the most part, Nehru's balance of power approach was focused less on pursuing a structured conversation with the great powers on China and more on publicly signalling that India had powerful friends. For instance, in November 1959, Nehru remarked in a press conference that the border problem with China would 'undoubtedly' come up during conversations with Eisenhower during the latter's visit to India. When asked about India's future approach to military assistance from the great powers, Nehru noted that in the unfortunate scenario of a war between India and China, 'such a thing will not remain an isolated, limited affair. The world is dragged into it.'[14] The following year, Nehru privately remarked that US fear of China had led it to view India 'as a balancing factor' and therefore 'more inclined to help' Delhi.[15]

Nehru felt that China would not risk a major war with India because 'the Soviet Union was dead opposed to it.'[16] More broadly, Nehru hoped that this public show of close Indo-Soviet and Indo-US relations would influence China and moderate its behaviour. He also felt that a US-Soviet détente would serve as a 'check' on China.[17]

In retrospect, however, all this was insufficient to help overcome India's asymmetry with China and could even have shaped Delhi's false sense of confidence in its subsequent dealings with Beijing. We also now know that the Soviet Union had informed India that they 'had done "as much as they were able to" in cautioning the Chinese to exercise restraint…the Russians were clearly not in a position to dictate to Beijing'.[18] When in February 1960 Nehru brought up the China issue and suggested an informal Soviet role in narrowing Sino-Indian differences, Khrushchev's response was instructive: 'We would not like our relations with either of our two friends to cool off.' Khrushchev declined a mediatory role and advised for a bilateral approach, 'It is possible for two wise men to agree among themselves. If the third man appears on the scene, he will only make matters worse...'[19]

Nevertheless, after 1960, India was receiving generous material support from both the superpowers even as China was getting increasingly isolated, which probably emboldened the Indian government to overestimate India's importance in the grand strategies of the superpowers of the Cold War period. The overall effect was that it created a belief that Chinese behaviour would be restrained, and, simultaneously might have reduced incentives for India to adopt a more reasonable negotiating position. In 1959, to the Lok Sabha, Nehru himself expressed a sense of confidence that the trouble with China had come at a time when India 'had the prestige' and 'wide friendship...in the world today.'[20]

Another anecdote exemplifies Indian thinking right upto the eve of armed conflict: On October 13, 1962, a week before the war, in an exchange between Foreign Secretary M.J. Desai and US Ambassador John Kenneth Galbraith, Desai remarked that there 'would be no extensive Chinese reaction because of their fear of the US – "It is you they really fear".'[21] Of course, by that time and unknown to Delhi, the Chinese had received assurances both from the US regarding a threat around the Taiwan Straits (June 23 and June 27) and from the Soviets (October 13–14) thereby freeing them to focus on the Indian front.

Assumptions About Chinese Non-use of Force

Nehru and his advisors continued to believe that the China threat was a long-range one that could be dealt with by India's industrial revival and that the 'Chinese could not sustain any major drive across the "great land barrier"'. India's Military Intelligence's assessment in 1959 was that a 'major incursion' by the Chinese was unlikely.[22] Even on the frontier, most stand-offs between the end of 1959 and the fall of 1962 were local and in most cases the Chinese had backed off without attacking Indian posts. These experiences shaped intelligence and military perceptions that the Chinese were not interested in a major conflagration. Even after the clashes at Longju in 1959, Nehru believed there was no 'real chance of a major conflict on the border but there is possibility of petty conflicts here and there.'[23]

Such a conviction was reinforced by a broader strategic belief that a limited high intensity war had become nearly impossible in a nuclearized bipolar system. So India's calculus was shaped by a one-step escalation scenario: any Chinese use of force would involve more-or-less a rapid escalation to the global nuclear level, and, the spectre of a global conflagration would deter a conflict on the Himalayan border.[24] The contrasting assessments of Nehru and Mao were evident from their October 1954 encounter. Nehru had argued that the nature of force had undergone a radical shift in a nuclear world, and that the next war would be truly global in both scope and destruction. Mao had rebutted this by saying that the nuclear revolution had not changed the basic nature of warfare, except that the casualties would henceforth be much higher. The role of force still mattered and could not be ruled out, Mao had claimed.[25] Clearly, there was a difference in strategic cultures and how each side viewed the relationship between military power and international politics. In a Lok Sabha speech in December 1961, Nehru remarked, 'one must not go by all the brave words that are said in these communications to us by the Chinese government. But other factors work also.'[26] This miscalculation is captured in Nehru's view as late as on October 2, 1962: 'he had good reasons to believe the Chinese would not take any strong action against us'.

Processing Intelligence

We now know that by October 1960, the Indian Army headquarters (henceforth, HQ) had provided a consolidated intelligence review that showed a Chinese build-up in Tibet that was three times the force levels in 1959. The Chinese were consolidating their hold over Tibet after a period of rebellion and violent unrest. By October 1961, the asymmetry was even greater with improving Chinese logistics and capacity for deeper deployment.[27] In short, India's political and military leadership were fully aware of the material asymmetry on the frontiers. Yet, it was in such a context that the Indian government decided to adopt an assertive posture by adopting the so-called 'forward policy'.

China's Great Leap Forward Strategy, a bold attempt to rapidly propel the economy on to a high-growth trajectory, had failed dramatically producing an economic and ideological crisis in its wake. In India, it led to policymakers over-reading Chinese threat perceptions. The assumption drawn was that given its deteriorating strategic environment after 1959 and economic crisis, China might bark but could not afford to resort to overwhelming force. Such an assessment, as we have seen in the previous section, reinforced Nehru's overall outlook to armed conflict in general where a large-scale war was deemed highly improbable in the nuclear era. The 1961 'forward policy' of staking claims to disputed pockets and showing the flag upto India's perception of the border in the western sector probably emanated from this overall geopolitical assessment that was deemed to be advantageous to India.

Until this new approach was decided in November 1961 and passed onto the regional commands in December 1961, the higher defence management and threat assessments had been mostly sound and prudent, and there was no mismatch between resources and objectives. After the bloody border skirmishes in 1959, Nehru had given explicit instructions for restraint and maintenance of the status quo:

'It should be clearly understood by our civil and military officers...that we must avoid armed conflict not only in a big way, but even in a small way. On no account should our forces fire unless they are actually fired at.' For the Aksai Chin area in eastern Ladakh, Nehru noted, 'For the present, we have to put up with the Chinese occupation of this North-East sector and their road across it.'[28] This political decision was reflected in a policy guidance regarding the China border that was laid down by Army HQ in November 1959. It 'stressed that the status quo that existed should be maintained and provocative action avoided.'[29]

As we can see, India's political and military posture prior to the introduction of the forward policy was pragmatic, defensive, and based on an avoidance of any provocation. The earlier strategy was based on a three-tier defence concept where forward posts were only intended for symbolic show of the flag and early-warning purposes, a middle line where these forward posts could retreat, and, finally a main rear base defence line from where counter-offensives could be launched against a logistically overstretched PLA in the event of a major conflict. What the forward policy – intended primarily for the western sector or eastern Ladakh area – did was to break the consistency between means and ends by dispersing resources toward forward posts and weakening the position in the rear. But these forward 'bases were no more than administrative centres with few troops.'[30]

This new policy was 'militarily unsound'. It 'virtually intended the establishing of posts to dominate the Chinese positions in occupied areas of Ladakh' and 'eventual domination of the Aksai Chin Highway', without providing the necessary power or deployments to the Western Army Command to underwrite these aims and enforce them if the Indian posture was challenged by the Chinese. In some cases, forward observation posts were also established despite the objections of the Western Command. Nevertheless, by July 1962 India had established several dozen thinly spread out forward posts in the western sector of the India-China border 'that had absorbed more than half the garrison strength in Ladakh'.[31]

Another reason perhaps why Indian intelligence inferred that the Chinese were not looking for a serious fight was the fact that since September 1959, China had reduced the intensity of its patrolling, and only resumed these in the summer of 1962. In early October 1959, Mao had assured the Soviet leadership that China would de-escalate tensions after the two Sino-Indian border skirmishes in that year. During that time, Mao took a decision where the PLA was instructed to cease patrolling in the forward zone within 20 kilometres of China's line of actual control (LAC).[32] Using this limited time period of a lull as their reference, the Intelligence Bureau assumed that the Chinese were unlikely to use force against any Indian post even if they were in a position to do so.[33] It was during this phase that India's forward policy of probing disputed areas in the western sector also found expression. The reality was that the Chinese had already accomplished most of their objectives by their own forward policies of 1956–59, and, by 1960, had established a 'line of actual control' in the western sector in the Aksai Chin area. They would henceforth adopt a holding pattern until the second half of 1962.

When China renewed its signalling through limited skirmishes and diplomatic channels to dispel Indian perceptions these were either ignored or misread. 'Chinese warnings had such a long history that their impact on Indian thinking was reduced in September and October (1962) – the final phase of Chinese preparation for attack. When the Chinese began to use significantly stronger language, the Indians viewed the threats as more of the same.'[34] From April 1962 onward the Chinese began a process of gradually responding to India's forward policy, a reaction with profound consequences because the PLA already possessed 'greater resources and easier communications' compared to the India Army.[35] Specifically, the measures included, 'ceasing withdrawal when confronted by Indian advances and adoption of a policy of "armed coexistence", acceleration of China's own advance, building positions surrounding, threatening, and cutting off Indian outposts, steady improvement of PLA logistic and other capabilities in the frontier region, increasingly strong and direct verbal warnings, and by September 1962, outright but small-scale PLA assaults on key Indian outposts.' Yet, none of these signals caused 'India to abandon its illusion of Chinese weakness.'[36] By the end of the summer of 1962, both sides were 'within striking distance of each other' and 'a small incident could spark off widespread hostilities.'[37] There is some evidence of India's political leadership attempting a thaw in July 1962. Largely driven by the Defence Minister, V.K. Krishna Menon, India sought a belated outreach to Beijing to restart talks on the dispute. The Indian envoy in Beijing was instructed to meet Zhou Enlai and inform him that Delhi would be prepared 'to send a ministerial-level delegation to Beijing to discuss, without preconditions, all bilateral problems and disputes.' The initiative was rebuffed by the Chinese who felt India was unlikely to put forward any new ideas.[38] On July 23, 1962, Menon also met China's Foreign Minister, Chen Yi, in Geneva. Hobbled by domestic pressure, however, Menon was unable to persuade Chen to allow India to maintain its forward posts around Aksai Chin. Convinced conflict was imminent, Chen briefed Zhou Enlai upon his return to China. 'It seems as though Nehru wants a war with us', stated Zhou. Chen concurred, 'Nehru's forward policy is a knife. He wants to put it in our heart. We cannot close our eyes and await death.'[39]

Meanwhile, although few and far between, there were candid assessments flowing from some Indian commanders on the ground to Army HQ in Delhi warning about an unsustainable situation developing on the frontiers. In particular,

Western Army Command began questioning the assumptions of the forward policy based on its own local intelligence and new patterns of Chinese activity in the western sector. These assessments were not heeded and, in some cases, rejected outright by Delhi. The first Chinese reaction to the forward policy in Ladakh was recorded on April 22, 1962 when a forward observation post was 'threatened and had to withdraw.'[40] In July 1962, there were a series of incidents in the western sector where the Chinese signalled their reaction by firing upon or intercepting Indian patrols. This caused considerable concern and prompted a reappraisal by the Western Army Commander General Daulet Singh via a letter on August 17, 1962 to Army Headquarters where he brought out the impending crisis to Delhi's attention. Since this is an important historical document, it is worth highlighting its salient features here. The essence of this recommendation was that given the unfavourable military situation in Ladakh, 'it was vital that we did not provoke the Chinese into an armed clash.' Furthermore, until additional deployments and Indian strength was built up, the forward policy should be held in 'abeyance'[41]:

> Assessments were undertaken before we embarked on the 'forward policy', since the inception of which, Chinese reaction has been sharp and significant. This reaction, I estimate, has led them to build up to a full division in Ladakh. Against this, we have been able, in three years, to build up to only two regular and two military battalions. It is obvious, therefore, that if we continue the present race for the establishment of posts, they will outrun us at every sector and at every stage. In fact, with the present quantum of forces and military capabilities on either side, it will be immeasurably to their advantage to entice us to continue this race…The present assessment, therefore, is an

> attempt to bring military logic to bear on a problem where, so far, military means have been grossly out of step with political needs. Our forward posts in Ladakh are nowhere tactically sighted, whereas the Chinese are everywhere. Our forward posts anchored to their designated zones, are tactically dominated by Chinese posts on higher ground...The Chinese deployment and buildup, on the other hand, shows clear evidence of a tactically sound military plan, in support of a declared objective. We do not as yet appear to have a clear-cut aim in Ladakh, or, if there is one, it is not served by adequate military means...
>
> In view of the forgoing, it is imperative that political direction is based on military means. If the two are not co-related, there is a danger of creating a situation where we may lose both in a material and moral sense much more than we already have. Thus, there is no short cut to military preparedness to enable us to pursue effectively our present policy aimed at refuting the illegal Chinese claim over our territory.[42]

The same army commander had earlier given an overarching strategic assessment. He had deduced from the experience of the previous three years that 'China does not wish war with India on the border issue provided we do not disturb the status quo.' He had also argued that, as the Aksai Chin road was a vital strategic link for the Chinese, they would react forcefully to Indian moves, which threatened it, however distantly.[43]

The above assessment and recommendation to strengthen force levels over the longer-term and lessen tension in the interim in the Ladakh area was brushed aside on September 5, 1962 by the Indian Army HQ. Instead, Army HQ reaffirmed the rationale for the forward policy, ironically contending 'that subsequent events had justified the policy adopted.' On September 20, the Army HQ ordered Western Command that surrounding of Indian forward posts by the Chinese would no longer be tolerated.[44] In the eastern sector, General Umrao Singh, 33 Corps Commander too argued for a less provocative and cautious posture as well as a defensive position in Tawang via a note on September 12, 1962. Yet, the course chosen by Delhi was to throw troops onto forward posts, which weakened positions in the rear. The entire military strategy, especially for the eastern sector was predicated on the assumption that there could only be limited skirmishes like the ones that had occurred in August and October 1959. Such a strategy dispersed forces that otherwise would have been available for effective defensive operations.[45]

It should be clear from the above discussion that opportunities for a policy course-correction were available and yet, fresh intelligence and strategic assessments in 1962, including communications from senior Army commanders advocating restraint and caution to Delhi did not prompt a reappraisal by the Army HQ or the political leadership on the main assumptions underlying the 'Forward Policy' or the policy itself. Finally, it is remarkable that between July 1961, when India's ambassador to Beijing G. Parthasarathi, was suddenly withdrawn as an act of displeasure to the deterioration in bilateral ties, and replaced by P.K. Banerjee, who was dispatched from his Counsellor post in Tokyo, the Indian envoy was neither briefed on his assignment nor was he 'called to Delhi even once during the build-up to the 1962 war.'[46]

Reluctance to Negotiate a Deal

From June 1954 to January 1957, Nehru engaged in several long exchanges with Zhou Enlai in Delhi and Beijing but the border issue was mostly excluded from their conversations. The underlying assumption was that highlighting the border issue would re-open the whole question and provide the Chinese an opportunity to start making unnecessary claims. For the Indian side, after the 1954 agreement, 'the clear presumption was that we had dealt with all outstanding matters and nothing remained and in the Treaty itself no reference was made to frontier claims or disputes.'[47]

It was only in December 1956 that the eastern section of the border was discussed in the context of the Sino-Burmese border. Zhou Enlai's response was that the McMahon Line was an 'accomplished fact' and both agreed that the 'minor' border problems with India should be settled soon. In early 1957, India invited the Chinese for talks to resolve these 'minor' disputes. But these never materialized and was quickly overshadowed by an escalating crisis in Tibet. And China's attempt to restore its authority in Tibet became inextricably linked with its attitude on the frontier with India.

Both sides would henceforth perceive each other with deep suspicion and mistrust: India for China's prevarication on the border, and China for India's open interference in its domestic affairs. Despite the dramatic setback to the relationship, there was an opportunity to settle the border question on reasonably acceptable terms. It was at this crucial juncture of the crisis where Nehru along with most of the Indian leadership erred.

In April 1960, Zhou Enlai, during his last visit to Delhi, had publicly stated that India should take a favourable view of the western sector in the same manner as China had accommodated India in the eastern sector.[48] Translating this principle into practice would have meant China accepting present-day Arunachal Pradesh as Indian territory in exchange for India accepting Aksai Chin as Chinese territory. Of course, the sincerity of Zhou's offer is unknowable – the overall circumstances China found itself in at the time suggest it *was* a credible offer – for the only way to test it was to engage in a serious negotiation with China. This was rejected by Delhi.

It was India's inability to equate the dispute in the eastern and western sectors that contributed to both sides getting locked in irreconcilable positions. Hobbled by fierce domestic opposition and his own emotional impulses, Nehru rejected a potential deal out of hand: 'there can be no question of horse trading in this matter – that you take this and we take that.' In April 1960, Nehru rebuffed Zhou Enlai's suggestion of both sides renouncing all territorial claims: 'Our accepting things as they are would mean that basically there is no dispute and the question ends there; that we are unable to do.'[49] For India, there was a certain legitimacy around their claims to the eastern sector that could not be matched by China's claims in the western sector. As one study notes, 'the Indian government was determined not to grant legitimacy to the concept of a Chinese "line of control" in Ladakh'.[50] This was despite Indian policymakers being fully aware that India's own claim to Aksai Chin was ambiguous at best. Nehru himself admitted this in 1959: 'It is a matter for argument which part belongs to us and which part belongs to somebody else. It is not clear.'

China's India War

In a *Global Times* article published to coincide with the 50th anniversary of the war, a scholar from the reputed Chinese Academy of Social Sciences remarked, 'Mao wanted to wake him (Nehru) up from the superpowers' influence by giving him a heavy punch, so that he would come to his senses and end the war. War is an extreme means of communication between civilizations.'[51] This rather blunt admission sums up the war from the Chinese perspective: 1962 was primarily a pre-emptive punitive strike intended to, in Mao's words, 'guarantee at least thirty years of peace' with India.[52] Liu Shaoqi, China's then-President, is reported to have told regional leaders in January 1963 that the Chinese had to show the Indians that China was a great power and, for this reason, had to 'punish' India once.[53]

After 1959, the dispute with India had become diplomatically costly. It impacted not only Beijing's growing differences with Moscow and ability to maintain prestige among other communist regimes but also China's standing across Asia and the non-aligned Third World countries. By the first half of 1960, the Soviets had withdrawn all their experts from China and suspended all economic contracts including nuclear cooperation.

In such a deteriorating strategic environment, the Standing Committee meeting of the Politburo, the highest decision-making body, in January 1960 adopted a more pragmatic line on the dispute with India and other unresolved frontier disputes with neighbouring countries. The PLA was ordered to follow a policy of restraint and avoid armed clashes. The Politburo also decided to avoid a public spat with the Soviet Union and attempts were made to prevent a further slide in Sino-Soviet relations. Importantly, the January 1960 Politburo meeting set out a guideline for Sino-American relations that were to be based on more flexibility.[54] The combined effect of this overall adjustment in Chinese foreign policy was China solving its boundary questions with North Korea, Myanmar (then Burma), Mongolia, Nepal, and Pakistan – a country allied with the West against China. The April 1960 Zhou Enlai visit to India occurred in such a backdrop of China demonstrating its willingness to defuse tensions with all its neighbours, including India.

By 1961, the consequences of the Great Leap Forward strategy in terms of economic crises, especially an agrarian crisis of declining production and a fall in industrial activity were being felt by the Chinese leadership. Between 1959 and 1962, China's GDP declined by 30 per cent! This prompted a further effort in foreign policy adjustment to help prevent a further slide in the economy. Attempts were made to overcome the ideological dispute with the Soviets by focusing on common national interests and on restoring elements of the economic relationship. By late 1961 and early 1962, however, China again perceived threats on its border regions, especially on its Southeastern coast vis-à-vis Taiwan, in Southeast Asia vis-à-vis an increasing American involvement in Vietnam, on the Sino-Soviet border in Central Asia/Xinjiang where 60,000 refugees fled across the border to Soviet Central Asia. The threat from India's forward probing was probably the least potent of these threats.

In January and February 1962, a struggle emerged within the CCP concerning the assessment of the Great Leap Forward. A faction led by Liu Shaoqi and supported by Deng Xiaoping criticized Mao's policies by seeking acknowledgement of the failure of the Great Leap Forward and advocating fundamental strategic adjustments in both economic and foreign policy. Mao absorbed the criticism and retreated to the second line of leadership, only to make a political counterstrike in August 1962, when he felt that criticism of the Great Leap Forward within the CCP had gone too far.[55] In an August 6 Central Committee meeting, Mao took on the 'revisionists', renewed his class struggle, and reversed the pragmatic foreign policy adjustment taken in January 1960. This marked an important inflexion point in the chronology of the Sino-Indian crisis, and, it is likely that the domestic ideological and power struggle within China spilled over into the international realm. In this situation, the October 1962 war worked as a sort of outlet and a demonstration of Mao's reassertion of his own domestic authority and policy shift toward a more radical direction.[56]

HOWEVER IRRATIONAL OR imprudent in retrospect, India's 'no-negotiation' stance with China was exacerbated by the reckless implementation of the forward policy, and, a rigid political and military leadership that failed to pause and reassess some of its core assumptions once a nimble Chinese PLA resumed its assertiveness in the spring of 1962. It was this latter development that converted what would have probably remained confined to a political argument into a military confrontation. On the Chinese side, Mao's deepening ideological struggle with the Soviet Union and its manifestation in domestic Chinese politics expressed via an intense struggle between radical Maoists and moderate pragmatists probably shaped the timing of the Chinese response, and, indeed the very decision to use overwhelming force. There is little doubt about this fact.

Looking back, the broader geopolitical context surrounding the years leading upto the war and the outlook and premises behind policymakers' choices and policies can offer the contemporary generation a glimpse into that tragic episode. The lessons are many and should not be confined merely through the prism of a military challenge. Today, India and China are too big to contemplate a major military confrontation on their disputed border. They are also militarily more secure – both are nuclear weapon-armed powers – and do not need to engage in risky brinksmanship to safeguard their territorial interests. The status quo has been stable for four-and-a-half decades, albeit punctuated by a handful of standoffs, with the 2017 Doklam crisis and the 2020 Ladakh crisis at the most serious so far. Today, the stakes are enormous. Nothing less than the future of Asia's resurgence and the development of their peoples is involved. Use of force must never be contemplated again in such a cavalier fashion as was done in the months leading upto October 1962.

3

CHANGING GEOPOLITICS AND NEGOTIATING POSTURES

The border dispute with China is so old but Indians are yet to come to grips with how this dispute can be resolved. The historical roots of the Sino-Indian frontiers have been narrated in several accounts. Understanding the historical variations and context around how China approaches the dispute has curiously received less attention. For, to make sense of the current scenario of India-China relations a focus on the intricacies of competing claims needs to be embedded in a geopolitical setting, which has been changing since the 1950s.

China Links the Border Issue to its Geopolitical Environment

Although the Chinese position provides the appearance of continuity, the actual bargaining posture has been one of extraordinary flux often shaped by geopolitical considerations that have little to do with the border itself. Let us explore each of these inflexion points in China's approach to the dispute.

In April 1960, Zhou Enlai embarked on an ambitious diplomatic mission to India to attempt a resolution. Let us recall the context. The previous year Sino-Soviet differences had come into view, ironically because Moscow publicly broke ranks with Beijing by taking a neutral position on the India-China dispute, and by the first half of 1960, Moscow had withdrawn its experts from China and suspended all economic contracts. The year 1959 had also witnessed two border skirmishes between India and China, including an especially nasty one in the western sector in Ladakh where nearly a dozen Indian security personnel were killed during a patrol in October 1959.

As a consequence, the Chinese had come under pressure, particularly from the Soviets. In a rather heated conversation between Khrushchev and Mao shortly after that skirmish, the Soviets came down hard on the Chinese for escalating the dispute.[1]

> Mao Zedong: 'Nehru also says that the events in Tibet occurred on our fault. Besides, in the Soviet Union they published a TASS declaration on the issue of conflict with India.'
>
> N.S. Khrushchev: 'Do you really want us to approve of your conflict with India? It would be stupid on our part.'
>
> N.S. Khrushchev: '...If you allow him (Dalai Lama) an opportunity to flee to India, then what has Nehru to do with it? We believe that the events in Tibet are the fault of the Communist Party of China, not Nehru's fault.'
>
> (After an intense exchange, Mao placates the Soviets and promises a peaceful settlement.)

> Mao Zedong: 'You will see for yourselves later that the McMahon line with India will be maintained, and the border conflict with India will end…The border issue with India will be decided through negotiations.'

It was in such a backdrop that Beijing made a decision in January 1960 to take a more pragmatic line on the dispute with India as well as other unresolved frontier disputes with neighbouring countries. The PLA was also ordered to adopt a policy of restraint and avoid armed clashes. Mao sensed clearly that China was facing a difficult international environment and therefore decided to seek a negotiated settlement.

This basic sense of insecurity is reflected in a May 1959 Chinese note to India, which might have been personally drafted by Mao.[2]

> The enemy of the Chinese people lies in the east – the US imperialists have many military based in Taiwan, in South Korea, Japan and in the Philippines which are all directed against China. China's main attention and policy to struggle are directed to the east, to the west Pacific region, to the vicious and aggressive US imperialism, and not to India or any other country in the southeast Asia and South Asia….our principal enemy is US imperialism…China will not be so foolish as to antagonize India in the west.
>
> Our Indian friends! What is [on] your mind? Will you be agreeing to our thinking regarding the view that China can only concentrate its main attention eastward of China, but not south-westwards of China, nor is it necessary for it to do so. Friends! It seems to us that you too cannot have two fronts. Is it not so? If it is, here then lies the meeting point of our two sides. Will you please think it over?

But Nehru felt this Chinese telegram had been 'discourteous' and he rebuffed the implied suggestion to stabilize the crisis with China. Foreign Minister Chen Yi was equally candid when he shared Chinese threat perceptions to Swaran Singh in April 1960. Chen candidly admitted, 'Our relations with the US and Japan in the east are tense. It would be stupid if we created a tense situation with India in the west also. The USA has its bases around us, atomic missiles and atomic weapons around us. Our dispute with India is very small…We are in a serious situation and need your friendship…The situation in the east being so tense we cannot afford to have trouble in the west also…If two ordinary countries are negotiating, they do not expose their difficulties to each other. (But) I am telling you about our difficulties… It would be best if we could reach some overall settlement, but if that is not possible some interim arrangement could be made.'[3]

Zhou's Delhi visit was an outcome of Beijing's policy to defuse tensions and arrest a worsening of its geopolitical environment. In his meeting with Nehru, Zhou Enlai explicitly offered that the line of actual control could form the basis of a settlement. But as we have reviewed and analysed the Indian position in the first two chapters, for India, how could there be any swapping of claims or 'horse trading' as Nehru put it, if all the territory, whether Arunachal Pradesh in the east or Aksai Chin in the west, were Indian? India spurned overtures from China between 1959 and 1960 to reach an amicable settlement. More importantly, policymakers completely misread India's relative position in the changing international environment. This proved costly with India sleepwalking into conflict with a radicalized Mao in 1962. Even more consequentially, in early 1962 China and Pakistan began border talks and announced their agreement in December 1962. And thus began the China-Pakistan strategic partnership.

ON NOVEMBER 19, a day before the sudden Chinese ceasefire, Nehru in a famous cable, prompted by a dire military collapse in the eastern sector, had practically invited President John F. Kennedy to intervene in the war. 'The situation that had developed is, however, really desperate. We have to have more comprehensive assistance if the Chinese are to be prevented from taking over the whole of eastern India. Any delay in this assistance reaching us will result in nothing short of a catastrophe for our country.' Nehru had requested for large-scale US air support to the tune of 12 fighter squadrons, air defence systems manned by US personnel as well as two squadrons of deep strike bombers that would enable India to target Chinese air bases and communication lines inside Tibet.[4] Washington's immediate reaction was to offer heavy lift capability to support Indian troop movements between sectors as well as supply emergency requirements. But on Nehru's invitation for a more expansive US role in resisting and pushing back the Chinese, the US was more circumspect. US thinking can be gauged in a November 19 cable from then US Secretary of State Dean Rusk to John Kenneth Galbraith, their ambassador in Delhi[5]:

'This involves for us the most far reaching political and strategic issues and we are not at all convinced that Indians are prepared to face the situation in the same terms.' Nehru's message was seen as not merely a proposal for a military alliance but complete commitment by the US to the ongoing war. Rusk noted that the proposal 'cannot be reconciled with any further pretense of non-alignment.'

However other geopolitical factors also played on US thinking. The US felt that active support to India might force the Soviets to support China. In fact, the Kennedy administration was beginning to debate options of adapting US's China policy. The key quid pro quo for Washington was that any US military assistance to India must be accompanied by Indian concessions to Pakistan. Rusk wrote, 'To put in the most brutal terms, India now may face the choice between Pakistan's assistance in the defense of India and some kind of satisfaction of Pakistan's interest in the Kashmir question.'[6] Indeed, given the pressure from the US and UK, India would soon enter into several rounds of talks with Pakistan over finding some settlement in Kashmir. They ended in a stalemate because the Indian side, despite its weakness at the time, was determined not to part with any critical territory.

Nevertheless, Indo-US discussions during November 1962 did establish a basis for future cooperation. In July 1963, this was mutually expanded to include 'US assistance in strengthening India's air defenses' in the scenario of a Chinese 'attack on India'. Interestingly, during discussions to establish the terms of implementation of this July 1963 agreement, John Kenneth Galbraith 'was at great pains to stress that participation of the US Air Force in the joint training ... would not, by itself, imply any commitment on the part of the US Government to the defence of India'. Galbraith 'also made it quite clear that the agreement' regarding US consultations with India 'in the event of a Chinese Communist attack on India' would 'not commit the US to any particular action'. US response to a crisis would 'depend upon the situation at that time'. In the 1965 war, when India was poised to take the upper hand over Pakistan and China issued a threat and along with forward deploying its troops, India requested the US for consultations as part of the 1963 Air Defence agreement but was refused.[7]

On the whole, the 1962 conflict and its immediate aftermath convinced India's policymakers that although they would need to adapt their foreign policy to draw more international support particularly for India's defence modernization, the cautious and transactional approach from the West including pressure being brought to bear on India's negotiating position on Kashmir as well as deep reluctance to confront China in the subcontinent strengthened the belief inside the Indian strategic establishment on the advantages of maintaining an independent foreign policy.

After the 1962 war, India and China would exist in a 'no war, no peace' type of relationship. Despite the 1967 Nathu La clashes, this phase would witness India asserting its position in the subcontinent by its performance in the 1965 and 1971 wars. Although India and China were in a state of a diplomatic freeze, China's domestic crises and simultaneous security challenges on its Russian and Southeast Asian frontiers made the India-China border relatively stable. The Himalayan border was largely unpatrolled – the Chinese had withdrawn to 20 km behind the LAC by 1963 and Indian forces too had pulled back. It was only in 1976 that the Indian cabinet took a decision to gradually resume patrolling on the LAC.

By the late 1960s, Prime Minister Indira Gandhi also signalled an adapted position on the border dispute. She decided to stop the publicizing of acrimonious demarches exchanged by both sides, as it 'would cool tempers down'.[8] In January 1969, Indira Gandhi hinted in a press conference that India's position on the dispute and relationship could not remain static. She remarked that India would be prepared to explore ways of solving differences with China through talks that were not based on any preconditions. Even in Parliament, the government noted that it would like to 'reduce tension' along the northern 'frontier'.

AFTER A HIATUS of 15 years, diplomatic relations were re-established in 1976 when Indira Gandhi decided to exchange ambassadors. The process was carried forward in 1979 when Atal Bihari Vajpayee, as the foreign minister, visited China.

From India's perspective, the visit was largely exploratory. Deng Xiaoping, unexpectedly, made a package proposal officially to Vajpayee without any prior diplomatic feelers. Deng told Vajpayee that a comprehensive settlement based on the exchange of claimed territories in the two sectors would settle matters for good. Deng ruled out a sector-by-sector approach[9] and used the expression 'package solution', to describe his proposal, one that would settle the dispute in one go. In his memoirs, Foreign Minster Huang Hua records that the package offer was again repeated in his talks with India's Foreign Minister P.V. Narasimha Rao in June 1981. Sharada Prasad records that Deng Xiaoping repeated the 'package deal' to Indira Gandhi's close advisor G. Parthasarathi in September 1982. Unfortunately, India was unable to even accept the swap principle let alone endorse it as the basis for a border settlement.

Let us, again, explore the geopolitical context underlying China's postures. While the ice had been broken in Sino-American ties in 1971, the normalization process assumed a greater impetus after Mao's demise and the arrival of a reformist Deng Xiaoping. A month before Vajpayee's February 1979 visit, Deng was in Washington engaging in candid exchanges with the Jimmy Carter administration on countering the 'Polar Bear'. Both sides were quite explicit that Sino-American geostrategy must seek to wean India away from its Soviet ally. US national security advisor, Zbigniew Brzezinski told Deng, 'The US has improved its relations with India' and 'it's important for Sino-Indian relations to improve as well'. Deng 'agreed' with this logic. On Pakistan, Deng urged Carter to provide 'solid assistance'.

Recall that Zhou Enlai's swap offer of April 1960 had emerged after the heated Khrushchev-Mao meeting in October 1959 when Soviets advised the Chinese to de-escalate and peacefully settle their problems with India. In 1979, the Chinese were now in the US camp and Deng's offer was part of the coordinated anti-Soviet containment posture adopted by China at the time, part of which was to pull India towards the US and Chinese side in the Cold War. Indian policymakers were generally conscious of Chinese motivations. As one note from 1976 conjectured, 'one of the reasons for China may be "the hope of detaching us from the USSR, or even turning us against her?" If so, we cannot oblige them. They seem to have greater hopes of influencing India…'[10]

In January 1980, Deng Xiaoping told visiting US Defense Secretary Harold Brown that 'after Pakistan has been strengthened, India will become a more stabilizing factor' in South Asia. Brown's comments to Chinese Vice-Premier Geng Biao are instructive: 'Indians must be brought to realize that there is no longer a concern about a threat from China. We think it is important that you renew a dialogue with the new Indian government and seek a compromise understanding on the border issue that would permit India to turn its attention elsewhere.' China's attempted rapprochement with India must be located in the wider geopolitics of the time as US and China sought to pull India away from the Soviets and isolate Moscow in South Asia.

So, China continued to repeat its swap offer in 1980, 1981, 1982 and continued to privately mention it until 1984. Indira Gandhi was interested in exploring such a deal but then, apparently, changed her mind at the last minute. Formal border talks were established after Foreign Minister Huang Hua's visit to Delhi in June 1981. Eight rounds of talks were held between December 1981 and 1988. During the initial rounds, both sides adhered to their bargaining playbooks: India sought to address the eastern sector first which it viewed as relatively solvable and hoped to create a positive atmosphere for discussions on the western sector. China favoured a 'comprehensive settlement'. Then, in the sixth round in November 1985, Chinese negotiators pressed claims in the eastern sector south of the McMahon Line. In an interview to Indian journalists in June 1986, China's Vice Foreign Minister Liu Shuqing, said 'the eastern sector is the biggest dispute and key to the overall situation'. The official Chinese statement after the seventh round in July 1986 stated, 'The Indian side noted a hardening of the Chinese stand…'.

Again, the changing geopolitical environment might explain the shift in Beijing's approach. By 1983, China was once again beginning to rebalance its foreign policy towards non-alignment after problems over Taiwan resurfaced in US-China relations. For its part, Moscow was attempting its own rapprochement with the post-Maoist leadership and offered to re-open border talks in February 1982. The post-Brezhnev Soviet leadership continued its China outreach with Huang Hua visiting Moscow in November 1982. Finally, in July 1986, Gorbachev sought to structurally transform the Sino-Soviet relationship and pave the way for a normalization process culminating in Gorbachev's 1989 China visit. During Gorbachev's India visit in November 1988, 'The Soviets made it clear that they wanted to normalize their relations with China, and called upon India to do likewise.' With Moscow assuming a neutral position on the India-China dispute, the impact on China's calculus was clear: it no longer felt the need to win India over to its side. By the time of the Rajiv Gandhi-Deng Xiaoping December 1988 summit, India's global geopolitical position had actually weakened with China no longer perceiving India through a triangular Sino-Soviet lens. Incidentally, the US through a backchannel had encouraged Rajiv Gandhi that Deng Xiaoping would reciprocate his overtures.[11]

The new geopolitical context after 1991 would prompt Delhi and Beijing to further stabilize their relationship and the border. The uncertainty and shared anxieties towards a new unipolar world, along with domestic changes in India and China, as both countries sought to promote economic reforms and domestic stability, would bring both to entertain a rapprochement. A major agreement in 1993 would de-link a settlement of the boundary 'from the maintenance of peace on the border' with both sides also formally renouncing 'the use of force to settle the issue.'[12]

What drove this shift? It is apparent that both sides had their backs to the wall during the early post-Cold War years. With China still under the scanner for its human rights record, and India too confronting major externally fuelled insurgencies in Punjab and Kashmir, both countries were able to normalize ties as well as craft substantive norms to stabilize the LAC. Reciprocating India's non-interference during the 1989 Tiananmen crisis, China too did not interfere in the escalating crisis in Kashmir during the early 1990s. Even during the Kargil conflict later that decade, Chinese called for the removal of Pakistani troops to their pre-conflict positions as part of ending the war.

The next big move came in April 2005 during Wen Jiabao's India visit. India and China signed a 'Political Parameters and Guiding Principles' Agreement, which constitutes a set of principles that finally reconciled hitherto competing positions, and importantly, albeit indirectly, implied a path to return towards a comprehensive swap deal with minor exchange of territory. Yet again, changing geopolitics appeared to be the underlying factor behind Beijing's surprising decision to formally endorse such an agreement. A new American policy to normalize the relationship with India and locate it in a wider Asian geopolitical setting may have prompted Beijing to raise its own game with India via the 2005 agreement. The follow through, however, quickly fizzled out for reasons that remain unclear. It has been suggested that Beijing was probing India's new orientation and the intentions of India's new strategic partners. Nevertheless, China shifted towards a passive-aggressive policy of simultaneous engagement and a gradual 'hardening' of their stand on the border dispute. For the past decade, this has been the general pattern of ties with engagement punctuated by a series of border crises and standoffs.

Will We See Another 'Swap Offer'?

We are now at yet another global inflexion point with a changing Chinese posture. US and China appear to be on a path of heightened international competition. The alignment with Russia has given China enhanced strategic depth to re-define its role and assume more great power characteristics than it could do alone. It is reasonable to postulate that China's geostrategy would prefer a cooperative India and stable Himalayan frontiers. But to what extent this would shape China's incentives to solve the dispute on reasonable terms remains unclear. After all, China is nowhere near as isolated, vulnerable or domestically divided as it was in previous episodes when a border resolution was viewed in Beijing as a positive lever to stabilize its southwestern periphery. China's deep economic interdependence with its neighbours and relatively swift recovery from the Covid-19 crisis is in sharp contrast to periods of greater domestic instability such as the late 1950s, late 1970s or the late 1980s. The power asymmetry with India is also wider than it was in those previous decades, again reducing the necessity for China to make concessions to buy India's cooperation. In fact, the recent 2020 Ladakh crisis has revealed that China can entertain more coercive and unilateral options to secure its security and territorial interests on the border with India.

The Indian elite for its part must enlighten the body politic that its original claims to Aksai Chin are not cast in stone and were too casually inserted into the border narrative and official negotiating position with consequences that are still with us. But India must also cast its gaze on global geopolitics and discern changing trends with a sober outlook and always with an eye on its own long-term interests. It would be a premature and even dangerous premise to visualize that India's relative global position enables it to actively play triangular or quadrilateral geopolitics with China. To 'swing' towards an anti-Chinese alignment and hope to be 'weaned away' by China is unlikely to work in practice. In fact, since 2015, this geostrategy has largely failed to produce the envisaged gains. A key reason and one that continues to elude many Indian geostrategists is China's negative or coercive leverage on India – both vis-à-vis Pakistan and structural superiority on the Himalayan frontiers – cannot be offset by an external balancer. Further, the so-called balancing partner, the US actually finds itself closer to China than India when it comes to Pakistan's domestic affairs and the basic balance of power and strategic stability in the subcontinent.

Bluntly put, it would be illogical for India to open a Cold War-style front with China when the potential costs would significantly outweigh the geopolitical gains. A more prudent course would be to maintain the present multi-directional engagement with China and its neighbours, and, simultaneously buttres the domestic sinews of our comprehensive national power along with elevating India's status in the neighbourhood by a more enlightened regional policy. That alone will gradually transform the regional environment and alter Chinese incentives to cultivate a serious and strategic equation with India.

The next opportunity for a border settlement will probably emerge as unexpectedly as they did during the previous episodes. If history teaches us one insight it is that opportunities to solve this question last for brief windows before the cycles of uncertainty rear their impact on India-China relations. It would require bold leadership and geopolitical acumen to convert fleeting moments into an enduring settlement.

4

INSTABILITY ON THE FRONTIER: 2013–2017

A series of border crises since 2013 have stretched the border management framework that was established by India and China in the 1990s. This can largely be attributed to a changing balance of power along the Himalayan frontiers as India and China have scrambled to develop infrastructure and adopt more assertive patrolling regimes. At the same time, the political will to reach a final settlement has dissipated in Delhi and Beijing.

Chinese Domestic Politics and the India–China Border

The year 2013 witnessed new developments on the unresolved India-China border dispute. Just as India's foreign policy elite was assessing the implications of a new leadership in Beijing, the Depsang incident occurred in April. On 15 April 2013, a small PLA contigent set up a camp 30 km south of Daulat Beg Oldi, in eastern Ladakh. The Indian Army responded by setting up another encampment a few hundred metres away. It would take over 20 days of high-level negotiations between Delhi and Beijing to resolve the face-off. On May 5, both militaries withdrew from the area.[1] No official assessment was undertaken to determine what prompted China to enliven the LAC by deploying a small contingent of PLA border guards for nearly three weeks in a disputed sector of eastern Ladakh.

Understanding the Depsang Valley Face-off

Analysts offered several interpretations. One view argued that China's civil-military system had become less coordinated and the Depsang incident was a local initiative by the regional PLA command. This view could explain away the incident, but there is little evidence to suggest that this is what actually happened. Several Sinologists recognize that the Xi Jinping regime is re-asserting its authority over the PLA, especially after the 2012 Bo Xilai scandal. Bo Xilai, a provincial leader who was subsequently expelled from the CCO, is known to have crafted an informal alliance with sections of the security services and the PLA leadership to establish decentralized, parallel power structures bypassing the formal party command structure in Beijing. Indeed, it is probably this development that prompted former President Hu Jintao to make way for Xi Jinping in a clean transfer of power. The Central Military Commission, the highest decision-making body on political-military matters, quickly came under the control of the new civilian leadership.

Another view held that China sought to impress its rising power upon India, and the ease with which it could present a fait accompli on the LAC by creating new facts on the ground or laying precedence for future claims. It is argued that such provocations are consistent with China's assertive posture across maritime East Asia.

A third view holds that the new regime in China has been confronting a complex geo-strategic environment, especially in East Asia, with an ongoing dispute with Japan and a larger strategic competition with the US. It is logical then for Beijing to ensure a stable and quiet southern periphery in order to engage with the larger political-military challenge from the east. Indeed, historically, Beijing has sought to forestall a geopolitical scenario of a united anti-China coalition from taking shape.

Finally, a fourth theory argued that the India-China dispute is *sui generis* with a dynamic on the LAC that creates periodic episodes of action-reaction by the two militaries. That the LAC has become a theatre of intense probing and patrolling by both sides since 2007 underscores that such a level of activism was perhaps waiting to come out into the open. As Defence Minister A.K. Antony told the Parliament in 2012, 'Indian security forces patrol up to all areas that fall within the Indian perception of the LAC.' There has, however, been no white paper or official statement by Delhi or Beijing on the frequency and intensity of transgressions on the LAC, and most public information is attributed to intelligence or Army leaks to the Indian media.

China's superior infrastructure and lines of communication to the border combined with more favourable topography enables the PLA to pursue a proactive peace-time patrolling posture that cannot be emulated by India. Forbidding terrain and decades of neglect of forward lines of communication suggest India cannot reverse this asymmetry anytime soon, although India's connectivity has been improving markedly since 2016.

Extending this logic would suggest that Beijing being the stronger actor on the border undertook the Depsang transgression to bring about a new operating environment and negotiate additional norms to stabilize the LAC. In fact, before the April 2013 incident, China had apparently been urging Delhi to negotiate new protocols to supplement the earlier norms that have been established in the agreements of 1993, 1996, 2005, and the MEA-led Border Mechanism of 2011, an initiative of the previous Chinese regime. The presumption behind Beijing's enthusiasm for new norms underscores that both sides were engaged in pro-active tactical border management that was perhaps getting detached from both sides' overall policy and strategic priority to ensure a stable frontier and a stable bilateral equation.

It was generally accepted that Beijing's signalling during the Ladakh incident was non-threatening and was intended to provoke a political rather than a military response from Delhi. On balance, China's rationale was probably to signal that the disputed zone was becoming a potential tinderbox, to probe India's civil-military relations and Delhi's control over India's border management system, and perhaps, to even gauge whether India was politically inclined to contemplate a settlement via an east-west swap by drawing Delhi into a renewed conversation on a potential settlement. In the Prime Ministers' meeting in October 2013, India and China signed the Border Defence Cooperation Agreement (BDCA) – another comprehensive set of military-to-military CBMs to ensure face-offs in 'areas where there is no common understanding of the line of actual control' are handled maturely and do not escalate into an unintended skirmish.

Himalayan Dispute, Back to the Fore

One of the ironies of the Depsang incident is that the border dispute has come back into the centre of the bilateral relationship, something India had always sought. India's traditional position is that other aspects of the bilateral relationship must not subsume the boundary question whereby the dispute goes into cold storage. Indeed, the 1988 modus vivendi accommodated India's position that an early solution to the dispute would remain a persistent effort. And India accepted China's position of expanding ties in other spheres that should not be impeded by the Himalayan stalemate, with the premise that the frontier would remain tranquil.

At one level Beijing has displayed a renewed willingness to solve the dispute, reflected in Xi Jinping's March 2013 remark that the border dispute should be resolved 'as soon as possible'.[2] Yet, since 2006 Beijing has held a hardened posture where it indicated that a settlement was nowhere in sight. In 2010, China even hinted a reversal of its neutral position on the Kashmir dispute by taking an anti-India position through some of its diplomatic actions. China has been blowing hot and cold, and, the deeper motivations and perceptions of the Chinese side can only be conjectured. It may suffice to say that China for realpolitik reasons could be exploring a settlement to stabilize its southwestern periphery and forestall a potentially unfriendly India in the emerging multipolar environment of Asia.

Whatever the causes of a flux in China's India policy, it behoves India to undertake a serious domestic conversation on the contours of a border settlement. Ever since the first Chinese offer of 1960 to settle the Himalayan question via an east-west swapping of claims, the essence of a deal remains remarkably unchanged. In 1979, Deng Xiaoping made a second formal offer for a 'package solution' to Foreign Minister Atal Bihari Vajpayee during the latter's visit to Beijing. Once again, the Indian side could not countenance a change in its traditional position, which would have required India to equate the eastern and western sectors of the disputed border. The mainstream narrative often neglects to stress that both sides already possess full administrative control over their core territorial interests. India holds the eastern sector, that is territory south of the McMahon alignment, and China holds the Aksai Chin in eastern Ladakh.

Sixteenth Round of Special Representatives Talks

In such a backdrop, National Security Advisor Shivshankar Menon met his new counterpart and former foreign minister, Chinese State Councillor Yang Jiechi in Beijing in June 2013. The lead negotiators have a dual objective to ensure a stable LAC underpinned by adherence to an agreed set of norms and move toward a final settlement.

Insofar as the latter goal is concerned, India and China have in fact attained a significant amount of common ground. The 2005 'Political Parameters and Guiding Principles' Agreement was a reflection that both sides had substantially converged their positions on the overarching principles that would guide a settlement. The 2005 agreement declared that a 'package settlement' is the only way forward along with a mutual recognition that this would involve minor territorial adjustments by both sides.

The Special Representatives (SR) continued their discusions on 'a framework for a resolution of the Boundary Question, which constitutes the second step of a three-stage process.'[3] The present stage of negotiations appears to be in a flux between accepted principles and a framework to attain a final deal. Menon had remarked that the stage of arriving at a framework was 'the most complex' since this directly translated 'into the line' on the ground. The challenge, therefore, had become more political than technical because there is little the SR can do to produce the wider political consensus necessary to legitimize an east-west swap.

A historical appraisal of the dispute suggests two obstacles to a settlement. One is that China has traditionally tied a settlement to geopolitical stability and a modicum of trust in India-China relations. The other constraining factor is India's national identity that is deeply entwined with its territorial integrity, which constrains any government from relinquishing the claim to Aksai Chin and meet China half-way.

Understanding the 2013 Standoff in Ladakh

In the cacophony of a media frenzy, a nuanced assessment of the 2013 Ladakh standoff had fallen by the wayside. Since the context was so important, it is worth exploring both the global and local causes for the standoff and understand the similarities or difference in the situation now.

The macro-narrative locates the standoff to China's stronger periphery control measures that are part of an increasingly sensitive and assertive China across its continental and maritime frontiers. China's perceptions and its approach to its entire periphery have undergone changes in recent years. The reasons can be attributed mostly to internal political dynamics where the Deng Xiaoping-era image of a passive and agreeable China has been trumped by a more assertive self-image of China as a great power during the time of Xi Jinping. The East Asian geopolitical dynamic, especially the US 'pivot' and renewed intra-allied cooperation in the US security network, only reinforces China's threat perceptions and its assertive posture. This is now an ongoing game as part of the evolving balance of power in the Asia Pacific.

To some extent, locating Chinese frontier activity with India in the context of its evolving worldview makes sense. Yet, the India-China border has a distinct dynamic and Chinese intentions here cannot be simply read-off from Beijing's geostrategic posture toward its eastern seaboard.

Missed Opportunities

There have been three opportunities since 1960 in resolving this dispute which we have reviewed in previous chapters. Zhou Enlai made an offer to solve the dispute via an east-west swapping of claims during his 1960 visit. India's reluctance to equate the two sectors would see this offer being rejected. In 1979, Deng Xiaoping made a formal offer for a 'package solution' to then Foreign Minister Vajpayee during the latter's visit to Beijing. This offer was repeated to Indira Gandhi's advisors in 1980–81. On both occasions, the Indian side could not countenance a change in its negotiating position. Indira Gandhi did, however, briefly consider seriously exploring the Chinese offer but it fell through because of disagreements in her national security team.[4] A third opening came with the April 2005 'Political Parameters and Guiding Principles' agreement, which indicated that both sides had substantially converged their positions on the overarching principles that would guide a settlement. The 2005 agreement declared that a 'package settlement' is the only way forward along with a mutual recognition that this would involve minor territorial adjustments by both sides.

The third time around it was China that would pull back by hardening its diplomatic position and adopting a more vigorous approach to border management via a strengthening of the PLA's logistical network across the plateau. Partly, these measures have been attributed to China's perceived insecurity over Tibet though this matters little because the potential spillover effects on India are real.

Lines of Actual Control

Despite having formally agreed to the principles in the 2005 agreement, the negotiating process has been stuck since 2006. Once the bargaining process lost steam, each side shifted its posture toward reasserting claims to their preferred LACs. In 2006, India took a major policy decision to upgrade road and air connectivity to the border areas.

Why are there conflicting LACs? In the east, the 1914 Line on which India bases its ground position was never formally demarcated. It was an alignment on a small-scale map. Both sides interpret the 1914 alignment differently creating 'a dispute within a dispute.' As former National Security Advisor M.K. Narayanan has noted, 'In the McMahon Line itself, because of modern cartography…There may be certain amount of changes with regard to the agreement that we may reach.'[5]

In the west, there is no accepted treaty arrangement, and, China by virtue of geography and necessity occupied most of its claim line by 1960, briefly challenged by India's forward policy of 1961–62, and then a reassertion over that area in the 1962 war. The 1992 Ministry of Defence's Official History of 1962 notes that China eliminated 'possible launch pads for any offensive against the Aksai Chin highway by eliminating Daulat Beg Oldie (DBO), Chushul and Demchok positions'.[6] Unsurprisingly, as these pockets are undemarcated they continue to witness intense probing by both sides.

After the April 23, 2013 flag meeting it became clear that both sides were engaged in probing up to their preferred LACs. Since 1995, both India and China's militaries have a mechanism to hold meetings near the border called Border Personnel Meetings (BPMs) that ensure regular consultation and interaction between the two sides. A BPM flag meeting is a meeting between the armies 'used to resolve local issues like patrols inadvertently crossing over and prevents flare-ups.'[7] China's intrusion into DBO was probably a reaction to India's probing elsewhere, which in turn is a reaction to the Chinese probing somewhere else. As Defence Minister A.K. Antony told the Parliament in 2012, 'Indian security forces patrol up to all areas that fall within the Indian perception of the LAC.' So there are always convergences of the Indian and Chinese probes on to undemarcated border areas.

In the 2000's, both sides had been adhering to the 'rules' of the game by avoiding frontal contacts. Each side would transgress into a disputed pocket and withdraw. Yet, the intensity of patrolling and frequent face-to-face encounters probably touched higher levels when China suggested in December 2010 that it would be good to establish a political-level device to supplement previous confidence-building agreements. This led to the civilian-led (headed by Joint-Secretary level official from the foreign ministries) Working Mechanism for Consultation and Coordination on Border Affairs (WMCC) established in January 2012. In the course of their meeting in 2012–13, an agreement had been reached to avoid tailing of patrols. The BDCA, signed in October 2013 would introduce this norm on no-tailing.

China's concern expressed at the flag meetings about new Indian border outposts being too close to disputed pockets compared to its own more extensive infrastructure in depth needs to be contextualized. Forbidding terrain on the Indian side makes the notion of a vertical logistical road-rail network running up from the plains to mountain points impossible. While Indian troops must negotiate treacherous terrain at times, the PLA can simply drive up to selected points. Hence, in order to preserve oversight on the LAC, India needs limited forward infrastructure to base some troops. China's flat terrain allows it the luxury of a defence in depth with the option of rapidly concentrating forces in any sector without having its troops deployed too close to the LAC.

Missing the Forest for the Trees

At some point intense forward probing can tend to undermine the bigger negotiating picture with both militaries seeking marginal improvements in their LACs. If political oversight from both sides over the local operational details is robust then this game can carry on a little longer. Overzealous tactical behaviour must not be allowed to dictate the strategy of seeking a negotiated settlement.

Paradoxically, the real incentive for intense probing is structurally built into the present negotiating process where each side aspires to put forward its preferred LAC since these cartographic positions will shape the bargaining over the precise nature of territorial adjustments during negotiations. In this sense, the militaries are following the logic of an excessively prolonged negotiation process.

If the present negotiation structure is leading to an endless scramble over legitimizing conflicting LACs, can the overall approach be amended? Yes, but this would require political will on both sides to bring both formal claims – Aksai Chin for India, Arunachal for China – and conflicting LACs claims into one single process of negotiations rather than the sequential approach of unilaterally establishing LACs and then bargaining. 'Give and take' would involve both swapping the formal claims – Aksai Chin for Arunachal Pradesh – and also simultaneously making mutual adjustments on the ground based on differing LACs. This presumes strategic trust because it would involve being sensitive to the other side's security perceptions and tactical requirements. It also requires bilateral stability at the political level of the relationship. That trust and sensitivity to each other's concerns has dissipated since 2017.

A Game of Chicken in the High Himalayas: The 2017 Doklam crisis

Another face-off at the Himalayan border surprised few. Since 2010, several thousand Chinese 'transgressions' have been recorded on the LAC, the undefined border zone between India and China. But the 2017 crisis was not a typical stand-off. The flashpoint, or area, of discord was unrelated to the main India-China territorial dispute. The stand-off site was at a 100 square km area called Doklam plateau, at the trijunction between India, Bhutan and China. It is surrounded by the Chumbi Valley, Bhutan's Ha Valley on the east and Sikkim on the west.

On June 16, 2017, PLA border troops reportedly brought construction equipment to the disputed area with an intention to extend a previously built road southward towards a Bhutanese Army camp near the Jampheri Ridge. Both China and Bhutan disagree on the border trijunction. A few days later, at the request of India's ally Bhutan, Indian troops intervened at Doklam and blocked the construction process. On June 30, the Ministry of External Affairs declared that, 'Such (Chinese) construction would represent a significant change of status quo with serious security implications for India.' Beijing, for its part, accused India of trespassing into sovereign territory and rejected India's right 'to interfere in or impede the boundary talks between China and Bhutan.'[8] In August 2017, China officially claimed it had notified India 'in advance' on the PLA's plan to construct in the area.

The Significance

According to Delhi, Indian involvement was aimed to prevent China from changing the status quo by building a road on territory claimed by Bhutan, India's closest ally in the subcontinent. By upholding the rights of its ally, Indian actions are intended to convey the importance Delhi attaches to its special relationship with Thimphu as well as to signal that it intends to preserve its traditional military advantages in the overall Sikkim sector. Beijing's motivations have been speculated to range from big power bullying as part of a general pattern of China's approach to its periphery, and driving a political wedge between India and Bhutan, to more mundane operational anxieties in a sector where India has traditionally held the higher ground. What made the crisis particularly dangerous compared to previous episodes on the border was the absence of an agreed definition of what was at stake. For China, it was about 'territorial sovereignty'; for India, it was about 'security implications' emanating from a potentially deeper Chinese foothold in the lower Chumbi valley.

Two broad schools of punditry sought to interpret the 2017 crisis. One argued that the unresolved Himalayan dispute, China's sensitivity over Tibet and the ensuing security dilemma was the main cause of recurring friction; the other claimed that wider geopolitics and threat perceptions have converted the frontier into an arena of competition to keep the other side off balance. Ideally, conflict management strategies should seek to address both these levels of the India-China dynamics of exchange. But with the level of mistrust and animosity at record highs, it seemed improbable that either side was interested in reassurance gestures. The indivisibility of the object of discord – in this case, China's territorial claims and India's conception of security of the Siliguri Corridor in northeastern India – made an exit ramp or de-escalation difficult. Both sides dug in their heels and signalled a commitment to their respective positions, the Chinese more explicitly and through a flurry of official pronouncements and unprecedented public media campaign that brought differences with India out into the open for its domestic and international audiences.

The Stalemate

By interposing itself in close proximity to Chinese border guards, India created a stalemate that could only be broken via one of three ways: one side backed off; either side tried to dislodge the other by force; or quiet diplomacy allowed both sides to save face. The first scenario seemed improbable given the crescendo of rhetoric surrounding the crisis. Rolling back the opponent's position was quickly realized as unviable because it would produce an escalation, whether in the local Sikkim theatre or along a wider front on the 3,488 km LAC. Some Indian commentators advocated responses where India's local military advantages were deemed to provide the ingredients of a compelling posture. However, unlike in the major disputed pockets of the LAC where brinksmanship might be entertained, coercing the PLA in an area where Beijing is convinced of its sovereignty and India's own territorial stakes were not even at play would almost certainly involve fierce reprisals in the form of vertical or horizontal escalation in military and other domains.

Confronting a prolonged stand-off with little prospect for a thaw, both sides evaluated their relative position in the international environment.

In 2017, the Chinese seemed to exude more confidence on this front. Beijing's relationships with its main rivals, the

US and Japan, seemed to be stabilizing. A divided Washington but with little bipartisan traction for a new adversarial posture with China implied that the Sino-American equation retained its complex stability. Moreover, US foreign policy remained focused on the Eurasian heartland threat from Russia rather than a rimland challenge from China. Japanese Prime Minister Shinzo Abe's bilateral encounter with Chinese President Xi Jinping at the 2017 G20 summit was also instructive. Abe was reported to have responded positively to China's BRI. Japanese officials noted that Abe held a 'very friendly' meeting with Xi and Beijing had shown 'goodwill from the top level' towards Tokyo.

The Calculations

In sum, while China's eastern front remained a zone of geopolitical competition, Chinese leverage in East Asia had reached a threshold where it could blunt a containment posture from the US-Japan alliance. As Chinese scholar Long Xingchun confidently opined at the time, 'Though the US and other Western countries have the intention to contain China through supporting India, they have a wide range of common interests with China.' The West is unlikely to 'unconditionally stand on the side of India'. When combined with the strategic depth that China was beginning to enjoy because of a stable strategic equation with Russia, the international environment from Beijing's eyes seem more comfortable and a far cry from the isolation China faced in the lead-up to the 1962 war or even the 1967 border crisis. Delhi probably knew this.

Ironically, the reasons for China's reluctance to escalate the crisis emanate from its strength and rising international profile. Outbreak of hostilities on the Himalayan border would taint

China's image and undermine the internationalism surrounding the BRI discourse. It would also fuel anti-Chinese sentiment in India, which both Washington and Tokyo would almost certainly profit from. Even on a sub-regional level, a conflict with India would steer China further towards an irredentist Pakistan as its sole partner, a suboptimal outcome for Beijing, which prefers a wider profile in the subcontinent.

From Delhi's vantage point, calculating India's relative position in 2017 was less straightforward. To be sure, policymakers had successfully navigated the uncertainty around Indo-US relations after the interlude of suspense since January 2017 when Trump assumed office. The bilateral relationship was soon stabilized. The summer 2017 Malabar exercises involving the Indian, Japanese and US navies in the Indian Ocean also offered psychological comfort to Delhi in the backdrop of the continental stand-off in the north. Some observers, however, exaggerated the geopolitical setting and imputed a wider dimension to Indo-US ties that might have faded since the Obama period.

Ultimately, both countries had much to lose in an armed clash and a new Cold War in the region. After a 72-day stand-off, at the end of August 2017, India and China simultaneously announced an understanding to pull their troops back from the face-off site in Doklam.

ALTHOUGH, AT THE outbreak of the Doklam crisis, both leaderships were already predisposed to perceiving the motives and actions of the other side through images of suspicion, hostility, and insecurity, they ultimately pulled back from the brink.

Ironically, the main reasons for a peaceful resolution to the stand-off had very little to do with the military balance on their frontiers. Although some observers have alluded to India's deterrent power as an important factor in China's calculus, India's actual military position on the frontiers remains asymmetric and presumes limited skirmishes or intense infantry combat as the probable warfighting scenario. Any deviation from that scenario – either as intensive vertical escalation in a single sector of the border or a wider horizontal escalation along the entire frontier – might bring Chinese geographical, logistical and technological advantages into play while simultaneously exposing India's vulnerabilities. So, it is unlikely that China's strategic restraint was primarily shaped by fear of reprisals or high direct repercussions of a military escalation.

It was the indirect costs and the positive facets of its interactions with India and South Asia that more likely shaped Chinese choices. Beijing was certainly conscious of US-India engagement during the preceding period. Another lesson from the crisis is that India and China discovered that they reside in a common neighbourhood, where other actors, albeit weaker and smaller, are also stakeholders in the region's affairs. In this case, it was Bhutan whose 'difficult position was on display during the crisis when it did not explicitly request Indian assistance and issued statements highlighting the bilateral nature of the dispute.'[9] But the basic dilemma of a common neighbour being caught in Sino-Indian crossfire could be a scenario extended across the subcontinent. And, it is in their common neighbourhood that both India and China have been projecting their developmental and geopolitical visions, a process that has also provided agency and options to the smaller actors. Consequently, Beijing and Delhi cannot ignore the consequences of a military conflict upsetting their regional policies and relationships. This remains relevant today.

Another reason that arguably arrested the path to conflict on the frontiers over Doklam in 2017 is the common order-building endeavours that have brought India and China together in recent years. Although non-Western multilateral institutions and networks – such as the Shanghai Cooperation Organisation (SCO) and BRICS (Brazil, Russia, India, China and South Africa) – have perennially been derided for years by commentators, they might have played a stronger influence in shaping China's calculus.

Unsatisfied with the Bretton Woods approach to development finance or the G7's stranglehold over the levers of global governance, China and India have discovered enduring reasons to promote new institutions that can make up the governance deficit with respect to the developing world, as well as create real bargaining leverage to persuade the West to reform its institutions and beliefs on the world order. Finally, bilateral economic interdependence, although still shallow and asymmetric, might have been sufficient to constrain more hardline postures from both sides. Indeed, the prospect of growing Chinese investment in India's infrastructure and manufacturing sectors has already expanded the stakeholders and policy influencers on both sides.

This is where the contrast with the 1962 crisis is sharp. In 1962, India and China had no real basis of cooperation or interdependence. The border dispute had been elevated as the sole feature of their relationship, and it was in that arena alone that both sides found themselves locked in an unconstrained zero-sum contest. In 2017, the depth of engagement and overlapping interests were enough for Beijing not only to assign value to its relationship with India, but also to worry about reputational costs in the subcontinent, an area where China seeks to gain prestige and influence.

5

A 'NEW NORMAL': LADAKH 2020 AND AFTER

The 2020 crisis in eastern Ladakh is the longest India-China stand-off in the post-Cold War era. The crisis also broke the four-decade record of stability and peace on the Himalayan frontier. It included a brutal skirmish on the night of June 15 that resulted in 20 Indian causalities and of an unknown number of PLA officers and soldiers. The crisis also included warning shots being fired by both sides in late August and early September in the Pangong Lake region on three separate occasions. At the peak of the crisis, nearly 100,000 troops from the Indian Army and PLA were mobilized and forward deployed in the western sector of the India-China border.

Peace and tranquility, however, has not suddenly disappeared but is part of a structural dynamic that has been taking shape over the past decade. Leaving the dispute unresolved has created unforeseen challenges in recent years.

WHEN WE CONSIDER the India-China border, the reader might get the impression that the entire stretch of the 3,488 km frontier is under stress. The 'disputed or sensitive' areas are actually fewer. These so-called grey zones are areas that overlap between the Indian perception of the LAC and the Chinese perception of the LAC. There are said to be about two-dozen such overlapping zones with potential friction points. During the India-China Joint Working Group meetings in the early 1990s, the Chinese had stated that the maintenance of peace and tranquility on the LAC did not automatically imply an agreement between Delhi and Beijing on the precise alignment of the LAC. Thus, ambiguity was inherent from the outset. What has changed is the capacity and intention to assert rights over these areas.

Over the past decade, there has been a shift in the way both sides approach the forward areas of the border. If we look back to the 1993 and 1996 CBMs that laid out a framework for a détente or 'peace and tranquility' on the border, a concept that stood out was both sides have a legitimate right to ensure the security of their frontiers. The asymmetry of the terrain and geography of the Tibetan plateau has endowed the Chinese with a more flexible option to border management, whereby the PLA does not need to develop extensive forward bases to maintain their control over the frontier. The quality and scale of interior lines of communications across Tibet enable Chinese forces to move back and forth, and, laterally across sectors. In contrast, India, which holds the lower ground, has been impelled to pursue new infrastructure closer to the LAC. In times of a crisis or even to maintain the symbolic showing of the flag, India could never reach up to its claim line in a reasonable time period until it had developed more efficient lines of communication.

In 2006, the Border Roads Organisation (BRO) was authorized to construct 61 roads of a total length of about 3,300 km along the border with China. After a slow start, where only 20 per cent of these projects had been completed by 2015, since 2018, 'the figure on finished roads had shot up to 2,486 km, with major gains in Jammu & Kashmir and Arunachal Pradesh.'[1] During this same period, India has increased its force levels for the border with China. 'In 2010, two new divisions were raised to strengthen deployment in Arunachal Pradesh, and additional formations were deployed in Ladakh. In 2013, the Indian government sanctioned the raising of a Mountain Strike Corps for the Northern border.'[2]

India, of course, has a legitimate right to improve its access to the forward areas. Where the problem has arisen is this narrowing asymmetry in logistical networks (although it is still very much in China's favour) has not led to an adjustment where both sides have been able to find common ground. The Chinese fear that this infrastructure spree is leading to further militarization of the frontier on both sides of the Himalayas. Ultimately, such a security dilemma dynamic will reduce security for both sides.

Forward Policies

In order to maintain their claims, both India and China engage in regular forward patrolling into the grey zones. 'Patrolling points (PPs) are designated spots on the LAC that are patrolled according to a pre-determined schedule by the security forces.'[3] The PPs – typically identified by 'prominent and identifiable geographical features, such as a pass, or a nala junction' or a numbered point with no prominent geographical feature – 'serve as a guide to the location of the LAC for the soldiers, acting as indicators of the extent of "actual control" exercised on the territory by India.' In India's case, these PPs were specified by the China Study Group[4] – a multi-agency forum of senior officials mandated to advise the government on China policy – in 1975 and subsequently reviewed in the 1990s.

As a consequence, the Indian Army has a defined politically-directed mandate on this subject. However, 'the frequency of patrolling to PPs is not specified by the CSG – it is finalized (in the annual patrolling programme) by the Army Headquarters in New Delhi, based on the recommendations made by the Army and ITBP (Indo Tibetan Border Police).'[5] According to a senior official, 'close observation of the LAC is ingrained in government procedure, and is done perhaps even more stringently than the Line of Control with Pakistan. The CSG is an integral part of that structure.'[6]

The instability has arisen from the growing ability of both militaries to undertake assertive patrolling postures. As both sides have improved their logistical networks and adopted forward policies, the two militaries are coming into more frequent contacts across sectors. If one compares the frequency of contact in the disputed pockets in the past decade, it is substantially more than in the late 1950s or even the 1980s. Since the late 2000's, after India's decision to expand its road and air connectivity, India's patrolling policy and assertion of presence has significantly improved. As India's former Special Representative notes, 'In almost all the contested areas, India's forces are more frequent visitors than the PLA.'[7] A former Army commander concurs, 'In many cases, the Chinese soldiers complained that they were being prevented from going up to areas that they had traditionally patrolled, but India was defending its perception of the LAC more robustly.'[8]

Yet, this growing capacity to pro-actively patrol was not intended to primarily advance security. Defence typically occurs in the rear, with both sides having in-depth capabilities and garrisons that are located some distance away from the front. So, the LAC transgressions always served a limited tactical purpose – to keep the dispute alive. Insofar as the most valuable pieces of territory are concerned, India and China are already in possession of that. China holds Aksai Chin, with the PLA's controls over that strategic area being robust. India holds Arunachal Pradesh, including Tawang. Thus, the areas that were historically central to the dispute are not really being challenged. But in a generally competitive context and one of mutual mistrust, the grey zones, those that lie near the highly valued real estate, have been the arena for intense jostling in recent years.

Most observers often forget that the parallel track of Special Representative (SR) talks and forward patrolling of the disputed sections of the border were part of a common and inter-linked dynamic that would eventually translate to more serious negotiations and an agreed framework that could then reconcile the precise concessions each side would make and where the boundary would eventually settle. But with that politically-led process more or less stalling since 2013, we have witnessed a tit-for-tat dynamic with each side scrambling for tactical advantages along the LAC.

The stakes have grown larger with each crisis since 2013. The 2017 Doklam stand-off led to aggressive posturing and even non-lethal contact like fisticuffs and minor injuries to soldiers from both sides. The 2020 Ladakh crisis escalated to lethal force (albeit without the actual use of firearms, ironically reflecting the resilience of the CBMs even in extreme face-offs, but nevertheless resulting in casualities on both sides). This is not a new normal that either leadership should be willing to accept. India and China are going to need more robust guidelines on how they exercise their forward policies, since the balance of power is very different from what it was during the 1990s.

More Robust CBMs

China still possesses significant advantages in terms of flatter terrain, superior infrastructure and advanced technology. This provides the PLA with flexibility and mobility that enables it to avoid a permanent forward presence on the LAC and yet maintain an efficient border management posture. India's geostrategic dilemma is the opposite: longer lines of communication over difficult terrain that shapes a very different border management posture requiring more regular forward deployments in the form of border outposts, often very near or at the LAC. This strategic effect of altitude and terrain have led to the adoption of different border management approaches for India and China:

> The difficulties of fighting at altitude – namely the long lead-time to move from garrison to the putative battlefield give both sides an incentive to make expensive preparations necessary to arrive quickly at the site of a dispute. India forward deploys much larger forces than China; locally garrisoned Indian soldiers outnumber the PLA both in the Sikkim and Ladakh sectors but as India has the 'downhill side' of the border in all sectors, the nearby units are often stationed at low altitudes. China, conversely, has far fewer soldiers permanently based near the disputed border sectors and has instead focused on developing expensive infrastructure to speed arrival of reinforcements, enabling smaller forces at the border to initiate and respond very quickly in a nascent dispute.[9]

CBMs need to reflect this asymmetrical reality for them to be effective and perceived to be fair. The 1993 agreement explicitly refers to the idea of 'mutual and equal security' rather than a parity approach. But this concept has never been discussed or explored in detail or implemented by both sides.[10] Nevertheless, given the trend of forward policing there is now a parallel imperative to devise more sophisticated conflict management channels to avoid escalation and faster resolutions to future LAC face-offs.

Historically, more responsive border management frameworks have emerged after major crises on the frontier. For example, after the assertive response by the Indian Army during the Sumdorong Chu Valley standoff in 1986, it 'sparked realisation on both sides that the boundary issue needed to be brought to the fore, and pending a settlement, some mechanism must be evolved to keep peace along the LAC.'[11] The 2020 Ladakh crisis should evoke a similar reaction from Delhi and Beijing. During their meeting to de-escalate the crisis, the foreign ministers from both sides 'agreed that as the situation eases, the two sides should expedite work to conclude new CBMs to maintain and enhance peace and tranquility in the border areas.'[12]

A Fraught Peace?

For the past decade, both sides have adopted forward policies matched by new connectivity links to the frontier. A belief that an array of CBMs would cushion this changing balance of power in the forward areas has been misplaced. It is clear that the next phase of the relationship depends on a peaceful frontier. But this should not mean merely a restoration of the status quo ante. If, by status quo, we mean two nuclear-armed neighbours with large conventional forces resuming their aggressive jostling and humiliating each other, that is unsustainable. To anyone who has viewed leaked videos of the border face-offs in recent years, the LAC grey zones have been transformed into a tinder box waiting to explode.

It is time now for stock-taking and re-envisioning a new conflict-management framework. There were two main reasons to engage in proactive probing in the grey zones – as a symbolic ritual of showing the flag to demonstrate consistency over claim lines, and, keeping an eye on each other so that nobody changes the status quo on the ground. Given the high altitude and mountainous terrain along the LAC in eastern Ladakh, it is not possible to man each forward post throughout the year, unlike the eastern sector where both sides maintain robust defensive control over their territories. Hence, any sustainable LAC border management system is predicated on a measure of India–China cooperation, based on precedence and predictable patterns of patrolling. Whenever this tacit understanding breaks down or one side perceives a change in patrolling intensity and unfavourable logistical developments, threat perceptions get heightened leading to stand-offs. This cycle has been playing out since 2013. This is also the main reason 'why tensions tend to flare up in the western sector much more frequently than in the eastern sector in recent years – there is more room for imagination, advancement, and alterations.'[13]

Now, this is where the complementary political element – the main conflict resolution channel – has abdicated its role. High-level talks between the SR's was intended to keep an eye on the bigger picture of a grand bargain and to lay out a framework within which each side would bring forward their claims for serious bargaining to commence. But with that political process stalling in recent years, tactical forward probing along the LAC has assumed a life of its own, disproportionate to the envisaged goals. Put another way, tactical initiatives and situations assumed a strategic life of its own, precipitating real threat perceptions on both sides.

Until a meaningful political-level track is revived, both sides will feel emboldened in future stand-offs as they keep acquiring the infrastructure and military heft to back it up. Leaving border management at the military level is not conducive to peace and tranquility. Military institutions are inclined to pursue security – their core mission is to hold territory – and not engage in diplomacy or conflict resolution. As a former army commander reflects, 'Only minor issues can be resolved by local military commanders, like behaviour of patrols and conduct of banner drills. When it develops into a major issue, resolution can only happen at the diplomatic level. We saw that at Demchok in 2013 and at Doklam in 2017'.[14]

Why can't both sides clarify the LAC? China has been reluctant to define the LAC for two reasons. First, it believes Indian incentives to pursue a final settlement would be reduced. From the experience of the early 2000's when maps pertaining to the middle sector were exchanged and were examined for the western sector, the process of defining the LAC incentivized both sides to exaggerate their claims of where the LAC lay, in effect negating the purpose of the exercise and converting it into a bargaining process for a boundary settlement. The clarification exercise is useful if it leads to a precise understanding of the disputed areas and followed by agreed mechanisms and norms to manage those grey zones. As a Chinese scholar remarked during a Track-2 dialogue few years ago, 'we are concerned about fixed lines as it would restrict the subsequent process of negotiations.' Second, a clarification of the LAC means the frontier becomes more stable and unambiguous without any geopolitical benefits or assurances from India on its future relationship with China.

For Beijing, there is little incentive to offer such a concession to India. In this respect, Tibet also plays a role in China's calculus and it is unlikely to make concessions on the question of defining the LAC until India's perceived involvement in the Tibet issue is resolved.

The empirical record of forward probing by China suggests an interesting pattern of activity, where the western sector has seen the most intense level of attention from China. Since 2015, nearly 75 per cent of the transgressions have taken place in the western sector of the LAC. The eastern sector (Arunachal Pradesh and Sikkim), in contrast, witnessed about 20 per cent of Chinese transgressions.[15] If we recall from the 1950s, the surrounding areas around Aksai Chin have always been viewed as highly strategic from Beijing's point of view, enough to even precipitate a war in 1962. When set against that historical backdrop, the Aksai Chin area remains a valued piece of real estate for China, and, the PLA's resolve to maintain its security in the western sector of the India-China border is higher than other sectors. This is because Aksai Chin 'offers the only direct road connection (National Highway G219) between China's Xinjiang Uyghur Autonomous Region and the Tibet Autonomous Region. In the event of major unrest in either area, which is home to millions of ethnic minorities, China will have to rely on G219 for access. Losing Aksai Chin, in other words, would jeopardize the stability of China's entire western frontier.'[16]

Today, the main territorial differences (the differences in LACs) in eastern Ladakh is the zone between China's November 1959 LAC and India's September 1962 pre-war LAC. Soon after the skirmishes with India in August and October 1959, Mao Zedong had ordered the PLA to cease patrolling in the forward zone within 20 km of China's LAC. Adopting a new forward policy in November 1961, India pushed eastwards into those vacated areas in eastern Ladakh, and by September 1962, had created its new LAC in the western sector. By virtue of its victory in October and November 1962, China re-established control over its (1959) LAC after the war with India. Subsequently, and as part of the ceasefire process after 1962, China again pulled back and did not permanently administer or patrol many parts west and southwest of Aksai Chin for decades.

The 2020 Ladakh crisis is a belated reassertion of China's original claims over that area, perhaps explaining the intensity and duration of the crisis. It is unclear what prompted China to react the way it did. It is possible that the Chinese have temporarily frozen the situation to negotiate a new normal, and, if unsuccessful in that goal, then establish a new status quo based on the 1959 claim line. Given the intensity of patrolling in recent years combined with a heightened threat perception on Aksai Chin in the post-Article 370 phase (after its revocation in August 2019), Beijing might have felt the need to dramatically make its claims felt as well as probe if India was really serious about recovering Aksai Chin.

Why can't Prime Minister Narendra Modi and President Xi Jinping settle the dispute? We still do not have a clear answer to this. After all, as the previous chapters have discussed, both sides hold most of their strategic real estate. The problem lies at the geopolitical level, which has also been analysed in previous chapters. Neither side is willing to make concessions to stabilize the relationship – a border settlement being a major and irreversible concession. However, stabilizing the frontier through new norms is possible and in the interests of both India and China. Creative approaches such as agreed buffer zones in the most contentious pockets and coordinated or restricted patrolling regimes to avoid violent scuffles should be integral to the new status quo. In 'the eastern sector, Indian and Chinese troops patrol contentious areas by weekly rotation, a formula that could be brought into play in eastern Ladakh as well.'[17] As the five-point understanding between the Indian and Chinese foreign ministers in September 2020 indicates, both sides have agreed to establish new CBMs once the crisis in eastern Ladakh is defused.

In their excitement or jingoism, many have declared a breaking point in India-China relations. This is precisely the time to avoid such hyperbole. The relationship has not suddenly gone south. The warning signs have been apparent for some time. It has been falsely claimed that Delhi has been oblivious to China's rise. In fact, Modi's China policy has been uncompromising across the board. From the BRI to maritime security to emerging high technologies such as 5G, Delhi has been bold in its rhetoric and actions. Even in the geopolitical arena, India has been unabashed and dogged in engaging the US, despite an unenthused president in the White House. Across Asia too, Delhi has been proactively tapping China's neighbours as a future countervailing hedge. With traditional ally Russia too, Modi's renewed outreach in recent years is reminiscent of the old geostrategy – promoting a balance of power in Eurasia.

If anything, India's policymakers could be critiqued for getting ahead of themselves and precipitating counter-balancing moves from China without having a credible strategy in place. But Delhi's real failure has been to not match its realpolitik words and deeds with a broader foreign policy framework where sustained engagement with China was also part of a grand strategy to emerge as a 'leading power' in a multipolar world. Instead, Delhi has found itself leaning against China with an empty treasury and unpredictable partners.

History shows that when India possessed strong and positive ties with the great powers, it was taken seriously by China. Yet, history also shows the clear limits of what leveraging that balance of power can do for India. The India-US and India-Soviet (Russia) ties worked to stabilize the India-China relationship when India remained firmly grounded in recognizing and pursuing its own interests rather than becoming an object in a great game. So only when two conditions simultaneously held was India able to shape a mutually beneficial relationship with China – shrewdly leveraging the international environment and maintaining a sophisticated China policy.

If history provides us with one lesson it is that the border issue is intrinsically interlinked with the broader geopolitics of the India-China relationship. As India's policymakers seek to cool down the heating frontier, they need to also pay attention to stabilizing the overall relationship, a theme that is covered in Section III.

II

GEOPOLITICS AND WORLD ORDER

This section will go beyond the border dispute to discuss the broader geopolitical context that shapes the India–China relationship. The question of a changing world order, the rocky transition towards a multipolar word, the competition between US and China, the resurgence of Eurasia, China's quest to establish its own network of power and influence in Eurasia and Asia, and the pursuit of non-western approaches to global governance. It is important for the reader to get a pulse of these broader themes since India's China policy will continue to evolve in a changing and turbulent international environment. Keeping an eye on world order questions is, thus, crucial for crafting sound policy as well as engaging in sophisticated debates on India–China relations.

1

WORLD ORDER WITHOUT HEGEMONY

Most Western thinkers presume that a titantic clash will occur during a power transition. But what if rising powers cannot assume the burden of underwriting the world order? We must contemplate alternate futures where a changing balance of power does not necessarily yield a new hegemony or a breakdown in the basic tenets of international order.[1]

At the heart of foreign policy debates today is the question of a changing balance of power. As Chinese President Xi Jinping pointed out recently, 'The changes we are encountering in the world are unseen in a century.'[2] In an important speech delivered in June 2018, the Indian prime minister too had alluded to global power shifts, uncertainty, and geopolitical competition. 'This world is at a crossroad. There are temptations of the worst lessons of history.'[3] How do we make sense of these power transitions? Is change possible without a violent confrontation?

Evoking a metaphor from the legendary Thucydides, it has been argued that in 12 of 16 cases from the past five centuries in which a rising power has confronted the dominant power, the result has been a violent struggle. The so-called 'Thucydides Trap' does appear to be a recurring pattern over a long span of history.[4] The sources or processes that bring about the power shifts are also a recurring historical phenomenon. The late Robert Gilpin illustrated this cycle with much insight: uneven growth rates and technological diffusion shifts power from the centre to the periphery of the system. Over time, this results in a disequilibrium between the burden of maintaining the existing world order and the material capacity available to the dominant power to supply public goods and enforce that order. 'From the perspective of rising powers, the perceived costs of changing the international system have declined relative to the potential benefits of doing so'.[5] The only way to resolve this disequilibrium is through some form of accommodation between the dominant and rising powers, or the functioning of the system itself will be imperilled. For most of history this bargaining process has ensued in a great struggle, often violent and nearly always contentious. The baton then passes to a new contender who resuscitates the overall structure and takes the onus of managing order and the global economy.[6]

The most famous instances of a peaceful power transition are actually quite extraordinary. The shift from British to American leadership, an uncontested passing of the baton between two culturally similar powers, and, the dramatic end of the Cold War in 1989 when the Soviet Union unilaterally decided to call a truce and end the ideological confrontation with the US. It then quickly obliged its rival by disappearing from the scene altogether. These instances of a peaceful power transition are very unusual. Will it be different this time around?

To begin with, we must immediately recognize that a structural feature from the first Cold War still persists. The largely stabilizing results of the nuclear revolution are firmly in place and make any notion of a violent assault on the existing order such as the one waged by Germany and Japan during the Second World War unthinkable. The status quo is resilient in that it cannot be militarily altered in a large-scale fashion. But strategic stability does not preclude competition or even limited conflicts. The Cold War witnessed several armed, if proxy, confrontations that were waged relentlessly despite the presence of nuclear weaponry as a restraining factor for large-scale war. Over the past decade, we have seen instances across Eurasia of rising powers defying the authority of the declining hegemon through limited military interventions or decisive strategic moves to alter the balance of power in several regions.

Mutual Accommodation

The renowned Edward Hallett Carr, during the 20 years' crisis leading up to Second World War, had laid out two necessary conditions for a peaceful power transition. First, the contending powers must possess the material leverage to bring pressures to bear on the dominant states for otherwise the latter would have few incentives to accept changes to the status quo. Second, the dominant states who draw the most benefits from the status quo have a moral obligation to make concessions so a successful and reasonable compromise can be reached.[7] More recently, theorists have added to Carr's appeal for 'a spirit of give and take' by suggesting that rising powers too have a moral responsibility to craft an accommodation because the power transition could otherwise 'generate so much insecurity that the threat of war comes not from the challenger or challengers, but from the dominant but declining power'.[8] Given the enormous stakes, 'both hegemon and aspirant must draw on some common stock of ideas in order to intentionally develop meaningful practices of accommodation'.[9] Thus, as Carr argued, 'peaceful change can only be achieved by a compromise between the utopian conception of a common feeling of right and the realist conception of a mechanical adjustment to a changed equilibrium of forces'.[10]

There would be contrasting opinions on whether these conditions apply to the contemporary setting. Given the mismatch between perceptions of relative strength between the US and its rivals as well as the absence of any constructive or far-sighted discourse in the West to channel its international policies towards reforming the world order other than merely a parochial quest to preserve its material privileges and unsustainable geopolitical commitments, the path to a peaceful accommodation does seem a bleak one.

Asia's rising powers, however, differ in several ways from their Western predecessors, making any extrapolation from European geopolitical history an untenable proposition. One key difference in the ongoing power transition, compared to previous eras, is the civilizational and cultural attributes that the new contenders exhibit in their basic international identities and behaviour. Asia's rising powers are more internally oriented, and their traumatic colonial or semi-colonial encounters have instilled a conception of sovereignty and an image of world order that is not in consonance with the roles played by traditional great powers of the Eurocentric mould.

Moreover, it is still unclear what distinct values and ideas the rising powers bring to bear on world order. If we dispassionately look at Chinese, Indian, and other discourses on globalization and world order we do not notice a revisionism – certainly not akin to a Germany or Japan from a century ago – nor a revolutionary spirit like that exhibited by Napoleonic France or by Mao's China during its radical phases, but rather a pragmatic and a largely rational outlook. One could even argue that the rising powers are changing their foreign policies and global roles more from reluctance and circumspection and in response to safeguarding their material interests that developed during the period of US preponderance. And, while there may well be a degree of exceptionalism and manifest destiny in elements of the strategic communities of rising powers, it does not even remotely resemble the proselytizing and ambitious geopolitical cultures of the Western powers during their rise.

Another key reason for rising powers' caution and restraint is that the domestic burdens of managing order in these continental-sized states are too vast to seriously entertain an aggressive or overly-ambitious geostrategy. The rising powers will be strong enough – or have already acquired that capacity – to veto key issues of global governance but they are not powerful enough and internally coherent enough to intellectually and materially assume the role of upholding the world order. So far, China's manifest destiny is about rejuvenating itself rather than any grand vision of remaking the world. There is a stark difference – between Western powers that typically possessed ideological and cultural motivations that underpinned ambitious internationalism and the very real and constraining effects that Asia and Eurasia's rising powers confront and will continue to do so during the power transition. It complicates the application of the theory of hegemonic stability that is premised on the expectation of a near total transfer of global responsibility from the declining hegemon to the rising power and the zero-sum struggle that ensues during this process.

Finally, we must address the question of legitimacy, that is, whether and to what extent the fundamental dimensions of the existing world order are seen as legitimate by the rising powers.

If they largely are on issues such as an open world economy and a rules-based multilateral trading system, respect for the commons, for norms on sovereignty and territorial integrity, on nuclear deterrence then the conundrum of a power transition is essentially one of mutual accommodation on the big table of global governance rather than one of radically revising the basic framework that underpins world order.

Recently, China's leading international relations scholar Yan Xuetong reflected on this fact. While declaring that 'the post-Cold War interregnum of US hegemony is over,' Yan admitted that, 'Beijing has no clear plan for filling (the) leadership vacuum and shaping new international norms from the ground up'.[11] He insists that 'China's ambitions for the coming years are much narrower' than assumed in Western security establishments, and that Beijing is 'in no hurry to become the sole object of Washington's apprehension and scorn, would much rather see a multipolar world in which other challenges – and challengers – force the United States to cooperate with China'.[12] In his year-end speech, Wang Yi, China's State Councillor and Foreign Minister, described a new era of competition restrained by interdependence:

> China and the United States do have some disagreements, which is only natural. And the existing problems between the two countries cannot be resolved overnight. However, their interwoven ties and intertwined interests also determine that China and the United States cannot be decoupled or completely isolated from each other.[13]

Rejecting Another Cold War

In this scenario, what could be said about India's predicament? A key assumption for India's strategic thinking in the post-

Cold War period has been the adjustment to the reality of one power centre that shaped political and economic life across the globe. This unbalanced structural setting – unipolarity as it was described by many – led to a policy of a sustained, albeit gradual at each step, integration into the US-led order and a transformation in bilateral relations with the US and its allies. It was a bipartisan effort and, for the most part, it could be claimed that Indian policymakers accomplished this process within the amorphous confines of strategic autonomy with some success.

But, given the diffusion of global power and disintegration of the unipolar consensus, should India reimagine its role and place in this changing world? There are some who argue that strategic autonomy is no longer viable in an age of complex interdependence further complicated by a resumption of great power competition, and that India must choose a side.

It is fascinating that Indian thinking, as reflected in joint statements or communiqués with the competing great powers, demonstrates a clear intention to uphold aspects of the international order that are in sync with India's interests. So, with the US, Delhi proclaims a commitment to an open and free order, with a particular focus on the integrity of the maritime commons. With Russia, it is committed to legitimizing multipolarity and inclusive security architectures as well as endorsing UN-centred norms on sovereignty. With China, India shares a common interest in a liberal economic order as well as constructing new development financial institutions responsive to the needs of the Global South. At the Wuhan talks, both agreed to build 'an open, multipolar, pluralist, and participatory global economic order'.[14] So it is not accurate at all when observers mock India for being all things to all powers, and argue that this balancing act is an exercise in delusion. Rather, India's multi-directional foreign policies should be seen as a reflection of the diffusion of global power and the fact that different great powers' interests, visions, and goals coincide with India's in different domains of power or issues, with each issue significant for India's domestic transformation or geopolitical security.

India's outlook to the power transition has, so far, been sensible:

> Asia of rivalry will hold us all back. Asia of cooperation will shape this century. So, each nation must ask itself: Are its choices building a more united world, or forcing new divisions? It is a responsibility that both existing and rising powers have. Competition is normal. But, contests must not turn into conflict.[15]

As a potential swing power, India must continue to reject a Cold War philosophy and play a responsible role in promoting and shaping a post-hegemonic world order. Power transitions in history have nearly always been disruptive. The ongoing phase is likely to be no exception. India's predicament is dealing with China's rise and ensuring it does not recreate a new hegemony in Asia, while also navigating the old and unsustainable world order towards new and more balanced horizons. This is a task for statesmen.

2

END OF THE LIBERAL WORLD ORDER?

Over the past four years there has been an animated debate in the US over the meaning of world order and its role in it. This struggle for ideas has not left other countries unscathed. In India, the response to these American contestations has been a mix of astonishment and fear, and policymakers and analysts appear to be clasping at binaries rather than unpacking the forces at play. Yet, when the dominant power is struggling to establish a legitimate consensus on the nature of its relationship with the rest of the world and, indeed, on how world politics itself should be regulated, there are no easy binaries to make sense of and resolve the contradictions of this phase of history. Any re-orientation of America's role in the world impacts India-China relations and alters the efficacy of different policy options and strategies. Thus, keeping an eye on US domestic politics and the spillover of its ideological fissures to the rest of the world will serve India well.[1]

The debate revolves around competing claims to some fundamental questions. What were the central motivations and concerns that drove American policymakers to envisage and design a liberal order after 1945? Does this 'liberal order' benefit the US and the rest of the world, or is there nostalgia for a world that never actually extended beyond a very small portion of the planet? And, is this order sustainable, that is, does the US possess the material capacity to uphold its traditional responsibilities and continue to supply public goods and open institutions?

Clashing Worldviews

The opposing camps on the emerging global order have been portrayed in several ways. No typology is devoid of value judgment, and yet each conveys some facet of the US's divide. We have the 'far right versus neoliberals' as a way to capture the contours of the political competition. 'Nationalists versus globalists' is another view being discussed. Joseph Nye, a proponent of the neoliberal camp, prefers the expression, 'populism vs globalization.' Since much of the debate is waged through rhetorical strategies aimed at de-legitimizing the opposing worldview, the underlying beliefs and conceptions of order are what should be most pertinent for unpacking this debate. One fascinating aspect is how each side seeks to advance their preferred image of the international system as a means to also advance their domestic agenda. The international and domestic have become entwined in their worldviews.

The nationalists fear a decaying industrial economy and an influx of immigrants as not merely an economic travesty, but a cultural assault on the US. They believe that persisting with the traditional course of US foreign policy will wither the US's economic and cultural foundations and heighten faultlines that have been latent for the past few decades when US material preponderance was undisputed. It would also overstretch American power and resources, producing an inevitable revolt at home. The advocates for the liberal international order, on the other hand, seem confident of the US's power capacities which, after some tactical adjustments, are seen as adequate to sustain an ambitious interventionist role. The globalists point out that the trends of interdependence are irreversible and the US must adapt to the new geoeconomic age of open borders and free trade rather than erect new walls. They also raise the spectre of chaos and catastrophes that would follow a world where the US was not directing the course of history. The globalists are also unperturbed by domestic stability arguments or that the US must preserve a distinct cultural and economic life at home. Indeed, they seek to radically change the US from within in order to maintain their vision of global primacy, shifting the old argument – that America's internationalism was intended to preserve its values at home – on its head.

So, we have two rival, almost irreconcilable, conceptions of order that pervade US domestic politics and the foreign policy discourse. When it comes to a 'buy-in' of their ideas, the nationalists from the right and, more recently, the progressive left, have been more on the money. And, this is for the most basic reasons of livelihood and identity. An overwhelming majority of Americans have been alienated in the otherwise dynamic age of globalization, and a distorted political system has utterly failed to salvage this structural decline of the middle class in the US.[2] The neoliberals have struggled to advance their global governance and trade ideas because they are, in many instances, the source of the problem. As a result, even more latent divides in the US – questions of race, identity and culture – have surfaced and increased the prospect of civil strife.

Historical Myths

The disdain by the Donald Trump administration for upholding long-cherished foreign policy ideas has led some observers 'to double down on historical myths'.[3] American foreign policy, it is asserted, found its groove during a 'golden age' of the 1940s when the ascendance of liberalism (and its final 'triumph' in 1989) drove US policymakers to remake the world. But, as Graham Allison pithily retorts, 'Had there been no Soviet threat, there would have been no Marshall Plan and no NATO.' It was the fear of an ideological counterpoise offered by the Soviet Union that drove American elites to envision and construct attractive institutions and offer non-reciprocal advantages to the shattered industrial centres of Western Europe and North East Asia that had become the arena for the ideological competition gravely threatening capitalism and Western security. Or, as Allan Bloom notes, it was 'Cold War sobriety' that disciplined Western states to raise their game and confront rival ideas in a way that would never have ensued if geopolitical rivalry had not prevailed. And, the prolonged great-power peace was a consequence of a balance of power between the superpowers, who not only held each other in check, but ensured their bloc followers eschewed the pursuit of narrow calculations of national interest in favour of a robust and interdependent economic and security community.

Nevertheless, a deeper liberal strand in Western strategic thinking was never absent and searching for its normative roots would aid our understanding of how we have reached the present impasse of the questions about the US capabilities in the current global scenario. Quinn Slobodian's fine intellectual history of neo-liberalism uncovers the central tenets of the rules-based world order. Neoliberal globalism sought to produce a 'doubled world' of sovereign states with limited autonomy and a supranational edifice of institutions and rules to govern the global economy and resuscitate the traditional interdependence that had prevailed before the devastating shocks of First World War, the economic crisis of the 1930s, and Second World War. At the heart of this project was a quest to insulate the world economy from 'mass demands for social justice and redistributive equality.' Neoliberals 'did not see capitalism and democracy as mutually reinforcing,' but viewed 'democracy as a problem', a threat that ranged 'from the white working class to the non-European decolonizing world'.[4] In short, neoliberal globalism was always about containing politics and populism at home and traditional geopolitics abroad.

Order for Whom?

In its utopian image, the liberal world order is one where the US supplies public goods in the form of norms, institutions, and military security to absorb the costs and undertake responsibilities so other states can benefit from such an open and predictable order. 'What proponents of the liberal international rules-based order really mean is an order that embodies good rules, ones that are equal or fair' and that others 'willingly embrace and sustain.' Legitimacy and the buy-in of the system by non-Western states, and the developing world more generally, is then central to the functioning of the order since it is not an empire and, therefore, cannot rest solely on coercion. Although it sounds altruistic, the order is envisaged to secure US hegemony and enable American capital and technology to access remote corners of the globe in a fashion that does not invite a revolt against the basic system by a return to either a 19th-century-style regionalized balance-of-power system or the Cold War spheres-of-influence order enshrined in the 1945 Yalta agreements.

But, 'Well before Trump, US foreign policy had to navigate between rival critiques, from Americans insisting that the international order was a hopelessly idealistic project with little in it for them and foreign critics who saw it as a euphemism for American hegemony.'[5] Over the past two decades, 'the political class that brought unending, unsuccessful wars in Afghanistan, Iraq, and Libya, as well as the financial crisis and Great Recession, had discredited itself'.[6] It would follow that Trump is a symptom rather than the cause of this disorder. Today, neoliberal globalists have an uphill task in taming US nationalism and the rising claims to economic security by Western societies, and a changing global balance of power where uncritical acceptance of neoliberal norms is at an all-time low. In short, it is a resistance on multiple fronts. Yet, '[d]espite his threats to overturn the old order, the power of the foreign policy establishment and its habitual ideas have steered Trump to quickly conform to the fundamentals of traditional US grand strategy'.[7]

The proponents of the status quo believe that 'were Washington to recommit to its previous foreign policy vision, the world would fall in line'.[8] This appears unlikely and the more sober critics are urging American elites to re-design the system and accommodate great-power rivals before it is too late. Further, 'The elements of the order that should be rebuilt need to be advocated for on their own terms.'[9] Ironically, it is the rising powers that have made some attempts at renovating the tattered order. For some time now, they have been insuring against a sudden reversal of their fortunes that to a large extent were brought about by engagement with an open economic order. BRICS is one manifestation of this trend, not to depose the old order but to re-imagine and reform it in ways that make the entire system more durable and equitable for the non-Western world. Other multilateral initiatives such as the China-initiated

Asia Infrastructure Investment Bank, which drew inspiration from BRICS and other developing world agendas, are also aimed at order-building in the face of a crisis in mainstream conceptions of globalization. In short, when India, China and others speak of upholding an open international order, they do so from a different prism, different identities and interests than the West, and yet no non-Western power seeks to topple the system altogether.

Since the advent of Trump, India's strategic discourse has lacked the subtlety to respond to the eroding bases of the neoliberal order and imagine alternative futures. To espouse that world order as the last word on global governance reflects a 'failure to comprehend the character of the post-war order, and the roles of race, empire and periphery war in it'.[10] For the past seven decades, the liberal world order has 'rested on the imperial prerogatives of a superpower that attempted to impose order by stepping outside rules and accommodating illiberal forces'.[11] And, beyond the 'north Atlantic core,' where this order flourished, the legacy has been 'far more complex and shallower' and evokes 'cynicism and suspicion' rather than the euphoria of being liberated by an enlightened force.[12] Finally, it fails to appreciate that the 'militant globalism' underlying neoliberal thought, and which purports to advance a seemingly noble endeavour of an interdependent world economy, is only made possible by disempowering politics and people, that is, containing true democracy and liberty itself. It should suffice to say that whatever intellectual framework follows the liberal international order, India's identity and interests would be most secure, to borrow John F. Kennedy's words, in a multipolar world made 'safe for diversity.'

For India, the transition from a neoliberal world order is an opportunity and a challenge. It is an opportunity because neoliberal internationalism was always inclined to tame state power and counteract the ability to develop national power and more balanced development. It is a challenge because the relatively more competitive world order framework that is likely to replace neoliberalism will impose pressures on the India-China relationship and constrain India's ability to draw benefits from the international environment.

3

US-CHINA: FROM CHIMERICA TO COLD WAR 2.0?

In July 1971, Richard Nixon instructed Henry Kissinger to undertake a secret mission to China via Pakistan. It immediately altered Asian politics and the course of the Cold War. The Sino-American rapprochement was as much a recognition of the limits of US power after the debacle in Vietnam, as it was a reflection of a divided Eurasia and collapse of the Sino-Soviet alliance. By the early 2010s, that chapter had closed and an evolving framework has yet to fully replace it. This chapter provides an insight into the shift towards acrimony and competition in the US China relationship. It also discusses why US-China ties might evolve differently and not resemble the typical expectation for two superpowers poised to collide. For India's policymakers, it is important that they get their forecasts right because strategic misjudgments on this complex relationship can be costly in the medium term.

Clashing Identities and Interests

It was the image of a common Soviet foe that brought America and China closer. That shared threat has not existed for nearly three decades. In fact, each is now deemed as the leading long-term challenge for the other. Not only are Washington and Beijing now defining their interests in competing terms in East Asia, their self-images and roles are making the process difficult to manage.

Let us first look at their interests. For Beijing, the direction of core geopolitical challenges is primarily from maritime Asia. Decades of smart diplomacy, periphery management, and importantly a gradual but sustained transformation in Sino-Russian relations have provided Beijing with tranquility and strategic depth on its inner-Asian frontiers not witnessed for centuries. Most of the perceived threats now emanate from the Pacific.

Japan's emerging identity as a normal state willing to adorn a military role in close concert with the US is the dominant challenge for Chinese geostrategists. China is gradually developing the capacity to increase its strategic space and claim greater influence on its maritime frontiers, which have been dominated by the US Navy since 1945. For America, its strategic interests are well established. It wants nothing to change. Washington seeks to preserve its forward-presence across the Western Pacific, access that enables it to influence Asian security and keep the political economy of the vast productive region linked with American capital and industry. In sum, America's idea of a status quo is being contested by China, which seeks a revision of how the East Asian order should be regulated.

While competing interests are manageable, when situated in the context of incompatible roles the bilateral dynamic becomes adversarial. The main reason why US and China did not have to confront dissonance for decades was because the China of Deng Xiaoping had accepted US global leadership primarily to buttress Beijing's domestic modernization. Deng was content with China's identity as a supporting actor in a world produced and directed by America. Even Deng's successors were remarkably restrained and offered no meaningful resistance to the renewed militarization of US global power after 2001.

This outlook changed dramatically in the 2010s as China's leaders sought a role more commensurate with its relative capacity and self-image. Ever since, China's great power identity has clashed with America's superpower identity. As Sinologist David Lampton remarked, in recent years 'an almost imperceptible tipping point nearly has been reached with respect to US assessments of China's internal and external policy direction.'[1]

Beijing's concept of 'a New Type of Major Power Relationship', first enunciated by Xi Jinping in February 2012, is essentially an attempt to persuade Washington to accept this new China. However, Washington is unlikely to voluntarily accommodate China's growing aspirations in Asian and global high politics.

US's domestic discourse is allergic to any re-orientation of an American role that eschews primacy and makes space for a rising power. Thus, any restructuring of the terms of engagement can only result from China's actual abilities to impose costs on vital American interests. And both in the economic and military realm, particularly in the Western Pacific, China's capabilities to impose limited or reciprocal costs on the US have been increasing over the past decade.

While the golden age of Sino-American cooperation has passed, it is premature to forecast unrestrained Sino-American competition.

For one, Chinese policymakers are still acutely aware of the fate of previous historical episodes of rising powers like Germany and Japan that recklessly challenged existing orders a century ago and self-destructed. Beijing still finds advantages from the open economic system that the West has sustained for decades. We will return to this theme below.

After three decades of industrialization, China's geoeconomic hand is now stronger despite the formidable internal restructuring challenges that lie ahead. Given China's economic base, interdependence is no longer a one-way street of asymmetry in favour of the West or Japan. Chinese policymakers will probably weigh their geopolitical moves against the potential cost of diminished access to Western markets, commercial technology and advantageous participation in transnational manufacturing supply chains. Recent trade statistics from East Asia tell us the trend. China is already emerging as a pillar of the Asian political economy. In 2019, ASEAN overtook the US to emerge as China's second largest trading partner with $644 billion in two-way commerce. During the first few months of 2020, ASEAN overtook the EU to become the largest trader with China. In the first seven months of 2020, China-ASEAN trade touched $362 billion. Having diversfied its external trade and expanded in regional footprint, China has less of an interest in making unilateral concessions to the US on trade and investment.

At the same time, as leading Chinese scholar Wang Jisi writes, 'In the foreseeable future, it is unrealistic to expect economic and trade cooperation to become the anchor and propeller of bilateral relations. However, a complete (US-China) decoupling of bilateral economic relations and technical cooperation is not in the interest of any party. The key strategic question lies in what areas and to what extent can and must economic and trade cooperation be maintained?'[2] The Chinese are prepared for a restructuring in the massive US-China economic relationship. It is quite possible that after the 2020 election cycle plays itself out in the US, a new administration with or without Trump at the helm will resume the hard bargaining with China. With nearly $700 billion in bilateral trade and a massive underlying two-way investment base supporting interdependent production value chains, both Beijing and Washington recognize the costs of recklessly disentangling their economies.[3] The Trump administration's economic offensive has 'cost the US economy nearly 300,000 jobs' with US companies losing '$1.7 trillion in the price of their stocks as a result of US tariffs imposed on imports from China.'[4] The US corporate sector is far more cautious. The most recent surveys conducted by the American Chamber of Commerce in China found that most companies remain concious of the cost and do not want to lose access to the Chinese market. Only about 4 pecent of companies might diversify or reshore their operations back to the US. But 70 per cent of the respondents 'had no plans to relocate any manufacturing out of China despite higher (US) tariffs'.[5]

The US too is not interested in a frontal collision with China whose opening with the West and Asia is now too deep to roll back. Ironically, despite the heightened image of discord, US and China do not actually have a direct dispute other than America's strategic commitments to allied states (that is, Taiwan, Japan, Philippines) that have bilateral disputes with China. In the normal course, neither Beijing nor Washington would risk seriously destabilizing these triangles to gain a costly advantage over each other.

Further, American policymakers, certainly those with a sense of history and strategy, are now sensitive to the US-Russia-China triangle and its evolving dynamics that could potentially complicate America's forward deployments and dilute US political alliances in East Asia and even elsewhere. US policy choices and military postures are directly shaping the nature of the Sino-Russian equation as part of a classic balance of power process. The prospect of Eurasia's geopolitical consolidation might restrain an overreaction by American strategists as they learn to devise more sophisticated means to shape China's choices and behaviour on its Pacific front.

Will US and China Wage Cold War 2.0?

In the summer of 2020, China's Foreign Minister Wang Yi declared that 'some political forces in the US' are pushing US and China 'to the brink of a new Cold War.' More recently, US National Security Advisor Robert C. O'Brien has called for the US and its allies to 'resist the Chinese Communist Party's efforts to manipulate our people and our governments, damage our economies, and undermine our sovereignty.'[6] Many observers have concluded that Washington and Beijing are poised for a contentious ideological struggle that could unravel the world as it exists today. The fact, however, is the US-China relationship is still in a flux. Neither Beijing nor Washington have truly come to terms with the next chapter in their interactions or its implications for the future international order. Each side will have a vote on the future course of the relationship.

Foreign offices around the world are trying to make sense of the deterioration in the Sino-American relationship. The uncertainty revolves around some fundmental questions: will the two erstwhile allies during the first Cold War, wage a similar struggle against one another? What will be the normative basis of their rivalry? Is it about power or incongruent visions of world order?

The Failure of America's Success?

The US national security advisor has recently articulated what has become the new conventional narrative on US's China policy in recent years:

> For decades, conventional wisdom in both US political parties, the business community, academia, and media, has held that it was only a matter of time before China would become more liberal, first economically and, then, politically. The more we opened our markets to China, the thinking went, the more we invested capital in China, the more we trained PRC bureaucrats, scientists, engineers, and even military officers, the more China would become like us... As China grew richer and stronger, we believed, the Chinese Communist Party would liberalize to meet the rising democratic aspirations of its people...Unfortunately, it turned out to be very naïve.[7]

The above claim is not entirely true. For the Americans, their China policy, from the outset, was a far more realistic, though still ambitious, enterprise. The goal envisaged by the American grand strategists four decades ago was precisely this: socialize a rising China into the mainstream international relations framework and embed it in a set of norms that were supported from within the Chinese political system. Contrary to popular belief, US strategy did not entirely fail. Bringing liberal democracy to China was never actually on the horizon of clear-eyed US policymakers. It would have been the icing on the cake but they knew it was near impossible. Besides, the Tiananmen Square crackdown in 1989 put an end to that delusion. Instead, the engagement was premised on expanding the avenues for US businesses along with re-orienting China's approach to world order and globalization after the end of the Cold War.

Claims that China failed to liberalize at home are all ex-post rationalizations to elude the fact that it is the US that finds itself unable to sustain the open international order and seeks revisions on how its benefits are allocated to key stakeholders. This is because the open liberal framework has accelerated the power transition and re-distributed economic power from the Atlantic to the Indo-Pacific. The American people no longer support a globalist venture that yields disproportionate material advantages to a tiny minority at home. US businesses are having to compete with a rival power on more and more technology fronts.

Since US policymakers cannot advance a plausible pretext for disrupting the open world order, the blame is placed on a failed experiment of promoting democracy, which was always peripheral to the overall conception of China policy and held by a few who were 'blinded by an idealistic if not narcissistic faith that the Chinese dream equaled their own.'[8] The nub of the problem is that China integrated into the post-1945 and subsequently the post-1991 order after the dissolution of the Soviet Union, not as a client or junior partner but as an independent state. It is this basic reality that the US elite cannot countenance. As the most recent US National Security Strategy candidly admits, US engagement with and inclusion of China into the international order was predicated on converting the latter into a 'benign' actor. This naïve expectation, if it was truly held, has been belied over the past decade.

This is where the debate on the US-China equation gets complicated. Is the main driver for competition merely to secure US national interests and preserve advantages that are seen to be fading away? Or is there a world order basis for the growing rivalry?

Those who advance the Cold War thesis to US-China relations naturally rely on indicating a deep normative struggle that is underway – between a democractic America and an authoritarian China. To assert that a difference in political systems, which of course is real, extends to clashing international visions, is less easy to argue. Unlike the US-Soviet rivalry that was built on a world order contest underpinned by zero-sum ideological visions and sharp dividing lines on the political economy, China's mixed economy, albeit state-led, has incorporated select capitalist precepts. These are to be found in China's economic governance framework as well as liberal ideas in its engagement with international institutions. Put another way, China's international identity is not a coherent whole but an amalgam of contradictions that cannot be confronted or 'othered' by relying on a simplistic Cold War rhetoric.

When stripped of its grandiose foreign policy discourse, China has been unable to truly distinguish its vision of world order. Claims to advance a universal community of shared benefits is not markedly different to the universalism of US liberalism. Ironically, China's attempt to reform the globalized order might even echo some of the ideas of liberals like Franklin D. Roosevelt who, in a not dissimilar context, advocated balancing a hard nosed out-of-control capitalism with principles to secure social stability and economic sustainability, a core priority for the Communist Party of China today. We often forget that FD Roosevelt's (FDR) 'vision was originally global in spirit and scope', and envisioned a concert of great powers managing the post-war order. The sudden outbreak of the Cold War propelled an alternative hegemonic vision of an 'American-led and Western-centred system'.[9] It is the latter imperial variant of US vision that China no longer supports. But China wants the basic tenets of the liberal world order to continue long after the decline of US hegemony and international primacy.

Chinese discourse reflects this. The 'vision espoused by China does not deviate much from the legal and political foundations of the existing international order but rather provides a moderate blueprint for the betterment of the international order.'[10] Broadly speaking, China seeks to maintain the open globalized framework after revising some rules and nudging the system towards a more sustainable course based on a balance of interests between the major powers. For example, in 'international finance, China certainly does not want to see the US dollar occupying a hegemonic position forever.'[11] In the geopolitical realm, China will not behave like Germany or Japan who have accepted a subordinated role in a world designed by the US. China does aspire for a privileged geopolitical position in Asia.

On a broader setting, China wants to make its mark felt, not by advancing radical ideas but ironically parroting what was heard not long ago by Western elites. Xi Jinping's famous Davos speech of 2017 is one of several instances where China has made a sharp distinction between 'two distinct outlooks'. One of a 'United States bent on "making America great again" by putting itself first, and, China who believes "what economic globalization needs now is not a bullet in the head, but a better compass in the hand.'[12] When Wang Yi recently remarked, 'China will firmly follow the path of socialism with Chinese characteristics that has been proven successful in practice, but will not export its system or development model', this was partly to reassure Cold Warriors in the West but it was also an admission – China does not even possess an exportable model after its own complex mutations of socialism.

Old Fashioned Competition

If the argument that China has accommodated itself to some key, though certainly not all, pillars of the open international order is plausible then the entire discourse on Sino-American competition needs to be recast. Can there really be another Cold War if the underlying ideological disagreements are less severe and not always discernible between the two? It is instructive that the White House strategy document on China that was released in May 2020 falls short of seeking to dislodge China's domestic system: 'Our approach is not premised on determining a particular end state for China…United States policies are not premised on an attempt to change the PRC's domestic governance model…'[13]

To be sure, US policymakers continue to espouse the democracy versus autocracy narrative to rally support within the US body politic and internationally to wean states towards the US. But the democracy argument is too tainted to be a normative fulcrum of a US-led charge on China. Few in Asia and the developing world will buy into that binary. Traditional US allies in Western Europe and East Asia too would merely pay lip service to such a mantra while continuing to do business with a rising China.[14] Germany's Chancellor Angela Merkel recently spoke of the European Union's 'great strategic interest' in maintaining 'constructive' cooperation with China. 'We Europeans will need to recognize the decisiveness with which China will claim a leading position in the existing structures of the international architecture'.[15]

We are witnessing something more in sync with the longue durée of history. A cycle of power transition that has played out in several instances. Some were peaceful and others intensely violent. The violent episodes like Napoleonic France or

Nazi Germany or imperial Japan all reflected one common feature: the rising power found no avenue to flourish and buttress its power potential under the prevailing international order. In contrast, China's rise has occurred within the liberal international order and a culture of interdependence enabled this process to occur. This negates the very meaning of a Cold War – a clash of irreconcilable ideas – towards competition over the reins of the international order. The script of how US-China competition will unfold is yet to be written.

The Sino-American relationship is *sui generis*. It will not follow the patterns of earlier clashes between Britain and Germany or the Cold War of the US and USSR. The present US policy is one of balancing against select components of Chinese power but 'remain open to constructive, results-oriented engagement and cooperation from China where our interests align.'

> We do not seek to contain China's development, nor do we wish to disengage from the Chinese people. The United States expects to engage in fair competition with the PRC, whereby both of our nations, businesses, and individuals can enjoy security and prosperity.[16]

World Order without a Hegemon

As other states grapple with the disruption in US-China relations, we should not lose sight of the broader historical need for a fresh outlook to organize international relations. The experience of past several centuries has accustomed us to accept that world order requires a hegemon – a central organizing power – and that such authority could only emerge from within the Euro-Atlantic community of states. While the post-1945 balance of power did reveal it was no longer possible to order the planet without cooperation with the non-Western world, we never really questioned the assumption that superpowers are pillars for international order.

So when the unipolar moment came, despite the discomfort and uncertainty it produced, few really challenged the notion that the world required a hegemon to supply public goods and enforce rules of the game for others to buy into. That premise broke down in the late 2000s with the relative decline in US material capacity to play such a role, the resurgence of Asia and Eurasia, and the misuse of the unipolar moment leading to a failure to create a true liberal and inclusive international order. The 2008 global economic crisis only strengthened this trend. And collectively, it led to the upheavals in the US body politic we can witness today as well as the collapse of the establishment consensus and authority inside the US.

However, this is where the power transition cycle is breaking with the patterns of past centuries, when the baton was passed from one Western power to another more capable Western power that resumed the responsibility of upholding order. All those previous power transitions were within the same cultural and intellectual milieu so to speak. Asia, and China in particular, has been unable and unwilling, to assume such a formidable and expansive role. Its complex identity constrains such a path and as the most astute observers of China recognize, Chinese internationalism is still too vague and couched in lofty rhetoric to be a true universal force.

As Chinese scholars admit, 'a hegemon must have a vision for the whole world's development and interests beyond its own geopolitical interests.' Yet, so far, China lacks such a 'broad, open, and progressive culture and an ideology of inclusiveness.'[17] That Beijing has renewed its focus on domestic stability and its regional periphery – exemplified most recently by violent incidents on the border with India – attests to China's inability to sustain a vision that can transcend its geopolitical interests. At any rate, China is unlikely to ever possess material power on a scale necessary to supply public goods on its own even if it could develop a universal or pan-Asian vision with finesse.

The only alternative normative pathway to a sustainable world order is a multipolar polycentric framework. Indian strategists and leaders have long sought such a world order, for it provides the maximum advantages for India's civilizational, geopolitical and geoeconomic resurgence. For this order to be stable and legitimate, it cannot be exclusive, bloc-based, or driven by norms that emanate from a few major states. It has to be open, plural, multi-civilizational, decentred and regionalized, and yet simultaneously global on issues like strategic stability, financial sustainability, and ecological security. Great powers that are most sensitive to this emerging and complex world and respond creatively with norms and public goods will become the pillars of the emerging world order.

4

INDIA AND THE GREAT POWERS

An exchange in 1964 between US diplomat Chester Bowles and Triloki Nath Kaul, India's then ambassador to Moscow, offers a fascinating insight into contemporary geopolitics. While discussing Southeast Asia, Bowles said, 'it would be a good thing if India could try to bring the Soviet and American points of view closer… India's friendship with both could act as a sort of bridge between them.' He 'hoped that it would be possible for [the] USA and USSR, with the help of India, to come to some kind of understanding about preventing Chinese expansionism and infiltration in Southeast Asia.' Kaul replied, 'India would be glad to bring the US and Soviet points of view closer as far as lay within our ability In fact this was our present policy.'[1] This response reflected India's then geostrategy to position itself as an area of agreement between the superpowers.

As Kaul's cable in September 1965 to Indira Gandhi subsequently explained: 'the interests of America, USSR and India, have a common feature of being aimed at the prevention of Chinese expansion in this area. This provides an opportunity for India to reap the maximum possible advantage from both sides and strengthen herself for the future.'[2]

History, however, followed a different course. As the 1960s unfolded, the Sino-Soviet ideological struggle culminated in an ugly spat in the Communist world. Ironically, both New Delhi and Washington perceived that trend differently and with contrasting ends in mind.

A Multipolar World

For Anglo-American policymakers, a long-cherished dream of isolating Russia and pulling China back into their orbit became a reality. For India, the spectre of an unfriendly China being checked through a shared understanding with Washington and Moscow fell by the wayside, and New Delhi was compelled to imagine new approaches to safeguard its interests and security. By 1969, the bipolar system had cracked open into a multipolar world. The US and China were on the cusp of a rapprochement, while New Delhi and Moscow had established strategic understanding at the highest level to respond to this disconcerting global re-alignment. December 1971 reaffirmed the new multipolar world with the Soviet Navy entering the Indian Ocean to stymie the Anglo-American attempt to disrupt India's military operations during the liberation of Bangladesh. That seminal period laid the foundation, as External Affairs Minister S. Jaishankar alluded to in Moscow in 2019, for a four-decade relationship that withstood further disruptions in international politics, including the end of the first Cold War in 1989 and the disappearance of the Soviet Union in 1991.

If we fast forward to recent years, historical patterns continue to have a robust afterlife. The US-Russia-China triangle still contains complex and counter-intuitive dynamics that often get obscured or distorted in India's strategic debates.

Does the contemporary environment enable a similar opportunity to again position India as an area of agreement between Washington and Moscow? To evaluate such a balance-of-power approach we need to examine the inner workings of the rapidly evolving US-Russia-China triangle, which defines the great power setting for Delhi.

Complex Dynamics

Despite the Donald Trump administration's aggressive posturing on China and its attempt to redefine the terms of that relationship, we do not yet see a credible and sustainable strategy to respond to China's rise. And growing Sino-Russian relations have not led to any fundamental reassessment in the US's thinking. In recent years, whether on the US's attempts to pressure North Korea or security in Northeast Asia or conflicts in the Middle East we have abundant evidence of Moscow and Beijing providing psychological and diplomatic support to each other. Even potentially contentious issues such as their Eurasian integration visions, that is, Russia's Eurasian Economic Union and China's BRI, have been projected in a spirit of co-existence and mutual respect, often disguising deeper questions of power and ambition. It is not that Moscow is oblivious to Beijing potentially squeezing Russian influence from parts of Eurasia but that Moscow's calculus is also shaped by the strategic necessity of a mutually beneficial partnership with Beijing in order to counter-balance a rigid and unfriendly West.

The Russia-China relationship is presently guided by, as noted scholar Dmitri Trenin suggests, the principle of 'never being against each other, but not necessarily always with each other'. This approach 'puts a premium on a solid partnership between Moscow and Beijing where their interests meet, eschews conflicts where they don't, and allows a lot of flexibility where interests overlap only partially'. For instance, we saw this nimbleness at the UN Security Council when Russia and China were on opposite sides in reacting to India's new Kashmir policy. We also saw this during the 2020 India-China border standoff in Ladakh where Moscow assumed a neutral yet constructive role in dissuading a more dangerous escalation after the June skirmishes along the Ladakh frontier.

The Asia Pivot

When mainstream American policymakers look at the big power triangle of the US-China-Russia, their unconcealed prejudice and geostrategic preferences are apparent to all. The door is still open to China whom the West would like to wean away from Russia to arrest America's deteriorating global position and arrive at a more favourable economic understanding to revive US industry and exports. New Delhi, of course, like in the 1960s, would prefer the opposite outcome: to wean Russia away from China or more realistically provide Russia with more options in its Asia pivot. India's foreign minister's remarks at the prestigious Valdai Club in Moscow in 2019 made such a case for the next chapter in India-Russia ties. In essence, he asserted that Asia's multipolar age has arrived; that the Indo-Pacific is not restricted to one conception: he distinguished India's independent approach that includes stable ties with Beijing from the US concept that some interpret as 'Chinese containment on the cheap'; and most importantly, Russia being a Pacific power with interests in the Indian Ocean should join the debate.

In substance and without openly ruffling Beijing's feathers, Russia is already shaping the geopolitics of the Indo-Pacific.

It has managed the rare feat of deep cooperation with rival parties in the South China Sea disputes. As Alexander Korolev, a scholar at the University of New South Wales, notes, the 'Russia-Vietnam partnership should not be underestimated, because it has been growing despite and independently of Russia-China relations'. Indeed, once Russia's advanced military and naval modernization assistance towards Indo-Pacific states such as India, Vietnam and Indonesia, along with Russia's own underrated Pacific Fleet whose area of responsibility extends to the Persian Gulf is accounted for, Moscow is already a player in Eurasia's rimland areas.

India's foreign policy challenge is to reassure Moscow that Delhi will not bandwagon with the US and remain genuinely committed to open and inclusive security and order building ideas. This would pursuade Russia to imagine a role in the Indo-Pacific that brings its vast diplomatic experience and strategic heft into the open.

Restoring India's Leverage in the Global Triangle

India's ability to exploit the global triangle and shape it in a direction that buttresses Indian strategic interests both in the sub-regional environment and in the extended Eurasian and Asian neighbourhood is challenging and implies the need for a more complex and nimble geostrategy.

While both US-India and Russia-India dyads do share a common concern about China's rise, India's two great power partners formulate their foreign policies on a much larger canvas aimed at system-shaping geopolitical goals. While resisting Beijing in the Western Pacific, Washington simultaneously seeks to wean China away from Russia, and thus decelerate the power transition towards multipolarity. While Russia too is concerned about China squeezing away Russian influence from parts of Eurasia, Moscow simultaneously values its global partnership with China to counter-balance the US who remains deeply suspicious of and reluctant to craft a mutually beneficial relationship with Russia. 'Paradoxically, a close Russia-China partnership should move India to broad-base relations with Russia (beyond the traditional defence and energy pillars). A strong stake in relations with India could reinforce Russia's reluctance (which still persists) to be a junior partner of China.'[3]

A simplistic balance of power approach formulated without a critical appraisal of the global chessboard will yield little, and more likely worsen India's strategic position. For example, a hard military alignment with the US will not only diminish India's freedom of manoeuver at a time of flux, but it would also produce adverse geopolitical futures that are bound to complicate India's rise and position in the region. Thus, the types of strategic choices Delhi makes in the larger framework guiding India's foreign policy will have ripple effects on how the global triangle manifests at the subcontinental and extended neighbourhood level. Restructuring and strengthening the India-Russia relationship, as part of a larger conversation on global and regional trends, is a key step towards stabilizing India's position vis-à-vis the global triangle. Russia's enduring interest in a balanced and multipolar Greater Eurasia and a shared interest in shaping China's rise will see Delhi and Moscow remaining close for years to come.

5

THE BELT AND ROAD INITIATIVE AND CHINA'S POLICY RE-ORIENTATION

The Belt and Road initiative (BRI) is an ambitious Chinese initiative that aims to develop connectivity and infrastructure linkages between China and vast parts of Asia and Eurasia, including surrounding areas of the subcontinent. It was enunciated soon after the Xi Jinping regime assumed power in 2012. BRI is part of a broader Chinese policy reorientation where its leaders are responding to the challenges and opportunities of a fraying US-led international order. Because the BRI included an objectionable corridor through Pakistan-occupied Kashmir, the debate in India has been, for the most part, a narrow one. Consequently, the big picture of China's geopolitical motives and attempts to change the existing world order has eluded mainstream Indian debates.[1]

The disintegration of the ancient Silk Route across Eurasia 600 years ago was a transformational event. Providing maritime powers with the upper hand, the collapse of the continental webs of communications altered the evolution of subsequent events in world history. Asia's later eclipse is often traced to the stasis of the Indian and Chinese empires leaving them in an unequal contest against a dynamic West. The developments of the 21st century have turned the tables dramatically, as Asian resurgence appears poised to restore these states to their historical positions as leading economic centres. Leading from the front is China, which has positioned itself to resume its role as the engine for Asia. Evoking admiration and fear in equal measure, the Chinese through their BRI idea are claiming to remake Eurasia's geoeconomic landscape.

A question being posed in every foreign office and corporate head office is: what are the Chinese motivations in this initiative? Some can be discerned overtly, while other drivers are less obvious. The BRI is a manifestation of a broader policy shift in China, where its leaders are responding to the challenges and opportunities of a fraying and unsustainable US-led international order. The context and timing of the idea's origins suggests that it was intended to gain strategic depth in hinterland and inner Asia, to counteract geostrategic pressure from the US-Japan alliance as well as to buy time to reform a highly imbalanced domestic political economy. The BRI should be understood as part of the 2013–14 foreign policy shifts that provided concurrent stress on development, security and regional order-building.

Geopolitical Depth

Most commentaries on the BRI have not provided the geopolitical, contextual or structural setting that led to Chinese leaders choosing a Eurasian-centred geostrategy. This is ironic because for most of the past decade it was the maritime realm that was expected to witness the thrust of China's strategic expansion. The BRI appears to be a culmination of internal Chinese debates on the type of geostrategy to counteract the US's geopolitical position around China's maritime periphery. It has led to a continental-centred order-building strategy with Eurasia emerging as the preferred arena to implement and test Chinese ideas. The Barack Obama administration's ambitious 2011 'Pacific pivot' had aimed to restore and expand US influence around China's eastern and southeastern periphery, both by strengthening traditional alliances in East Asia as well as by building new maritime partnerships.[2] By June 2012, the military dimensions of this 'rebalancing' to Asia was also enunciated by US policymakers who declared an intention to devote substantial naval power to the Western Pacific.[3] These moves had heightened Chinese threat perceptions with several analysts viewing the pivot as an attempt to divide Asia and build a regional coalition against China.[4] Interestingly, initial Chinese responses to the US pivot were 'cautious' with a 'wait-and-see' approach. Michael Swaine suggests that the impending 2012 leadership transition, unwillingness to heighten regional tensions, which would play into the hands of the US, and general uncertainty regarding the staying power of the US's Pacific ambitions, all combined to stay Beijing's hand.[5] Even China's diplomatic and military assertiveness on its maritime periphery was restrained by an overarching posture of 'avoiding conflict' with the US and its frontline allies.[6] By 2012, the idea that a Pacific expansion was a natural path for China's geopolitical rise was being questioned by influential scholars such as Wang Jisi, who urged it to 'look beyond the traditional problems of the coastal territory.'[7]

Wang argued that a geostrategy based on maritime assertiveness would fuel security dilemmas and risk a headlong collision with the US in a theatre where China held a weaker hand. Instead, a march West strategy would enable China to shape an area that was not defined by 'a US-dominated regional order or a pre-existing economic integration mechanism.' Wang described his geostrategy as 'rebalancing' rather than abandoning East Asia, and with 'a parallel pursuit of both sea power and land power'.[8] To be sure, the Grand Western Development strategy in 2000 had also aimed at developing China's Western provinces to correct the internal imbalances vis-à-vis the richer coastal provinces. But, the altered international context of 2012 and growing Sino-US friction in East Asia ensured that renewed arguments for China to shift its gaze towards its inner Asian frontiers and beyond found traction in Beijing. Wang argued that it would also help 'balance the Sino-American relations' as there is 'immense space for both sides to cooperate on subjects like investment, energy security, anti-terrorism, maintain stability and peace ... And there are no risks of military confrontation between China and America in this area. Instead, the US needs China's help'.[9]

The course correction or adaptation came in October 2013 after intense debates about the wider direction for Chinese foreign policy. In a major forum on foreign policy, the entire Chinese leadership deliberated on establishing the 'strategic objectives' and 'basic principles' on China's approach towards its periphery for the following decade.[10] Essentially, the new leadership decided to decrease their emphasis on the older approach of Deng Xiaoping from the 1980s and 1990s, which had eschewed leadership as part of a low profile, in favour of a proactive stance to shape the external environment, with the periphery deemed to constitute the core zone of attention. One facet of this new posture has been to demonstrate more resolve towards issues of sovereignty and territorial disputes. Another facet 'is the emphasis on using China's growing economic clout to develop an enduring, integrated set of relationships with periphery states that will eventually alter their incentive structure in ways that benefit China and themselves'.[11] This is where the BRI initiative fits in: as a means to secure and socialize the periphery and advance the possibility of a regional order that connects different sub-regions of Asia. During the 2013 Work Conference on peripheral diplomacy, Xi Jinping had remarked, 'Maintaining stability in China's neighbourhood is the key objective of peripheral diplomacy. We must encourage and participate in the process of regional economic integration, speed up the process of building up infrastructure and connectivity. We must build the Silk Road Economic Belt and the 21st century Maritime Silk Road, creating a new regional economic order.'[12]

By 2014, the Xi Jinping regime had further outlined its foreign policy agenda and expressed views on the changing international environment. In a Foreign Affairs Work Conference in November 2014, Beijing gave further expression to the October 2013 forum on periphery diplomacy. A central theme in Xi's speech was the emphasis on China's deep linkages with the international system:

> China's relations with the rest of the world are going through profound changes; its interactions with the international community have become closer than ever before. China's dependence on the world and its involvement in international affairs are deepening, so are the world's dependence on China and its impact on China.[13]

Although espousing interdependence has been a feature of Chinese official rhetoric in the past, this assessment underscored that the nature of interdependence was becoming more symmetrical, providing new opportunities. Marking a clear shift from Hu Jintao's 'cautious and conservative' 2006 line, the 2014 line was that 'China's growing strength and influence in an increasingly interdependent relationship with the world is a major feature that must be incorporated into Beijing's diplomacy going forward'.[14]

In his speech, Xi called for China to 'develop a distinctive diplomatic approach befitting its role of a major country'.[15] According to one interpretation of this post-Dengist strategic thinking, an international system with 'dispersed pattern of global economic power combined with the deepening involvement of a stronger and more influential – yet increasingly dependent – China apparently means for Xi that Chinese foreign policy must become more sophisticated, strategic, and dynamic in order to advance Chinese interests.' Foreign policy, thus, has acquired a function beyond an instrument for economic development to also 'minimize the threats and maximize the benefits presented by a more complex and challenging environment'.[16] Some Chinese analysts have been quite categorical in locating the BRI as one of the means of counteracting pressure from the US. According to this view, it is 'not merely a series of engineering projects, but a strategic concept meant to break through US attempts to "strangle China."' By choosing to direct Chinese geoeconomic power towards Eurasia, the BRI avoids a direct and costly 'collision course with the US' and gains strategic depth for China's continued development and security.[17]

Political Economy

The problem of under-absorption, that is, China's inability to fully absorb its supply-side production capacity has been an inherent feature of China's economic story. Since the 2008 global economic crisis, China's investment-intensive export-oriented model, relying on massive reciprocal import demand in the high income economies to absorb Chinese production, has been widely acknowledged as unsustainable. The steel sector has become symbolic of this overcapacity. Today, China can produce 1.2 billion metric tons of steel, 50 per cent more than what is required for domestic and export markets.[18] The accumulation of imbalances and excess capacity over the previous period has a part to play in China's BRI strategy. Yet, as a former senior Chinese banking official recently remarked, the BRI is not a solution for China's excess capacity problem. Given that China already runs a $600 billion per year trade surplus with the rest of the world, it is unlikely that net exports can grow at a sufficient rate to absorb domestic overcapacity.[19] This issue can only be addressed by painful supply-side reforms, which were announced by Xi Jinping in 2017.

To understand the deeper drivers for the BRI, one needs to look beyond the overcapacity question and focus on the political economy dynamic inside China. The changes in China's mixed economy over the past three decades, the dramatic growth of private Chinese capital that occurred during this period, and the contradictions that it has produced within China's political system, are arguably important drivers in the very choice and design of the 'going out' strategy. It is generally recognized that the CCP now represents mixed economy interests that emerged during the privatization and opening of sectors to the non-state economic actors in the reform era. To be sure, Xi Jinping's 'unwavering commitment to the dominant position of public ownership suggests that there will not be large-scale Reagan- or Thatcher-style privatization in China'.[20] But, the reality of a mixed economy cannot now be reversed. Privately-owned businesses now account for 60 per cent of China's GDP and for 88 per cent of all manufacturing investment. State-owned enterprises, in contrast, account for about 20 per cent of GDP and 35 per cent fixed-asset investment.[21]

During the pre-crisis period, the pre-2008 high growth phase, China could handle these contradictions because everyone was making money.[22] Further, the massive stimulus via the state sector in the post-2008 period to compensate for the contraction in net exports and domestic demand diminished the relative position of private capital inside China.[23] Xi's centralization of power and party-strengthening strategies must also confront the reality of non-state economic interests that have accumulated inside China. Could the conception of the BRI be linked with the aim of externalizing the accumulation of private and state capital, and safeguarding the basic domestic structure and primacy of the CCP-led one-party system?

The 'going out' strategy could be aimed at accommodating neoliberal reformist factions by offering private Chinese capital a credible alternative to expand abroad. By facilitating external options for private capital, domestic factional contestations may have been contained enabling a more durable intra-party consensus on the next phase of China's domestic governance. Some Chinese scholars have called the BRI 'an upgraded version of the reform and opening up, an upgraded version of China's international trade, and an ungraded version of China's "going out"'.[24] Wang Yiwei, in particular, makes an interesting observation when he notes that the BRI 'is not an extension of China's efforts to deepen reform, it is needed to support further reform. In China, there are still many forces attempting to undermine the construction of the Belt and Road.'[25]

Although the domestic realm cannot be fundamentally disturbed, the global realm offers a vast space for externalizing China's domestic contradictions. The Chinese have stressed that, in addition to state capital, they are 'looking to stimulate Chinese and non-Chinese private capital' through the BRI.[26] For example, some of the recent big investment projects in Southeast Asia – steel sector in Thailand, hydropower in Indonesia – are by private Chinese actors. In 2015, private Chinese companies pushed $51 billion in outbound investment compared to the state sector's $157 billion. In 2016, China's private sector completed about $60 billion in outbound mergers and acquisitions and other direct investment, such as project finance. The mixed political economy structure appears to have created incentives inside the party to carve out room for the non-state private sector as a 'go out' strategy, including in the BRI initiative.[27]

In sum, domestic imbalances and the political economy contradictions vis-à vis state and private economic actors need an external realm to accommodate and stabilize the diversity and conflicts of interest that have emerged inside China in the reform era. Within the national arena, these struggles could become explosive, as we have seen in periodic crises during the evolution of China's opening-up process since the 1980s. Opening the external valve enables the preservation of the one-party system, promotes cooperation between state and private capital, and simultaneously staves off a stasis of the type that ensued after the 14th century when China turned inward.

THE PHASE OF China as a so-called free rider in a US-led order, content merely with capital accumulation and integration into a pre-existing system, has passed. The BRI is as much a consequence of a global power transition as it is an attempt to shape that transition in ways that can buttress China's regional and international position as well as preserve stability in the domestic realm. From a geopolitical perspective, a Eurasiacentred geostrategy – which the BRI now embodies – appears as a pragmatic choice to avoid a headlong confrontation with the US in the Western Pacific. An inside-out political economy interpretation, on the other hand, suggests that the CCP is engaging in ambitious order-building at home to accommodate, and perhaps even transcend, the contradictions that have emerged during the first reform era. The external realm with which China has become interdependent is seen as vital to regulate internal contradictions and stave off an existential crisis in the governance system. An outward-bound posture is now the key to preserving the fundamental characteristics in the domestic realm. Since the Chinese define order and security holistically, the pursuit of multiple goals through the BRI may not be seen as a contradiction. The dual aspect of the BRI, as an internal and external stabilizing strategy, suggests that this is the clearest sequel to Deng Xiaoping's template for managing China's domestic and foreign policy.

Understanding the geopolitical context and domestic political economy that is driving China to re-establish multiple lines of communication – similar to the ancient Silk Routes centuries ago – with its neighbours in Asia and Eurasia will help India to navigate the changes and even disruptions this process will inevitably produce in the years ahead. As Section III will remind readers, India has always been a part of the various transnational trade routes and cultural networks that entwined different regions of Eurasia and Asia. For India to profit from these wider shifts in connections or re-connections in the neighbourhood while safeguarding its interests in a stable and secure region, it will need to recover some of its own history as a power that was always at the crossroads of many thriving civilizations and socio-economic networks. We will discuss more of this in Section III.

6

BRICS AND A NEW DEVELOPMENT VISION FOR A MULTIPOLAR WORLD

It has become customary for Indian analysts to deride multilateral networks that have not emerged from the Bretton Woods womb. BRICS, or the combined forum of Brazil, Russia, India, China and South Africa, invites particular scorn. Yet, if India's economic elites can get over their prejudices, they will discover that BRICS is fuelled by both a normative impulse to buttress national and civilizational identities, and, an instrumental strategy to reverse the north-south divide. This is precisely the opportunity before BRICS today: to promote a narrative for the international community and the broader Global South that can break from the stale discourse on global governance and development that has been seriously discredited over the past decade.

The first BRICS[1] summit was held in 2009 in the backdrop of a Western financial crisis and a deep global recession coupled with geopolitical instability across the Eurasian continent. The need for global governance in general, and especially on the management of geoeconomic and geopolitical questions was palpable. BRICS emerged onto the global scene at a tumultuous juncture where the status quo powers were losing their erstwhile dominance over the world economy and high politics. Each successive summit has expanded the scope of issues and the inclusion of South Africa in the 2011 Sanya summit has made BRICS a truly 'transcontinental' and multi-civilizational network of states.

Often missing in the post-Cold War discourse is the acknowledgement that unipolarity and neoliberal globalization of the 2000s was an internationalist phenomenon that sought to subsume rising power identities and nationalisms. The geopolitical and geoeconomic disruptions over the past decade, however, have re-opened an identity challenge for rising powers. The question of where these states fit in the emerging world order is again becoming relevant.

As long as the Bretton Woods order could cede space and sustain the legitimate aspirations of its new entrants, this identity problem could be and was set aside in favour of international integration by the rising powers. But with the decline in America's capacity, leadership and consequent inability to co-opt non-Western states into the old order, rising powers began re-asserting their national identities in the 2010s. As they reset their equations with the West, it is not surprising that BRICS states have found friction with the US, albeit in different degrees, and in the case of India and China between themselves too.

BRICS is one platform for its members to project their distinct national identities and roles on a global stage without the pressures of socialization and conformity that engagement within Western-dominated institutions has typically entailed.

But BRICS is also driven by instrumental reasons. For many, an anti-BRICS posture is essentially 'a cut India's nose to spite China's face' argument. To be sure, there *are* challenges such as preventing a capital surplus China from throwing its weight in BRICS institutions. The norm of equality has been established as a conscious antithesis to the hierarchical Bretton Woods format. The critics, however, have missed the woods for the trees. For the past decade, the BRICS has been a 'stabilizer', not a 'disruptor'. Rather 'than seeking to sideline existing arrangements and institutions, the BRICS have openly advocated the need to reinforce multilateralism and strengthen the global institutions in the face of mounting protectionist pressures. In other words, rather than aiming to substitute existing global institutions the BRICS are creating new arrangements that complement and reinforce the existing institutional framework of the global economy via addressing some of the weaker links and gaps in global governance.'[2] This is hardly a revolutionary group but a pragmatic venture led by a group of rising powers that seek a more sustainable multipolar world order.

As for China's evolving role, ironically, there is some similarity between Beijing's approach to BRICS and historical US policies in shaping the post-1945 economic order. After the Second World War, the US emerged as a capital surplus country with massive financial claims on the ravaged but then still industrially-advanced Western Europe. The US invested in institutions to share power and decision-making authority with its former economic rivals to forge a rule-based economic community. While the extraordinary asymmetry between America and the rest of the world after 1945 is not valid in today's context, the logic for stronger rising powers such as China to initiate a similar process of sharing power and authority to create durable institutions exists. While China has struggled to acquire a sophisticated internationalist vision, it is finding it beneficial to invest in multilateral institutions where its relative economic weight may not yield immediate national payoffs. The proof is in the pudding. After all, other rising powers, including India, are only buying into this process because it is based on 'democratic governance structures' and has demonstrated the ability to deliver the goods.

For some observers and analysts, this is a mere temporary expedience before China reverts to traditional geopolitical behaviour by steering BRICS to become a Chinese handmaiden. But this argument presumes BRICS minus China is doomed to fail and Moscow, Delhi, Cape Town and Brasilia lack the agency and skill to shape their destinies and defend the shared norms that underpin BRICS. The answer to the dilemma of power asymmetries between states is more sophisticated multilateralism, not less.

An optimal path for BRICS would be that Bretton Woods institutions gradually recognize their folly and seek to create a genuinely reflective and responsive governance system. Here BRICS would be the ideal partner and vehicle to bridge the Western and non-Western worlds and, the North and South. Paradoxically, it is BRICS' success that might change Western attitudes to global governance. Plainly put, BRICS would need to demonstrate the efficacy of a second alternative governance structure to reform the dominant one. To influence the global discourse, however, BRICS needs to articulate their development norms and construct institutions that reflect these norms.

According to World Bank data, developing countries now trade more with each other than with the advanced economies. China has played a central role in this expansion of South-South trade. But it has also produced imbalances. Although China runs surpluses with all its BRICS partners, Russia and Brazil as mineral, commodity and energy rich exporters can compensate for inward Chinese manufacturing. India's problem is unique in that it lacks surplus natural resources to pay for its China imports. It also lacks manufacturing depth with the lowest share of manufacturing-GDP ratio among major developing economies at 16 per cent. Until the 2008 global economic crisis, India had been walking a tightrope by absorbing large capital inflows to pay for its industrial imports. As easy money dried up over the past decade, and India's domestic savings proved inadequate to sustain the state and private sectors, India's structural problems have become all too apparent.

The New Development Bank (NDB), founded in 2015, offers an ambitious solution. Since the heart of the problem is the asymmetry in supply-side manufacturing capabilities between the BRICS economies, the NDB will 'mobilize resources for infrastructure and sustainable development projects in BRICS and other emerging economies'. Conceived during the March 2012 Delhi summit, the NDB was built on the idea of pooling capital and channelling it towards sectors that were starved of productive capacity and investment. By breaking the Bretton Woods monopoly on developmental finance, which merely addresses a fraction of the social and infrastructure investment needs in the Global South, the NDB was envisioned as a cost-effective option for BRICS members and potentially for low-income economies too. In the next two decades, according to one study, the NDB could reach a 'stock of loans of up to US$350 billion' exceeding World Bank finance.[3] In 2019, major rating agencies such as the S&P and Fitch, 'reaffirmed the Bank's AA+ international credit rating. The Bank has also obtained a AAA international credit rating from the Japan Credit Rating Agency.' This places the NDB at par with major multilateral development banks and extremely competitive in the cost of credit.[4]

The chapter will take the readers on to the multilateral side of India-China relations, and how the disruptions in globalization over the past decade is bringing these competing powers to also cooperate in setting the agenda for a post-Western dominated world order. Many in India believe this is futile and a distraction from the immediate security priorities on the frontiers and in the region. But since India's prospects as a potential major power are inextricably linked to the fate of the global economy, it is too vital to be set aside in national debates. The risk of an inward-looking India is all too real in the years ahead, and BRICS is one of the platforms to keep Delhi engaged in pursuit of a progressive world order discourse.

Why is the post-1945 open liberal economic order constructed by the US in deep structural crisis? Will globalization survive the end of US-led unipolarity? Can BRICS envisage an alternative world order and thereby modify globalization to ensure equality and sustainability? Can BRICS promote a discourse that addresses the formidable developmental challenges that confront the Global South, including its own members? This chapter reflects on these questions and attempts to rescue BRICS from the narrow images that have been painted in recent years.

The Decline of the Ancien Régime

The current international economic architecture originated in the aftermath of the Second World War. The US emerged as the undisputed leader of the capitalist North, and, post-War foreign policies of the US were shaped by the overarching goal to salvage the global economy after the bloody power transition. With a share of 50 per cent of global GDP, the US towered over the remaining industrial centres. The US constructed new institutions and expended an extraordinary amount of capital and aid that helped resuscitate the economies of Western Europe and Japan.

The Bretton Woods Institutions – the International Monetary Fund (IMF), the International Bank of Reconstruction and Development (the World Bank) – the General Agreement on Tariffs and Trade (GATT) and several other agencies of the United Nations were erected in such a geopolitical context to ensure the transition to a smooth functioning of interdependence in the Organization for Economic Cooperation and Development (OECD) world. And, it was the US as the 'security community's' leader and manager who promoted and underwrote this economic and security interdependence.

The end of the Cold War accelerated the process of economic globalization. The OECD's economic division of labour was from here on extended to economies on the periphery. This interdependence was only promoted because of the unprecedented advantages of the North – high-tech industrial infrastructure, a strong innovation and R&D base, established multinational corporations (MNCs), powerful brands and a consumption value-chain close to home. These entities sought access to inexpensive labour and processing industries to keep the industrialized core running. Such resources were available in abundance in emerging economies. It is instructive to note the empirical effects of this interdependence: in 1996, core industrial economies ran a total current account surplus of US$42 billion compared to the total current-account deficit of US$90 billion by the South. By 2004, geoeconomic patterns had reversed. Industrial economies ran a total deficit of US$400 billion (a US$666 billion external deficit by the US alone) versus emerging economies that ran a current account surplus of US$327 billion. The fundamental change was that the North was channelling much of its production – largely low-end manufacturing and offshored portions of high-tech value chains – through the emerging South and this was reflected in the latter's trade surpluses.

In many respects, globalization raced ahead not only of the institutions that were meant to regulate it, but it also ventured outside the US-led hierarchy into nation-states that had not been socialized or integrated into the Western security system. This phenomenon is captured by Thomas Friedman's triumphalist quip in 1999: 'the most basic truth about globalization is this: No one is in charge'.[5] For example, in a previous phase of global imbalances in the early 1980s, the US could assemble the G-5 and implement the Plaza Accord in 1985 to create a readjustment in the terms of trade between the US and the next three biggest economies at the time – West Germany, UK, and Japan – and compel the latter to bear the burden of the global adjustment. Between 1985 and 1987, the dollar depreciated by 51 per cent vis-à-vis the Japanese yen enabling the US to rapidly improve its current account deficit. In the current geopolitical context of globalization this is no longer possible. There are now nation-states that have become important members of the global division of labour without being part of the Western or Northern security community. Thus, for example, China cannot be coerced or cajoled to the same extent or with the same tools that were applied to Japan two decades ago to bear the burden of a global re-adjustment. The US-China trade war since 2018 attests to this.

The Bretton Woods institutions were also established in a context when the state was a major actor in the global economy. The Cold War Keynesian capitalist model that relied on a compact between big capital, big labour and big government gave way in the 1970s and 1980s to a wave of deregulations and privatizations that transferred industrial capacities into private oligopolies and MNCs. Over the past decade, MNCs have accounted for over two-thirds of world exports of goods and services, of which a significant share is intra-firm trade. It is estimated that 35 per cent of global trade is accounted for by intra-firm commerce.

Global governance institutions have not kept pace with these developments. For instance, there is no reliable data regularly published on global MNC supply chains to discover the true extent of 'interdependence'. This is truly astonishing because we have exhaustive data that scrutinizes national economies and the quantum of interaction between states but very little on the oligopolies that dominate the commanding heights of the global economy today. Institutions are, therefore, lagging behind and unable to monitor or regulate geoeconomic trends. This was reflected in the 2013 Durban declaration: 'The prevailing global governance architecture is regulated by institutions which were conceived in circumstances when the international landscape in all its aspects was characterized by very different challenges and opportunities.'

Another central feature of the post-2008 crisis economy has been the inability of the American and European household in general to pay for the consumption of offshored manufacturing that is produced in the low-cost locales of the Asia Pacific. In the US, both the state and private households have been living beyond their means; in most of the Eurozone, the state accumulated more debt given its relatively higher social obligations.

Trade and financial globalization, therefore, became intrinsically linked with capital flows into the US becoming a corollary to its high structural trade deficits. Despite being the world's largest debtor, the US itself supplies the principal reserve currency – the US dollar – for its creditors thereby transferring the vulnerability of this imbalance onto the latter. One of the major causes of the present crisis is the systematic abuse of its reserve currency status by the US and the asymmetric costs that it is imposing on the rest of the world. The unrestrained monetary expansion via the massive printing of dollars by the US Federal Reserve has meant that other countries integrated with international finance have two policy options: first, let the values of their own currencies rise, relative to the dollar, which means a fall in aggregate (export) demand and a rise in unemployment. Second, undertake a monetary expansion (print more domestic currency) to match the depreciating dollar, which ultimately feeds into inflation of goods and assets. Essentially, the choice is really between nominal and real exchange rate appreciation. US monetary expansion has also created asset bubbles and volatility in emerging markets across assets such as oil, real estate, commodities, and gold as investors divert surplus liquidity into higher-yielding assets that do little to actually upgrade the capacity of the real economy.

The asymmetry of this 'exorbitant privilege' has reached a level where the entire basis of exchanging real wealth (exports of merchandise into the US) for paper money (accumulating US debt) is being questioned. The growing use of regional currencies for trade and investment is a rational response of emerging economies who are most exposed to the ineluctable devaluation of the US dollar. It was also in such a context that the BRICS Delhi Declaration of March 28, 2012 called for a 'just international monetary system that can serve the interests of all countries and support the development of emerging and developing economies.' In 2015, The New Development Bank (NDB), proposed the use of national currencies in trade and investment. In the April 2020 meeting with BRICS finance ministers, K.V. Kamath, the president of NDB, disclosed that between 2016 and 2019,

$15 billion of approved financial assistance had been offered by the bank, of this figure 25 per cent had been denominated in local currencies (mainly Rand and RMB). He also said, '50 per cent (of projects) should be local currency financed'.[6] Recently, the BRICS members 'also discussed creating a common cryptocurrency for mutual payments, as the grouping was reducing the share of payments in the US dollar.'[7]

The legitimacy of US leadership was underpinned by its role as a guarantor of global stability and its ability to provide asymmetric benefits to new members in the global economy through predictable access to markets, capital and technology. It was the US's ability to transcend interstate competition, temper the structural motivation for relative gains, and, promote investment and commerce on the promise of a mutually beneficial global economy. Of course, the US was the biggest beneficiary of this seemingly benevolent hegemony. But others too with domestic policy frameworks and robust state capacity could benefit too. In recent decades, however, the US position in the global economy has transformed into one of a 'free rider' where both core industrial regions, such as Europe and Japan, and developing and the BRICS economies are being compelled to underwrite American profligacy by bearing immediate or medium-term national costs.

The fact that the US is unable to sustain its original mission or role as a supplier of public goods exemplifies that the post-1945 arrangements must be adapted, reformed, and, in some cases, supplanted to reflect a new reality. As the late political economist Giovanni Arrighi observed, 'the breakdown of any given hegemonic order is ultimately due to the fact that the increase in the volume and dynamic density of the system outgrows the organizational capabilities of the particular hegemonic complex that had created the conditions of the systemic expansion'.[8] In other words, the present cycle of economic globalization sowed the seeds of its own crisis.

After Hegemony, What?

Many thinkers in the US warn that as the 'unipolar moment' fades away with the relative decline of the West, a 'multipolar chaos' will ensue that will unravel the economic and geopolitical stability that American predominance provided to the international system. Indeed, the concept of hegemonic stability that is derived from such a discourse maintains that stability of a system requires a single hegemon to articulate and enforce the rules of interaction among the leading actors. Is this a self-serving narrative that emanates from a West unwilling and unable to contemplate a course of world history that might not conform to the 500-year cycle of Western capitalism and its guarantor – Western geopolitical preeminence?

To be sure, recent centuries of Western predominance have seen cycles of power transitions where one hegemon was replaced by another rising power, usually after a period of intense struggle and conflict. Each successive hegemonic power transition involved an expansion of the global economy both in complexity and geographic scale with the new dominant state underwriting the interdependence of the era. Each new hegemonic order was 'endowed with greater systemic capabilities than the old hegemonic complex' to resume the process of economic globalization after a period of turmoil.[9]

Given such a historical development of global capitalism, it is not surprising that mainstream conversations anticipate the rise of another hegemon to resume the 'longue durée' of capitalism. Such predictions are wrong. The present transition from *pax Americana* to a new regime of global governance, however, cannot replay the historical mode of a violent power transition that paves the way for a more capable hegemonic state or bloc.

For one, we are witnessing a bifurcation of the international system where the overall military balance still favours the declining US-led bloc while the more dynamic economic centres of capital accumulation are mostly emerging outside this US-led hierarchy, led of course by the BRICS economies. This represents a historical break from all previous cycles where the ascendant power(s) not only demonstrated greater dynamism than the incumbent powers but also developed military and geopolitical strength to match that economic vitality. According to present trends, the emerging powers will not be in a position to militarily dominate the US-led North even after the denouement of Western hegemony.

One way to resolve this bifurcation of the international system has been the rather ingenious suggestion by some Western scholars to forge a 'G-2': a grand coalition between the US and China that could salvage the present phase of globalization and much of the geopolitical status quo. Indeed, the second Obama administration seemed to have toyed with such an idea but soon found the geopolitical and even geoeconomic contradictions impossible to overcome. China, for its part, probably recognized that the degree of geopolitical concessions from the West that could induce it to forge such a global compact would have been unpalatable to the West making the entire idea too far-fetched to merit debate. Anyhow, China's state identity, which has always relied on an anti-hegemonic narrative, would constrain even the most ardent cooperative leadership in Beijing from changing China's international role to an open collaborator with the West.

The second reason why the historical trend of a hegemonic power transition cannot be replayed is because the military-technological environment rules out a violent power struggle.

The defining feature of the nuclear age is that revolutionary war has become impossible. Consequently, the rising regional powers will have fewer opportunities to leverage their growing capabilities to displace the extant great powers through use or threats of use of force. Naturally, the logic of strategic deterrence works both ways. The declining hegemon too, cannot leverage its conventional superiority to reorder and salvage the present system through either conquest or coercion. This is the unambiguous lesson of the past two decades.

The notion that BRICS can emerge as a geopolitical bloc to replace the declining US-led bloc is, therefore, an erroneous prediction, and a digression from the central purpose of BRICS. Instead, what we must prepare for is a fragmenting and decentralized global system that cannot be salvaged by relying on a new hegemonic bloc, however loosely it is structured. A democratized concept of world order is then the only viable alternative to a prolonged period of turmoil and chaotic adjustment by the leading states. As the renowned political economist Robert Cox once said, 'the new order will have to be built from the bottom up, when the present order falters in its attempt to hold things in place from the top down'.[10]

The emerging balance of power would not necessarily produce uncontrolled competition and a zero-sum world if the rising poles choose to focus on system-level problems such as security of the commons, re-designing and regulating global finance to make it less destabilizing and more development conducive, strengthening and reforming collective security institutions such as the UN, UNSC and the more nascent regional institutions like the Shanghai Cooperation Organisation (SCO). As multipolarity gains momentum, the 'moral hazard problem' that leads to free riding would be replaced by new incentives that impel rising powers to shoulder more responsibility, especially in supplying public goods to their own regions and investing in innovative multilateral initiatives.

Ironically, what unipolarity, ultimately, could not enforce – realigning national policies to system level problems – might see a better chance in a world where power and thus responsibility is diffused. The main ideational challenge will be to overcome the epistemic bias in mainstream discourse, particularly in India, that prevents us from visualizing a multilateral and democratized regime of global governance that does not require a hegemonic hierarchy to regulate and sustain it.

After Globalization, What?

Some optimistically view BRICS as an opportunity to resurrect the present mode of globalization with minor tactical reforms. The main issue is that the implicit offer to emerging economies was a disingenuous one, namely, share a rising burden for rebalancing and stabilizing the global economy but within an institutional structure that does not actually empower the Global South. Thus, the essence of global reform must begin with adjustments by the North who still benefit disproportionately from globalization (even though the backlash against globalization within western societies suggests the main benefits have been secured by a small minority).

Nevertheless, it is important to debate whether BRICS, assuming they have the capability, should restore globalization to its earlier avatar, which has been in a semi-crisis state since 2008. Some economists seem to tentatively support BRICS on the premise that these economies will assist in jump-starting the globalization and growth process. According to this argument, since BRICS members have flourished in the phase of globalization that is now under stress, it is in their self-interest to shore up the system that underpins their growth. Indeed, since 2001, BRICS have accounted for over 30 per cent of global economic growth and today BRICS account for over a third of global GDP.[11] On the surface, the argument sounds compelling.

However, if we undertake a dispassionate and far-sighted cost-benefit analysis of the structure of growth that emerging economies have actually witnessed, such as, investigating the consequences on social inequality, human capital development, ecological degradation, indigenous innovation, urban-rural imbalances, and financial instability, we will conclude that BRICS too has an ugly underbelly that reflects their active participation in the imbalanced and unequal neoliberal global model. In fact, some BRICS members, including India, are seriously lagging behind even low-income economies in the Global South on per capita human capital and socio-economic indicators even as absolute statistics advertise national success.

Sections of the policy elite of BRICS have acknowledged these contradictions though there is still no consensus on the broader lesson of the global economic crisis, which is that replicating Western capitalism is ultimately suicidal both nationally and for the entire planet. Resource constraints are such that BRICS, who account for 43 per cent of the world's population, cannot assume per capita consumption levels of non-renewable energy and other natural resources at the level of the high-income North without severely undermining the planet's and their own ecological stability. Plainly put, BRICS cannot emulate the 'ecological footprint' of the North in their future development strategies.

Furthermore, the present spectrum of available technological solutions to overcome 'Malthusian' type shortages is resource and fossil fuel-intensive in its applications, thus, imposing even greater demands on the finite resources available. It is also in this context that the present agenda of climate change is inadequate for it merely seeks to limit the growth potential of the South without fundamentally altering the essence of the present fossil fuel-dependent technological mode of industrialization or modifying the global capital accumulation structure itself. Logically, it is imperative to envision a completely new spectrum of technological solutions to sustain growth in a resource-constrained world. Suffice it to say, this can only be a collaborative effort and the initial intent could be discerned from the 2012 BRICS Delhi Declaration, which called for 'flow of knowledge amongst our research institutions' in 'priority areas of food, pharma, health and energy' and 'fields of nanotechnology, biotechnology, advanced materials science'.

Clearly, there is a need to construct a new discourse, which encourages regulated capital accumulation and simultaneously accords equal priority to sustainability and human capital development. It is now apparent that the scale of growth witnessed in recent decades would have been impossible to attain without ravaging the ecological system and degrading (underpricing) the value of labour and human initiative, and, with most of these costs being borne disproportionately by the Southern economies. A path-breaking study has provided rare empirical evidence for the period between 1990 and 2015. 'Value added per tonne of raw material embodied in exports is 11 times higher in high-income countries than in those with the lowest income, and 28 times higher per unit of embodied labor…On aggregate, ecologically unequal exchange allows high-income countries to simultaneously appropriate resources and to generate a monetary surplus through international trade.'[12] It is still not a flat world!

Hence, BRICS has a strategic self-interest in producing a discourse that both disincentivizes such unrestrained capital accumulation and corrects the unequal capacities to convert identical resources and inputs into surpluses. This means replacing the intellectual uniformity around the present conversations on the future of globalization with policy diversity, 'policy space', and experiments with decentralized and bottom-up solutions more in sync with local and regional realities.

For BRICS, Change Begins at Home

For BRICS to be an agent of change, resolving their domestic imbalances should find policy priority. The impact of the global crisis from 2008 onwards has made this unavoidable.

As alluded to earlier, globalization involved low and some medium-end labour-intensive manufacturing and services processes, previously located solely in the North, being off-shored and subcontracted to emerging economies. This fragmentation created what economists call 'under-absorption' in Asia, where production exceeds consumption, and 'over-absorption' in the West, where consumption exceeds income. The trade surpluses in the former and deficits in the latter were an empirical expression of this global division of labour.

The global economic crisis, which has continued for more than a decade now, has called this arrangement into question for two reasons. First, de-industrialization and the consequent adverse effects of unemployment in the North has made further offshoring politically contentious. Second, the massive build up of sovereign and private household debt in the North implies it can no longer fully absorb the export-oriented manufacturing infrastructure that its own MNCs have established in the emerging South.

The question that logically arises is what happens to the South's, including BRICS', production infrastructure whose *raison d'etre* has been to primarily supply the North?

Emerging economies will have to both retrench and divert their manufacturing and trading systems to cater to domestic and regional demand. One of the consequences of developing an export-oriented structure is that domestic savings invariably rise to finance manufacturing and related infrastructure, and wages are suppressed to make the labour force attractive to international capital. Consumption naturally declines. China has come to exemplify such a model. For instance, China's share of GDP contributed by the household sector, that is wages and consumption, had fallen to 35 per cent in 2010 compared to its peak of 56 per cent in 1983. In 2010, Chinese workers' salaries were equivalent to 25 per cent of GDP, versus the world average of 55 per cent. A rise in wages, and thus income, is a basic step in reviving domestic consumption. By 2015, workers' share of national GDP had risen to 50 per cent with domestic consumption also accounting for half of the national economy (in 2018), underscoring the rebalancing process underway in China.[13]

At a philosophical level, what BRICS members need is re-defining the metrics for economic progress and re-questioning the concept of development.

First, one of the enduring insights from North-South interdependence is that as emerging economies plugged into globalization they found capital accumulation easier than 'intellectual accumulation', the latter strategically guarded by Northern MNCs. To overcome this, BRICS' elites should end their overriding obsession with GDP growth rates, and focus more on outcome-oriented metrics that actually gauge social realities, human capital, innovation and the technological potential of their economies. In most BRICS economies – particularly in India – and, across the Global South in general, we observe that despite high GDP growth rates, there has been modest progress on human development indicators, food security and nutrition, science and technology, and, healthcare and education systems. Furthermore, if BRICS economies aim to improve the terms of trade with the North, that is move up the value chain by increasing the share of local value addition, it is people-centric development as described above that alone will sustain the resurgence of the emerging South.

Second, BRICS as an institution can promote a discourse whereby the logic of unrestrained profit accumulation inherent in capitalism is balanced by a dynamic, responsive, and strategic state. The latter issue is important as there is an implicit or even open contempt for the state in some BRICS economies. For instance, the emergence of an anti-statist ideology in India in the post-Cold War era, ironically, undermined the prospects of big capital, which is discovering that the receding of the state in socio-economic life diminishes the long-term prospects for capital accumulation! As the developed world's history shows, the dichotomy of 'state versus market' is a contemporary and erroneous invention emanating from the Reagan and Thatcherite retreat from statism after the 1970s, and historically, both elements have been indispensable for a dynamic and sustainable capitalism to function. Without a robust state, there can be no governance, no agency to establish and enforce property rights, and nobody to ensure the development and systematic flow of commodities, labour, and capital. Indeed, as some historians like Immanuel Wallerstein argue, the Westphalian state was the most enduring legacy of European capitalism.

Third, there is little doubt that the interdependence between Northern capital and labour in BRICS nations has adversely affected the latter's workers. Indeed, the workers in BRICS nations could not be faulted for wondering why their hard-earned savings have not been reinvested in domestic productive capital or social infrastructure but 'recycled' back into Western debt to finance Western consumption with the state mediating this process. What is required is an ideological reconstruction of capitalism and a new compact between capital and labour akin to the 'New Deal' forged during the 1930s in the US as a response to the crisis of 'over accumulation'.[14] The difference being that the present crisis requires such a compact to be on a global scale. The state along with several multilateral institutions will inevitably assume a central role in regulating and sustaining this new deal. Unsurprisingly, the political economy of the North, particularly in countries like the US, rejects such a 'New Deal' and its implied redistributive features not only as ideologically abhorrent but also because it would imply ceding wealth, and thus power, to the emerging South.

BRICS, however, cannot rebalance their own economies without forging a sustainable compact between capital and labour. And the fact that BRICS provides both the spatial, resource and human capital inputs vital to global production, it potentially represents a bargaining leverage that the BRICS states can collectively use to improve the terms of economic exchange between the high-income economies and the Global South.

THE ONGOING FLUX in the international political economy suggests both an ideological crisis and a geopolitical and geoeconomic one, as the crisis that the North seeks to grapple with is intricately linked with the 'interdependence' and the attendant diffusion of wealth that advanced economies themselves initiated. Globalization was so 'successful' that systemic instability emerged sooner than anticipated. By 'successful' it is meant that relative growth rate differentials and future trends between the industrialized North and the emerging South have become significant enough to produce resistance in the developed world's body politic. BRICS is an expression of this diffusion of wealth and power. Today, BRICS accounts for almost a third of global GDP (when measured at purchasing power parity). By 2018, BRICS had surpassed the G7 on this indicator.[15]

Having acquired its present material position, BRICS should play an active role in shaping the post-crisis world order by crafting an alternative discourse that seeks to modify globalization. One of the legitimate grievances of BRICS elites is that they were either excluded from or simply ignored in the aftermath of the Second World War when most of the contemporary governance institutions were conceived and erected. Now, to be at an inflexion point and perhaps on the eve of another tumultuous global adjustment, BRICS cannot excuse itself from fashioning a transformative vision.

Ultimately, the most important contribution of BRICS to international relations should not be simply to balance material power, which of course is essential to preserve a semblance of global order and to counteract the reactionary impulses of the West, but to promote new norms and attendant institutions that reflect the near absence of global governance today. To be sure, only when inter-governmental networks such as BRICS attain a level of cohesiveness, capability, legitimacy and credibility to address systemic issues and thereby pose an institutional competition to the older arrangements will emerging powers be in a position to bargain for alternatives. For now, BRICS may not display all these prerequisites. But the group is acquiring the internationalist vision and practical experience to manage the disruptions in the global economic system. The question that should, however, be debated is the future direction and role that BRICS should take. It would be truly tragic if BRICS became a platform for parochial power seekers or a symbol of cosmetic change.

Finally, the questions for India are equally profound. If India can leverage the ongoing global power transition to increase its developmental options why should it squander that opportunity? If the US, Europe and Japan can compete fiercely among their industrial and consumer MNCs without compromising on their common strategic agenda to preserve their asymmetric advantages in the global terms of trade why can BRICS not reconcile the logic of competition with their parallel strategic collectivism to reshape the rules of the world economy in favour of the Global South? We need a more sophisticated conversation in India. Let us also remember that the trend lines are for an interdependent if chaotic multipolar world, not a Sino-centric Middle Kingdom. For a world deprived of governance, BRICS might just supply a modicum of order and ideas. India can and must step up to the plate, even if its motivations are derived from the narrow perspective of accumulating more national power and enhancing the well-being of its polity.

III

STRATEGY AND POLICY

This final section engages with the broader debates in India by weighing in on high policy and strategy including debates over military doctrines that are most relevant for managing regional security. This theme is also closely linked to the type of roles that India wants to play in the emerging world order. It also examines the recent connectivity ideas and plans that have emerged as new faultlines but also possible opportunities for innovative cooperation between India and China in the future. Finally, the section delves into the challenges, opportunities and risks confronting India's policymakers as they look at various options in crafting a new equilibrium with a rising China.

1

INDIA'S GEOSTRATEGY AND CHINA: MACKINDER VERSUS MAHAN?

In 2013, it was reported that Chinese submarines had been conducting forays into the Indian Ocean that were apparently picked up by US Navy sonar.[1] A few weeks later, there was a Chinese intrusion in the western sector of the India-China border where a platoon of Chinese troops entered the Depsang Valley area of eastern Ladakh.[2] While the status quo ante was peacefully attained, the 2013 Ladakh standoff was a vivid reminder of the abiding implications of an unresolved Himalayan dispute. Collectively, what both these events also evoked was a deeper contestation in India's geostrategy vis-à-vis China. India's geostrategy is being contested by two somewhat competing images: the Mackinder image – or the idea that continental spaces are what really matter in power politics – and the Mahanian image – or the idea that maritime spaces in the seas are what ultimately account for the power of states. The

2020 Ladakh crisis brought this geopolitical dilemma back to the forefront of India's debate on a viable geostrategy.

The Mahanian Delusion

The typical Mahanian solution to the China challenge is that India can overcome some of its continental disadvantages vis-à-vis China by posing a nuisance to China's sea lines of communication (SLOCs), or even involving itself in East Asian disputes in the South China Sea. Indeed, during the 2020 Ladakh crisis India deployed a frontline warship in the South China Sea area in coordination with the US navy.[3] The underlying logic stemmed from the idea of horizontal escalation where asymmetry in one theatre can sought to be overcome by escalating the conflict to a wider geographical domain. In sum, if China pursues adventurism in the mountains, India can respond on the high seas.

While conceptually intuitive linkage requires equivalence in that Beijing must value the integrity of its SLOCs enough to change its calculus on the mountains. Naval blockades are also complicated operations and the time horizon for success, to the point that China would find its resource security threatened, would be significantly longer than a swift and limited continental operation pursued to permanently change the LAC or for punitive reasons. China's growing Strategic Petroleum Reserve, though intended to offset market disruptions, will also be an asset in such a situation. Finally, China's pursuit of new Eurasian lines of communication, both with growing energy linkages with Russia and connectivity through Central Asia, indicate a potential declining dependence on Indian Ocean SLOCs, at least for some strategic resources.[4] As for the idea of signalling some sort of pressure in the South China Sea by an individual or a coordinated deployment with the US, China's natural strengths in the area are adequate for such a move. We will return to this later in the chapter.

Clearly, China must perceive the game similarly, and there is nothing to suggest it does other than the Indian maritime strategist's preference for such a game. Plainly put, a 'core interest' cannot be secured by peripheral horizontal actions.

Dealing with Continental Pressure

How can India deter serious conventional pressure from being applied on its frontiers? There are no alternatives to deterrence capabilities in the continental realm where India's core interests (territorial integrity or maintenance of the status quo in disputed area) can be pressured. Perhaps, a more systematic way to develop deterrence options is through a two-fold process.

First, strengthening India's frontier tripwires at key passes across the LAC by enhancing logistics, heavy-lift capabilities, and intelligence, surveillance and reconnaissance (ISR) capabilities to increase the ability to move forces forward toward vulnerable mountain passes. This would raise some costs for China. To be sure, there are inherent geographical limits to how efficient and flexible the logistics chain can become and India can never match China's advantages that involve a relatively flexible approach to border management, given the advantages of the Tibetan terrain that is generally flatter and thus easier to manoeuver.

Over the past decade, India has been attempting to narrow the gap. In 2006, the BRO was authorized to construct 61 roads of a total length of about 3,300 km along the border with China. After a slow start, where only 20 per cent of these projects had been completed by 2015, since 2018, 'the figure on finished roads had shot up to 2,486 km, with major gains in

Jammu & Kashmir and Arunachal Pradesh.'[5] In 2010, the Indian Army Headquarters had identified 28 strategic rail routes for access to India's border areas, 14 of which were prioritized by the Ministry of Defence in November 2010. Yet, none of these projects had seen progress by 2016.[6]

While this spurt of infrastructure activities has certainly improved India's access to forward areas along the LAC, the logistical networks are still constrained by geography and modern infrastructure. Currently, India is not even close to reaching the viable limits of what would constitute a modicum of modern logistics and ISR network within the constrained topography. To appreciate how formidable the logistical constraints are for high altitude areas on the India-China border, note the following assessment:

> After acclimatization, soldiers move slower at high altitudes than they do at sea level, must carry lighter loads, and consume more calories to sustain themselves. The diesel engines that power trucks and armored vehicles, likewise, are less efficient and less powerful at 4,000 meters. Resupplying soldiers under these conditions is a massive undertaking… for Sino-Indian border contingencies, the most important measure of distance is not kilometers from the engagement, but meters below the engagement, because the tightest logistical constraint upon arrival at the battlefield is acclimatization time, not driving distance.[7]

It could be argued that the absence of modern logistics and a connectivity network may have inadvertently led to an over-emphasis on forward patrolling of disputed posts on the LAC. In other words, the prevailing approach to border management appears to be a quick fix to compensate for the decades-old structural problems in the rear: such as infrastructure, logistical chain, and technology-based ISR. If some of these measures, including monitoring capabilities, were strengthened, border management would be transformed. But in the absence of a serious transformation of the rear logistical network leading upto the mountains, India will always remain hostage to a Chinese fait accompli on a disputed pocket on the LAC. The strategic effect of altitude and terrain have led to the adoption of different border management approaches for India and China:

> The difficulties of fighting at altitude – namely the long lead-time to move from garrison to the putative battlefield – give both sides an incentive to make expensive preparations necessary to arrive quickly at the site of a dispute. India forward deploys much larger forces than China; locally garrisoned Indian soldiers outnumber the PLA both in the Sikkim and Ladakh sectors but as India has the 'downhill side' of the border in all sectors, the nearby units are often stationed at low altitudes. China, conversely, has far fewer soldiers permanently based near the disputed border sectors and has instead focused on developing expensive infrastructure to speed arrival of reinforcements, enabling smaller forces at the border to initiate and respond very quickly in a nascent dispute.[8]

China's 'posture has been facilitated by the impressive development of China's highway and high-speed railway networks, particularly the extension of the Qinghai–Tibet railway.' Today, 'Beijing could dispatch several divisions to the LAC within a few days.'[9] In other words, China possesses the flexibility to rapidly concentrate forces during a standoff or crisis to any point on the long frontier. The PLA also enjoys 'a much more robust, multilayered communications architecture, having laid fiber-optic cabling and installed numerous small-aperture terminal satellite stations.' In addition, because of the high elevations of the Plateau of Tibet, Chinese ground forces benefit from some commanding advantages – they overlook many Indian forward positions, rendering surveillance and artillery operations easier to execute.'[10]

The 2020 Ladakh crisis reflected such a scenario where the PLA was able to leverage its advantages to swiftly move military forces into disputed grey zones along the LAC and alter the status quo, despite India's infrastructure modernizations in recent years.

Second, rather than escalation in peripheral domains, the ability to escalate vertically (that is, in the same area) and horizontally (in a broader theatre) the levels of violence is an important element of enhancing deterrence. China is capable of amassing a large volume of forces and firepower to any sector of the LAC at short notice.[11] To deter such a blitzkrieg scenario, India can signal capabilities and a doctrine that enables it to degrade targets deep inside Tibet and in a domain that China truly values – important provinces and industrially significant cities in the continental heartland in eastern China.

This implies that India requires stand-off deterrent systems – such as longer-range missiles and greater reach in its strategic and tactical air power. Some of these capabilities already exist but they have not been directed toward deterrence objectives by a central policymaker. Consequently, the services – Army and Air Force in this case – have been left to indulge their parochial preferences that preclude a joint land-air doctrine. The Army had remained wedded to a manpower-intensive approach to deterrence and the Air Force has yet to construct a modern and integrated air-defence network like China possesses on the other side. Nor does India possess the inventory of missiles that have transformed the PLA's ability to strike at a range of targets on its periphery.

Perhaps it was from such a fragmented assessment that a widely-read 2012 policy document advocated asymmetric deterrence by preparing to 'trigger an effective insurgency in the areas occupied by Chinese forces' in the event of an invasion.[12] China is not even remotely going to oblige the Indian strategist's plans for a protracted war near the foothills, where most of India's forces are garrisoned. In fact, it can be argued that a manpower-dominated modernization approach to frontier defence rather than enhancing deterrence might inadvertently undermine it by sending the wrong signal to Beijing, and, simultaneously, delude the Indian political and military leadership into believing that an 'active defence' type posture is coming into being.[13]

Peacetime Challenges and Limited War

The China challenge on the frontiers should be clearly deconstructed. In the absence of an unresolved boundary, one challenge is to ensure the disputed LAC zone does not widen because of China's logistic ability to pursue an activist peacetime patrolling posture. This can only be dealt with by the alluded focus on logistics and monitoring capabilities along with a streamlined approach to border management. Further, since India holds the lower ground, it should also leverage CBMs and jointly negotiate new norms to constrain some of China's flexibility and superior patrolling capabilities. If leveraged prudently, CBMs can assist in the management of a stable status quo. This is easier said than done, given the stress to the existing CBMs and agreements since 2013. Standoffs have grown more and more complex in their duration and scale with the 73-day

Doklam crisis and the 2020 Ladakh crisis as the most serious in a chain of incidents over the past decade.

Furthermore, there is the classic scenario of a limited conflict ensuing from a deterioration in bilateral relations. This goes to the heart of a viable deterrence strategy based on the geopolitical nature of the Himalayan battlefield. A deterrence-by-denial strategy is a flawed approach in a nuclear world. In fact, the asymmetry can be turned to India's advantage. Instead of relying on a flexible response strategy, which plays to China's strengths, given its superior logistics and geostrategic advantages of the higher ground, India's doctrine should be based on deterrence-by-punishment. It is futile and expensive to prepare to engage China at all levels in the entire spectrum of violence. If there is one lesson from the India-Pakistan dyad this is it. The conventionally weaker actor can negate asymmetry by politically leveraging its strategic capabilities and doctrine. A credible and thoughtfully signalled nuclear doctrine correlated to a joint theatre-wide conventional doctrine might enable India to stave off a scenario of Chinese adventurism and a larger military conflict.

Whose Doctrine is it Anyway?

The key point is that the existent military doctrine is emerging from institutional inertia and parochial preferences rather than through a carefully debated plan overseen by the political leadership. If the goal is to create deterrence under high-tech conventional and nuclear conditions, then investing in manpower to engage in a hypothetical battle in Tibet is a sub-optimal strategy that would exacerbate the India-China security dilemma without increasing India's security on the frontier. Given China's geostrategic, technological and logistical advantages an active defence posture by India is simply not a credible aspiration.

A deterrence-by-punishment strategy combined with robust holding capabilities is preferable to pursuing the illusion of an active defence doctrine. Such a strategy requires stand-off precision long-range systems, space-based domain awareness, fourth and fifth generational air power capabilities, and a modern air-defence network. Again, some of the underlying ingredients are already scattered across the services but have not been honed toward joint doctrinal goals.

The heart of the problem is not the dearth of strategic thought but the diversity of strategic perceptions and doctrines that are vying for individual relevance, and even primacy. While the Mahanians belittle the continentalists for clinging to outdated geopolitical images, the continentalists have struggled to internalize the implications of a post-nuclear high-technological environment, where deterrence must be the principal purpose of military strategy. The military dimensions of grand strategy cannot be additive where different stakeholders – in this case the multiple wings of defence services – suggest autonomous means to confront the same threats or even reconstruct threats to suit the means and then the strategist is tasked with adding these doctrines up.

Strategy is not about throwing money into a bottomless pit but dynamically and creatively honing the most appropriate instruments toward threats the way they are likely to appear based on the opponent's political goals and military doctrine, and not how and where they should appear. India's political elite must accept the lion's share of the blame since it is apathy and abdication at that level that has condoned the bottom-up and fragmented approach to strategy with no central planner willing to set the terms of the agenda.

India's Priority: Continental China or Maritime China?

India should focus more on continental China rather than maritime China; and it is the balance of power and influence on the subcontinental periphery that needs constant strategic attention. China's lines of communication with South Asia emanate from continental China. The corridor to Central Asia, trans-Karakoram linkages through Pakistan or the corridor through Myanmar are all part of a continental geostrategy by China to secure its peripheral regions and integrate its neighbours. The extension and further potential of these lines of communication into the northern Indian Ocean – Bay of Bengal or the Arabian Sea – cannot be tapped without Indian strategic acquiescence and cooperation.

The maritime realm between India and China, contrary to the observation of most analysts[14], is not a zero-sum theatre where 'core' interests for both countries are at stake. The geopolitical reality is that China's SLOCs traverse near Indian naval deployments, with more than 85 per cent of Chinese oil imports flowing through Indian Ocean sea lanes. Similarly, more than 50 per cent of India's trade now goes through the Malacca and Singapore Straits. Rather than becoming a source of contention this should form the basis of an accommodative maritime relationship.

In an interdependent international political economy, the idea of unilateral security over SLOCs is illogical. The 'Indo-Pacific' commons fell under the sway of a single superpower – the US – under unique historical conditions that are not likely to prevail indefinitely. While it is premature to pre-judge the evolution of the 'Indo-Pacific' maritime system, it cannot but be a collective endeavour where no single power can be excluded from the management of the commons. Within that logic, it is probable that different regional powers will assume greater burdens in their geopolitical peripheries. But as long as inter-regional commerce and resource exchanges underpin the global economy the commons cannot become a closed security system. The historical lessons from the Anglo-German maritime rivalry over a century ago attests to the futility of a zero-sum contest. That rivalry produced an uncontrollable arms race that shattered British maritime dominance and, ultimately, Germany's own pretensions to European hegemony. None of these states have recovered from these strategic misjudgments.

In fact, the evolution of military technology underscores that Mahanian ideas are nearly obsolete. The historical Mahanian logic of offensive sea control – 'defined as the ability to use the seas in defiance of the will of others'[15] – via large surface fleets is passé. The original Mahanian prescriptions of sea control were derived from a specific historical, industrial and technological context that no longer prevails given the evolution of the military-technological environment and diffusion of asymmetric capabilities. In current times, continental-based extended-range missile forces; fourth and fifth generation aerospace capabilities; undersea capabilities like attack submarines; land, air and space-based ISR and targeting capabilities; anti-satellite weapons (ASAT) and cyber capabilities make the idea of sea-control a deeply contested concept. Actually, sea denial along with limited power-projection capabilities is perhaps the most that contemporary rising powers can realistically aspire to. The maritime force structure of tomorrow is likely to trend towards disaggregated and less vulnerable platforms rather than concentrated firepower in large carrier-based fleets.

It would be more appropriate to describe the current Chinese military strategy as a regional sea-denial approach than a quest for global maritime power.[16] Land-based systems play an integral part in shaping China's naval modernization, that is, not emulating the large surface fleets in the Anglo-American tradition, despite having the economic and industrial base to pursue such a force structure. As one Western assessment notes, 'the Chinese navy's main purpose is still to protect China from US sea-based strike power.'[17] As an authoritative US study finds, 'China's new navy relies more on unmanned cruise and ballistic missiles than on manned aircraft, and more on submarines than surface vessels.'[18]

This was exemplified by China's August 2020 test of its long-range anti-ship missiles – so-called 'carrier-killers' – seen by many observers as a strong message to the US navy, which has been the dominant military player in the Western Pacific. China claimed the tests demonstrated advanced capabilities that could 'detect, track and lock on' to enemy warships.[19] Given this situation, it is ironic then that India's strategic discourse invokes the Mahanian image of China's two aircraft carriers (the second domestic-built carrier entered service in December 2019 and is still developing its capabilities) as a symbol and guide for China's maritime strategy.[20]

It is true that in quantitative terms, the People's Liberation Army Navy (PLAN) has surpassed the US navy. According to the US Department of Defense 2020 report, the PLAN has about 350 ships and submarines including over 130 major surface combatants. The US navy, in comparison, has about 293 ships. Qualitatively and technologically, however, the PLAN is focused on threats on China's eastern seaboard where the competition led by the US presents a formidable challenge. As the US government report notes, China has over '1,250 ground-launched ballistic missiles (GLBMs) and ground-launched cruise missiles (GLCMs) with ranges between 500 and 5,500 kilometers' including 'one of the world's largest forces of advanced long-range surface-to-air systems.'[21] This inventory of defensive and offensive firepower reveals China's focus. 'The PLA is developing capabilities to provide options for the PRC to dissuade, deter, or, if ordered, defeat third-party intervention during a large-scale, theater campaign such as a Taiwan contingency.'[22]

Blue water projection beyond regional seas, in particular the first island chain consisting of strategic areas like the South China Sea and the Taiwan Straits, is of secondary priority for Beijing. In 2020, China has been conducting more complex military exercises including simultaneous drills in the four sea regions on its maritime periphery, 'to signal its readiness to handle confrontation with the United States and self-ruled Taiwan.'[23] Despite a full treasury and an industrial capacity to expand its navy for global roles, the core objective of Chinese military strategy for the foreseeable future is on sea denial focused on the Western Pacific and the US Navy.

The US Navy recognizes that it can no longer operate unhindered in the maritime peripheries of several regional powers, and much of US strategic discourse is animated by the asymmetric anti-access challenge ranging from regions such as West Asia to the Korean Peninsula.[24] Such disruptive technologies that provide asymmetric options to regional powers are here to stay, and as these capabilities are fielded by the Eurasian rimland powers, the Mahanian conversation will be radically altered in the coming years.

In sum, while continental states such as India and China can raise the operating costs for other maritime powers – including each other – in their respective regions, they cannot unilaterally acquire the sea control necessary to secure blue water SLOCs, which are the lifelines for their economies. Therein lies the logic of competition and cooperation. Self-help strategies can co-exist with cooperative burden-sharing norms to enable stability of the wider commons.

Taming the Mahanians for a Continental-first Geostrategy

The irony is that Chinese influence in the Indian Ocean littoral has not emerged because the PLAN is perceived as a security provider, but because China's economic and military-technical assistance has ensured a political space for China. India's naval instrument can only be one of an ensemble of means to restore Indian influence. Insofar as Indian influence in East Asia is concerned, emulating China's own practices of creating economic and political presence in these countries is more viable than premature military forays into theatres where India will have to face the brunt of Chinese firepower. For example, Indian influence is advanced more by buttressing Vietnam's own capability to asymmetrically balance an assertive China than a direct footprint in the South China Sea.

The Mahanians have been urging India to discard its continental images and envisage an expansive maritime role for itself and become a 'net security provider' in other regions. The analysis thus far would suggest this is not a prudent strategy for India. Given the extraordinary investment and lead-time for a naval modernization, it is vital that Indian strategists get this right.

The Mahanians in some respects do reflect the wider changes in India's economic and diplomatic profile that have dispersed Indian interests across the globe. It is true that a globalizing India has an economic and cultural footprint in several continents and India's institutions should reflect this. But it is by no means clear whether the maritime instrument, often projected as a potential guarantor of India's expanding global interests, should be leading this process. And it is certainly not evident that India should pursue an extra-regional role before producing a modicum of security and influence in its own region, where Indian regional aspirations remain contested, and attaining stability, if not, a final border settlement with China.

For the foreseeable future, India's 'core interests' should remain continental and must be pursued via a continental-first geostrategy. A secondary maritime role closely linked to enhancing Indian deterrence and influence in the sub-continental realm seems more in tune not only with India's national challenges but also with the geostrategic direction of pressures that keep recurring.

In the 1950s, Nehru had remarked, 'To be secure on land, we must be supreme at sea'. This assertion reflected an uncritical acceptance of an old British adage despite a vastly different geopolitical context. Separated from continental great powers, the British and Americans could shape the balance of power at sea without worrying about their land frontiers. For India, continental geopolitics can never be compensated by a maritime geostrategy.

2

SHOULD INDIA 'BE EAST' OR BE EURASIAN?

For the past decade, Western security commentaries have portrayed India as a natural member of East Asia's political life. The impetus for this narrative began in November 2010 when President Barack Obama, in his address to a joint session of Parliament, urged India's lawmakers to 'not only "look East" but "engage East"'. In the ensuing years, American diplomats have prodded India towards a 'Be East' policy, perhaps reflecting impatience with the pace of India's Pacific rendezvous.[1]

India, in fact, elected to look East back in the early 1990s, long before Washington's courting began. And simply because the West has been encouraging this, does not mean that India should do the opposite. However, what India's political and strategic community should debate is a geostrategy that is consistent with the geopolitical context of South Asia.

It can be argued that by diverting India's geostrategic attention eastwards, Washington has been attempting to re-orient Indian threat perceptions away from Pakistan. And it is not difficult to discern why. Drawing India's strategic focus away from the subcontinent would enable Washington to maintain its South Asia policy of increasing investments in both India and Pakistan without their bilateral contradictions undermining its regional strategy. This pattern recurred throughout the Cold War, and continues to be a potential nuisance to US foreign policy.

Now, China is undoubtedly both a regional and a geostrategic challenge to Indian security and most analysts have viewed the US promoting India's 'East Asia' credentials as an opportunity that should be leveraged both to enhance Indian influence and perhaps even increase its bargaining leverage in relation to China.

But it is arguably not an overriding factor that should compel India to abandon its multi-vector worldview, which seeks to expand Indian influence in West Asia, Southeast Asia and the Indian Ocean littoral. Plainly put, by looking eastwards neither will the reality of Pakistan disappear, and thus, nor would the opportunity of a pressure point on India that a Pakistani proxy offer to its benefactors gets removed.

By exclusively and openly focusing on a future Chinese threat, India would merely invite a larger deployment of Chinese offensive forces in Tibet requiring an Indian counter-response, thus producing an action-reaction dynamic that can hardly enhance Indian security. It would presumably also give the Pakistani military a window of opportunity to rehabilitate itself and maintain its position as a regional balancer, ironically a situation that would favour China.[2]

In fact, a *threat-based* assessment goes against the very grain of contemporary strategic discourse in security establishments today. The mantra of *capability-based* military modernization is now preferred by most aspiring powers, including India in a post-Cold War era where the dissolution of entrenched ideological and material conflicts is reducing the salience of the notion of permanent threats.

What does this essentially mean? A focus on capabilities rather than threats is advantageous because threats may be transient and continue to assume different avatars, and, a grand strategy or military modernization programme that tailors itself exclusively to preconceived threats will usually find itself behind the curve. In contrast, focusing on capabilities will offer more flexibility to re-divert or re-deploy national instruments toward dynamic threat contingencies. This has become particularly pertinent at a time when India's adversaries are employing unconventional means to destabilize or coerce India. Pakistan's proxy war and its well-documented mission of instigating turmoil and insurrection in the Kashmir valley is a case in point. Similarly, China despite the rhetoric of stability continues to question India's territorial integrity and challenge Indian influence across the subcontinent.

To be sure, capabilities are not acquired in a vacuum. Capabilities require a context and a reference point if they are to be acquired and honed efficiently. This context is derived from a country's self-image of its place in international life, the geopolitical location of the state, the material and military attributes of its peers, and the desired zone of influence.

Returning to the contemporary flux in India's political and security posture, what geostrategic orientation should India assume to channel its grand strategic agenda? India's potential and aspiration to be a pole in the international system coupled with the complex geopolitical reality that includes at least two uncooperative states on its periphery implies that it would be imprudent to focus on Pacific China as an exclusive symbol of India's rise. From India's perspective, its core interests are in South Asia and it is continental China rather than naval China that remains a priority, and it is the balance of power on the Himalayan frontiers that India must seek foremost to improve.

Thus, deconstructing the 'China threat' from an Indian perspective requires greater nuance. China is both a battlefield threat with regard to the defence of India's northern frontiers and a regional challenge as an unchecked Chinese power in South Asia will inevitably reduce Indian influence in the subcontinent and reshape the politics and foreign policies of India's neighbours.

The former does not require India to deploy its entire military and diplomatic apparatus as a counter-response. A focused strategy of conventional and strategic deterrence will deny China the opportunity to implement a policy of coercion against India on the border, thus creating a theatre of balance of power on the Himalayan front. Responding to China's potential for coercion on the Himalayan front would require the Indian armed forces to transform their mission and doctrines from an attritional orientation that is predicated on waging an extended campaign with the PLA on Indian territory to a more flexible orientation in force structures and war-fighting doctrines.[3]

This implies that India requires stand-off deterrent systems – such as longer-range missiles, greater reach in air power and better intelligence, surveillance and reconnaissance capabilities (ISR) – to improve its situational awareness of the entire Himalayan theatre. In other words, deterrence would be achieved not by luring the enemy deep into Indian territory and waging a high casualty war but by demonstrating the capability to degrade China's offensive forces at the earliest sign of a forward mobilization.

Simultaneously, the overall conventional asymmetry in respect to China – both in terms of comprehensive national power and combat war-fighting capabilities – must also be counteracted with an equal priority accorded to operationalizing a credible second-strike nuclear capability implying the deployment of long-range ballistic missiles that cover China's eastern seaboard. Without this attendant development, India would have fewer options in deterring a Chinese conventional escalation should India's conventional strategy fail in its deterrence mission. Bluntly put, India must have the capability to raise the levels of violence should the 'vertical escalation' game ever arise.[4]

Insofar as balancing Chinese influence in the sub-Himalayan space is concerned, that can only be effectively dealt with by a policy of internal balancing or building India's domestic capabilities – improving governance, economic and social connectivity across the subcontinent, adopting an economic model that produces true pan-Indian development – and a more astute and nimble regional policy.

In the broader Asian arena, India recognizes the challenge that surrounds China's rise and is keen to participate in diverse bilateral and multilateral initiatives that can both serve as a hedge against a more assertive China, and, advance the search for a stable equilibrium and a plural multi-polar status quo. India's abiding belief that a bloc-based system usually produces lesser security for all implies that India's vision for Asian security is broader than that of the status quo actors in East Asia and the Western Pacific. As India's former NSA Shivshankar Menon had once remarked an Asian security system 'should be plural. No one-size solution or simplistic prescription will work. We should learn from the failure of Cold War alliance systems in the area, and of earlier Asian Collective Security proposals'. The NSA had further argued that a new Asian order must include 'the entire Eurasian landmass' from the 'Suez to the Pacific'.[5]

The underlying logic for such an open security system is underscored by the global political economy. The economic interdependence within Asia, especially in East Asia, and the complex web of extra-regional trade and investment linkages that connect Asia to Western economies only emphasizes the need for an open economic and security system. Despite the US-China trade and economic competition, geoeconomic linkages between the West and China continue to be deep and complex and include the participation of a multitude of state and corporate actors from across East Asia. India's perfunctory contribution to this division of labour is the true failure of its 'look east policy'.[6]

Geopolitical Foundations of Indian Foreign Policy

The contemporary question among some strategists is whether India should steer its military modernization towards land warfare (including air power) capabilities or become a 'hybrid' power with land and sea capabilities to reflect the 'continentality' and 'maritimity' that characterizes South Asia's geopolitical setting.

India's growing share of international trade and rising hydrocarbon imports have increased the importance of the maritime domain for the country, and it now has a vital interest in ensuring its own energy sea lanes remain open (oil import dependence close to 90 per cent). Thus, the trajectory of economic and industrial development has made the search for natural resources in West Asia and lines of communication to the Indian heartland a new geopolitical variable that will inevitably shape Indian foreign policy. India also has interests in developing partnerships in Southeast Asia, particularly with nations like Vietnam that are seeking to maintain their autonomy in the face of the rise of China.

These geoeconomic and strategic imperatives, however, cannot come at the cost of neglecting the complex continental challenges to the Indian heartland. The search for new lines of communication to other centres of resources outside for which Indian maritime capabilities will be an indispensable instrument of the state will have to be balanced by securing and strengthening the heartland itself where India's core interests lie.[7]

Even today, the geopolitical context requires the Indian state to pay adequate strategic attention to the continental dimensions of its national security: the proxy war by Pakistan, multidimensional challenges to the territorial integrity of Jammu & Kashmir, an unresolved border dispute with China, covert cooperation between China and Pakistan, prospects for stability in Tibet and its potential to spill over into the sub-Himalayan space, and, enhancing economic and political linkages within the subcontinent. Clearly, as far as India is concerned, 'border pressure' is greater on its land frontiers than sea frontiers.[8] Ultimately the response to the geopolitical pressure on its continental frontiers that will determine its emergence as a serious player in the Asian and global arena.

In the final analysis, India's geopolitical location requires a corresponding multi-vector geostrategy, where no one region or location must overwhelm or negate its priorities, interests, and projection of influence in other directions. So yes, look East, but do not stop looking over your shoulder too. This would produce a manageable relationship with China and its neighbours without compromising the strategic flexibility and options relating to Pakistan and West Asia; especially when that region is primed to witness tumultuous change in this current decade.

India's geopolitical location makes it a Eurasian power, and the country's foreign policy must reflect that.

3

INDIA'S ROLE IN ASIA

Geopolitically, Asia is churning. How can India make sense of the uncertainties and carve out a regional role? Policymakers and analysts are grappling with the Asian puzzle in which the pacifying effects of economic interdependence are receding. The materialism that informs liberal theories about the logic between interdependence and peace is being questioned. The missing link can be traced to ideas and emotions that conventional scholarship dismisses as 'irrational'.

Perceptive observers now recognize that Asia's transition is a dynamic of both power and identity. Gilbert Rozman, a professor at Princeton University, argues that East Asia is undergoing an identity flux, where foreign policies are being shaped by the search for stable national identities and roles in the emerging order.

East Asia's history has made this process even more boisterous. China's history with Japan is well known. It is hardly surprising that Chinese leaders during their visits to India invoke the image of Dwarkanath Kotnis, a selfless Indian doctor, who treated Chinese troops in their independence struggle against Japan in the 1930s. The Korean peninsula, too, has a past with Japanese annexation that still shapes perceptions. Though it is the North Korean regime that has a self-image as the vanguard of Korea's independent anti-colonial identity, South Korea, too, has struggled with its role as security partner of its former colonizer.

India's 'Look East' discourse mostly ignores such perceptual and identity factors vis-à-vis the history of Japanese militarism. The post-1945 reconstruction of Japanese identity was an extraordinary exercise in which the victor socialized the vanquished into a new role that was firmly in place once the Pacific Cold War erupted in the 1950s. Over the past two decades, China's rapid rise reopened the question of Japan's resumption of normal sovereign rights.

Perhaps the most India can do is empathize with regional perceptions of militarist Japan's legacy, and simultaneously recognize that its diminished geopolitical role since 1947 probably makes it tough for Japanese politics to objectively assess its militarist past that was purged from Japanese institutions after its defeat. Interestingly, the Japanese defence minister's remarks at the Shangri-La Dialogue some years ago that 'Japan caused tremendous damage and suffering to…Asian nations' is a positive sign.

It is unclear whether the US can sustain its role of regional manager indefinitely. Arguably, despite the rhetoric of a Pacific 'pivot', the structural trend is of formerly subordinated states assuming more control of their destinies. This is unlikely to be a smooth ride and Washington should responsibly secure its interests rather than exploit identity politics for transient benefits.

China's rise also has implications for the regulation of the emerging multipolar order. What ideas will inform the future order? History offers few viable templates.

The pre-nineteenth century Sinic-world order relied on a hierarchical principle with China as the 'Middle Kingdom'. This order was based less on military coercion than on a self-image of Confucian moral superiority, and Chinese emperors expended much treasure to socialize the region to China's cultural hegemony. It collapsed with the entry of the European powers that shocked China out of its 'Middle Kingdom' complex.

The other image of regional order is of an aggressive Japan-style rise of a regional contender leveraging its industrialization to overwhelm the Western Pacific and continental East Asia.

Clearly, history offers more lessons than solutions. This is where India can make a normative contribution. India has always believed that bloc-based systems destabilize a region and perpetuate security dilemmas. India's official pronouncements must remain committed to an open, inclusive and plural security architecture and not a closed hierarchical system led by one major power and at the expense of other great and middle powers. This is a realist rather than a post-modern insight, and India's Cold War experience attests to this.

This also implies eschewing securitizing the 'Indo-Pacific' via narrow images of some maritime strategists who rarely articulate the ingredients of a sustainable order. Going forward, India should interpret the 'Indo-Pacific' concept holistically by constructing a role to shape and benefit from inter-regional economic and security interdependence. Finally, by recognizing the relevance of history in shaping contemporary East Asia's identity politics, India can craft a more sophisticated regional policy.

Factors that Should Inform India's Indo-Pacific policy

First, do not become a spoke in the hub: that is, do not get roped into a collective security bloc with rigid political and military commitments. India's traditional preference for open and inclusive security architectures is well known and it must adhere to that concept rather than drift into a closed security grouping dominated by one or more states.

Second, recognize that the Indo-Pacific is an immensely complex theatre where old histories continue to cast their shadow over contemporary power politics. Conflicting identities – China-Japan, South Korea-Japan, North Korea-Japan, Russia-Japan, China-Vietnam, China and the South China Sea littorals – continue to animate East Asia's international relations.

Both China and Japan have a complicated equation with their neighbours. For China's neighbours, it is the prospect of reviving a 'Middle Kingdom' suffocating nation-states on its periphery that fuels insecurity. For Japan, it is an undiminished colonial history affecting the national identities of the Korean peninsula, China, and much of the Western Pacific. Japan's quest to acquire the sinews of a normal state has only heightened the shadows of its past role in Asia.

In sum, both China and Japan are struggling to define a role that can carry the rest of Asia along with them. Ironically, and in a strange way, India legitimizes both China and Japan's role in Asia. For Japan, India is the only state without the stain of colonial oppression, and one that is eager for a larger Japanese role in Asia's future.

For China, India is a relatively stable neighbour in contrast to rising antagonisms with a U.S.-led Pacific bloc. India's independent role and a relatively clean slate in Asia, despite an unresolved dispute with China, provide India with leverage and space if used sensibly.

Third, Russia and China have forged a mutually beneficial global partnership primarily to counteract the unilateralist impulses of Washington. Whether it was the Iran nuclear issue, the Syrian civil war, or the tussle between Russia and the West over Ukraine's alignment, or the security situation on the Korean peninsula, Moscow and Beijing have been on virtually the same page. As a Chinese scholar once remarked, 'When China is confronted by US, we think Russia is with us – and vice versa. It boosts us psychologically.' Indeed, in a gesture to Beijing, Russia has already conducted sophisticated naval exercises with China in the East China Sea as a deliberate signal to Washington that it could complicate America's forward presence in the Western Pacific.

While the Kremlin is by no means misty-eyed about its partnership with Beijing – indeed it worries about a future imbalance in Eurasia – Washington's policy of crude containment has left Russian President Vladimir Putin with few options but to seek strategic and economic depth with Russia's largest neighbour. Anyhow, the Russians hardly need lessons on geopolitics from others – they have always played a hand better than the cards they were dealt.

For Indian policymakers, it is imperative they recognize these broader realities and avoid postures and policies that could entangle India in larger power struggles in which it has no direct interests or stakes.

India Re-defines its Role

Recent foreign policy moves by Delhi do indicate a flux. Combining orthodox ideas from the Cold War era along with 21st century pragmatism, it appears that India has decided that the emerging multipolar world is becoming far too complicated for the binary choices and easy solutions that some had envisioned for the country's foreign policy. Not only has it recast its approach to the maritime Indo-Pacific but as recent

Shanghai Cooperation Organisation (SCO) summits have exemplified, it is also building deeper and more constructive links with continental Eurasia.

Setting a New Tone

Prime Minister Narendra Modi's speech at the Shangri-La Dialogue in Singapore in June 2018 laid out a framework that is likely to be a template for future policymakers.[1] The speech was dominated by four themes that collectively tell us about the evolving foreign policy. First, the central theme was that at a time when the world is facing power shifts, uncertainty and competition over geopolitical ideas and political models, India would project itself as an independent power and actor across Asia. One of the most important parts of the speech was when Modi described India's ties with the three great powers. Russia and the US were called as partners with whom India has relationships based on overlapping interests in international and Asian geopolitics. And, India-China relations were portrayed in complex terms as having 'many layers' but with a positive undertone that stability in that relationship is important for India and the world.

The intended signal to all major capitals was that India will not be part of a closed group of nations or aggregate Indian power in a bloc but will chart out its own course based on its own capacity and ideas. Notice, for example, the following phrases: 'our friendships are not alliances of containment' or 'when nations stand on the side of principles, not behind one power or the other, they earn the respect of the world and a voice in international affairs'. For some this portends a renewed emphasis on non-alignment. The prime minister himself used the more agreeable term 'strategic autonomy'. In essence, what it really means is that India has become too big to be part of any political-military camp whose design and role in Asian affairs is being conceived elsewhere, upon ideas that India might not fully share, and where India has a marginal role in strategy and policy implementation.

The China Factor

While the rise of China has undoubtedly increased the demand and space for India to increase its region-wide engagement, India's role in the vast Indo-Pacific is no longer envisaged as a China-centric one. Thus, as his second point, Modi removed any lingering impression of an impeding crusade or an ideological subtext to India's Act East policy in the coming years when he remarked, 'India does not see the Indo-Pacific Region as a strategy or as a club of limited members. Nor as a grouping that seeks to dominate.' If anybody imagined that India's identity as a democracy would position it naturally towards one side in the emerging world order, Modi clarified that misperception quite emphatically: 'India's own engagement in the Indo-Pacific Region – from the shores of Africa to that of the Americas – will be inclusive... That is the foundation of our civilizational ethos – of pluralism, co-existence, openness and dialogue. The ideals of democracy that define us as a nation also shape the way we engage the world.'

India's Ambassador to Beijing expressed a similar message on the eve of the 2018 SCO summit: big countries 'can peacefully coexist despite differences in their systems and that they can work together'. In other words, India's democracy is far more comfortable with a world of diversity than the spectre of a clash of civilizations or great powers locked in ideological contests.

Third, despite this policy adjustment, India's approach to the region is not going to be a hands-off policy or one devoid of norms. We continued to hear an emphasis on a 'free, open, inclusive region' and a 'common rules-based' Indo-Pacific order. Some believe this is aimed squarely at China but it is more accurate to interpret such rhetoric as directed at the type of order India would like to see and actively support. Significantly, Modi asserted that such 'rules and norms should be based on the consent of all, not on the power of the few'. Again, this underscored Delhi's belief that the normative basis of the region's future political-security architecture would only find legitimacy if it were based on a consensus among all stakeholders.

Finally, without mentioning either, Modi urged both the US and China to manage their rivalry and prevent their 'normal' competition from descending into conflict. 'Asia of rivalry will hold us all back. Asia of cooperation will shape this century. So, each nation must ask itself: Are its choices building a more united world, or forcing new divisions? It is a responsibility that both existing and rising powers have.' He made it clear that while India would pursue many partnerships 'in the region and beyond', it was not going to choose 'one side of a divide or the other' but would remain wedded to its principles and values that emphasize inclusiveness, diversity and of course, its own interests.

The overall message in Modi's speech was unmistakable. Rapid changes in the international environment are prompting Delhi to rediscover a posture and policy for a multipolar world as well as assume greater responsibility for its own future and destiny. Reflecting its unique geographical position at the rimland of Eurasia and at the mouth of the Indo-Pacific, India's foreign policy is likely to be driven by a dual attention to the balance of power and order building in the continental and maritime environment around the subcontinent.

4

INDIA, CHINA AND THE NEW SILK ROUTES

In 2013–2014, China made a series of foreign policy declarations on a new approach to engaging and connecting with its inner Asian heartland and maritime periphery. At its core was a new connectivity vision, unveiled in 2013 by Xi Jinping in Kazakhstan and Indonesia, sites chosen for their symbolic reference to Janus-faced directions of China's new Silk Roads, more or less tracing the ancient routes a millennia ago, but backed by power and purpose. Xi Jinping's 2013 speeches were infused with such symbolism. In Astana, Xi evoked the memory of the ancient Silk Route:

'As I stand here and look back at history, I seem to hear the camel bells echoing in the mountains and see the wisps of smoke rising from the dessert, and this gives me a special feeling...This land has borne witness to a steady stream of envoys, caravans, travelers, scholars and artisans traveling between the East and the West.'[1] In Jakarta, Xi spoke of Southeast Asia's heritage as 'an important hub along the ancient Maritime Silk Road...Ours is a diversified region where various civilizations have assimilated and interacted with one another.'[2]

Referred originally as the One Belt, One Road and eventually as simply the BRI, the plan envisages extensive continental and maritime infrastructure investments such as ports, high-speed railroads, highways and pipelines linking China with its western neighbours in the Eurasian heartland like Russia, Central Asia, Europe and Iran, and, its eastern neighbours in South and Southeast Asia. (See Chapter 5 in Section II for the main structural reasons that drove China to contemplate such a geostrategy).

In India, these developments have been viewed with a mix of curiosity, trepidation and awe. The spectre of a China reviving the old Silk Routes echoes some of India's own aspirations to re-connect with its surrounding regions after the colonial disruptions of the past centuries and the severing of landward connections because of Partition. This chapter will trace Indian worldviews and thinking as it has evolved between 2014 and 2019. It will also look back at the ancient Indian Ocean system to offer lessons for India and China to navigate their rivalry in a more positive-sum direction. Finally, I make the case for a more sophisticated Indian policy response to the BRI, one that if conceived and executed intelligently, could re-shape China's geoeconomic engagement in South Asia.

IN MAY 2014, China through its official news agency *Xinhua,* unveiled maps showing ambitious Land and Maritime Silk Roads (MSR). The MSR envisioned an 'economic cooperation area' stretching from the Western Pacific to the Baltic Sea as a sort of maritime highway buttressed by Chinese-supported infrastructure and port facilities in states straddling maritime routes along which China's trade and natural resources flow.

The *Xinhua* map traced this silk road commencing in Quanzhou (Fujian province), touching Guangzhou (Guangdong province), Beihai (Guangxi) and Haikou (Hainan) before heading south to the Malacca Strait. From Kuala Lumpur, the MSR headed to Kolkata, and then crossed the northern Indian Ocean to Nairobi, Kenya. From Nairobi, the map showed the MSR moving north around the Horn of Africa and through the Red Sea into the Mediterranean, with a stop in Athens before meeting another land-based trans-Eurasian route in Venice.[3]

Debating China's BRI

According to a former Indian diplomat, China has been seeking to consolidate her presence and ties to her South and West. They now extend beyond Southeast and South Asia and go across the Indian Ocean and Central Asia to the Mediterranean and Europe. A principal focus has been on establishing connectivity by every mode of transport.[4] The MSR idea is part of this wider attempt by China to construct multiple lines of communication to its economic heartland in eastern China since the early 2000s. The underlying aim of such a geostrategy is also to develop inner Chinese provinces and shape China's regional periphery by exercising economic, political and cultural influence.

India was formally invited to join the MSR at the 17th round of Special Representatives (SRs) Talks in New Delhi in February 2014. The Indian response was lukewarm, and certainly not one of immediate acceptance. The Chinese Foreign Ministry spokesperson elaborated on the MSR:

> This initiative is just an idea for cooperation. It is an open-ended platform. The purpose is to integrate all kinds of ongoing cooperation especially cooperation on connectivity in

> the spirit of (ancient) silk road so that they can connect with each other and promote each other and accelerate regional countries' common development... China adopts an open attitude. We also hope to see good suggestions from other countries so as to substantiate this idea.[5]

India's position on the broader BRI initiative (of which the MSR is one component) has been of generally staying away from it and publicly opposing some of its continental variants because of the China-Pakistan Economic Corridor (CPEC) that traverses Indian claimed areas of Jammu & Kashmir. While the official position has been linked to sovereignty (regarding the CPEC) and sustainability and transparency around Chinese investments, an analysis of different worldviews and perceptions on China's connectivity plans will be useful for the reader. Since it is possible that India's interests evolve in the coming years as the BRI adapts to international scrutiny and critiques, it would be important to get a sense of the thinking in India's strategic community.

Although this chapter focuses on the maritime component of the BRI, it can be taken to also represent how the BRI was broadly perceived in the initial stages of its launch in the middle of the past decade. Broadly speaking, there are four schools of thought – held by former policymakers, diplomats, strategic analysts, maritime and naval analysts and scholars – in India.

It's Geopolitics, Stupid!

According to this view, the MSR should be understood as part of a rising China's attempt to 'reorder Asia' and 'undermine American alliances' in the region. China is attempting to create trade and economic relationships with Association of

Southeast Asian Nations (ASEAN) countries through trade, port and continental land bridges to countervail US influence and to draw the Indian Ocean Region (IOR) littorals within its sphere of influence. Chinese proposals to develop the Kunming Railway that will connect China-Singapore and other countries in Southeast Asia, as also the recently commissioned oil and gas pipelines and proposed railway line connecting the Rakhine coast of Myanmar with Kunming, underscore this strategy. The MSR proposal, thus, compliments such infrastructural initiatives and enables landlocked south-west China to access markets in Southeast Asia.

Some analysts also locate the MSR as part of a Chinese reassurance posture to 'diffuse the tension' on China's maritime periphery after a period of uncertainty over Chinese maritime behaviour. It is also viewed as a policy to complicate the US' rebalancing strategy by 'softening' the renewed interest of ASEAN elites in reaching out to the US, Japan and perhaps, even India. The Indian dilemma is as follows. The fact that China is promoting two corridors (continental and MSR) as part of its evolving regional geostrategy and that 'India lies on both the MSR and the Southern Silk Route'[6] poses opportunities and challenges for India in light of other potentially alternative economic options via strategic partnerships with Japan and the US. Some also argue that India can, simultaneously, conceptualize other strategic options with Japan and ASEAN to present alternative regional initiatives. Given the pace of China's MSR diplomacy, India must project its own ideas to influence the final contours of China's initiative. According to this view, Delhi should interpret all Chinese actions as a 'clinical assessment of Asia's rapidly evolving geopolitics and its consequences for Indian security....But Delhi appears a long way from developing an appropriate strategy.'[7] If India 'could come up with a counter of our own which would naturally be less threatening but which would also allow us the excuse to expand our naval reach into these areas, then we would have used the Chinese opportunity.'[8] Although the Indo-Pacific concept has evolved in recent years in terms of India's naval and strategic outreach to East Asian countries, its geoeconomic dimension remains underdeveloped.

Foreign Policy Traditionalists or Neorealists

The entire proposal should be seen in the context of Indian national interests and implications for India's role in the IOR and South Asia. The unstated, underlying strategic objectives of MSR raise questions about Chinese intentions. China is attempting to expand its influence in the Bay of Bengal and Arabian Sea by seeking port facilities in Sri Lanka, Pakistan and Bangladesh, apart from other Indian Ocean littoral states, through a strategy generally referred to as 'String of Pearls'. Pakistan, Bangladesh and Sri Lanka have pledged support to Xi Jinping's MSR initiative. If the MSR leads to important neighbours like Bangladesh and Sri Lanka drifting into the Chinese orbit – it has not happened so far – it would represent a serious setback to India's traditional conception of the subcontinent as a privileged sphere.

Another perception is that South Asian states have already discovered the option and ability to play the 'China card', that is, exploit Sino-Indian mistrust to advance their national and developmental objectives. For India's neighbours, the MSR is perhaps another potential opportunity to play the 'China card' in their strategic bargaining with India. A former diplomat, however, argues:

> [I]t would be premature to view the concept of MSR in purely strategic terms. The sovereign decisions of littoral states

on scope and extent of Chinese investments should not be underestimated. No one would like to get sucked into military conflict or armed confrontations arising from port developments undertaken by the Chinese as part of the exercise.[9]

Nevertheless, one of the reasons for the regional outreach of the Modi government in recent years is to attempt to decelerate such a possibility by re-establishing Indian credibility with its neighbours.

Interestingly, while the *Xinhua* MSR map excluded Gwadar, Indian analysts offer competing interpretations. One view is that China is hedging against an unstable Gwadar corridor, which begins from Xinjiang and passes through Pakistan-occupied Kashmir. Given the potential for deeper instability in the AfPak region and Baluchistan province after the drawdown of Western forces, China is shifting its priority to other maritime routes in the IOR.

Another view is that China will pursue both *continental* and *maritime* lines of communication. If the MSR loses traction or is delayed, the land corridor to Gwadar can become an important commercial hub for both China and Pakistan. Gwadar's proximity to the Persian Gulf and its ability to support both naval and commercial activity in the Arabian Sea makes this Silk Road too attractive to be dismissed. Indeed, Sino-Pakistani diplomatic activity suggests the Kashgar–Gwadar corridor is still in play. During a visit to China, a Pakistani minister had noted that 'Gwadar is the gateway to the economic corridor and it will be developed into a modern port city.'[10]

Therefore, despite China's original MSR map bypassing Pakistan, the planned Chinese investments in Pakistan are indicative of a sustained strategy. The omission in the map was probably deliberate to prevent adverse reactions from India's strategic community and make the MSR appear less contentious in Indian debates.

As of late 2019, 'Gwadar still remains a remote, provincial city with its port currently under development. It is very poorly connected to the rest of the country, it is not an economic hub by any standard, and so far faces very mundane problems, such as a shortage of water and power (not to speak of the threat for Baloch armed groups, which in May 2019 have shown the capacity to strike targets even within Gwadar city).' Since the MSR will be a long-drawn process, India will need to scale up its own investment in its immediate neighbourhood in precisely those capacities where China is investing (ports, logistics, shipbuilding) to dissuade India's neighbours such as Bangladesh, Myanmar and Sri Lanka from becoming Chinese 'political outposts'.[11]

Mahanians

Although the MSR is couched as an economic initiative, to the maritime analyst, it has deeper, particularly security-related, implications. What troubles Indian strategists is the fact that China's long-term ambition of establishing permanence of presence is being aided by the structure of 'outposts' from Myanmar to Bangladesh, Sri Lanka, Maldives, Pakistan, Sudan, Tanzania, Seychelles, Mozambique, and a couple of others in the pipeline. While these 'outposts' have been built in the guise of developmental assistance, the MSR is perceived as the final cog in the wheel that will make Chinese warships easily supportable in terms of logistics and operational turnaround, a prerequisite for the People's Liberation Army Navy (PLAN) to forward deploy in IOR.[12] China has invested over US$ 1 billion in Hambantota and Gwadar ports, and is also developing the

Colombo South Port project. Such development in the 'String of Pearls' was intended as a return on upfront investments – places if not bases – for the PLAN and other Chinese vessels.[13]

Another maritime analyst dismisses the 'String of Pearls' theory 'as purely speculative and over-hyped...China's port development activities' are to 'ensure that its Sea Lines of Communication (SLOCs) were net-worked and constantly replenished.'[14] Another question posed is whether the MSR is part of China's attempt to neutralize its 'Malacca Dilemma'. In 2003, Hu Jintao had publicly expressed the 'Malacca Dilemma', which describes the vulnerable SLOCs crucial to China's trade and their potential to interdiction from another state.[15] China's long and vulnerable SLOCs extend from West Asia and East Africa to China's eastern seaboard. Eighty-five per cent of China's oil imports flow through the northern Indian Ocean in close proximity to Indian naval deployments. So far, the PLAN does not possess the strategic basing rights to secure its IOR SLOCs. As of 2020, China has established a sole military base at Djibouti that provides the PLAN an ability to secure Chinese investments and energy flows from Africa and the Middle East.[16]

There are two aspects to this. First, China's growing SLOCs can potentially convert the IOR into a contested space. Indian analysts take the official Chinese discourse seriously: that China's economic growth and high dependence on West Asian and African resources would translate into an expansion of Chinese naval power in the long term, requiring capabilities to accomplish missions in the IOR as well. For some, this is the logic that is driving PLAN to gradually extend its operational range from the first and the second island chains to 'far seas' that stretch from the east of the IOR to the east coast of Africa.[17] It is this broader impulse of projecting power up to and beyond 1,000 nautical miles from its territorial waters that is driving

China's maritime force development and possible deployment of nuclear attack submarines and carrier-based task forces in IOR.

Second, Indian strategists know that China is aware of the fact that the Indian Navy eyes Chinese SLOCs through the Malacca Strait as its 'Achilles heel' and that a detour through the Sunda or Lombok Straits will not ensure complete security for China's strategic commodity trade because, ultimately, Chinese SLOCs traverse near the Indian peninsula.[18] Another strategist argues, 'The Chinese weakness lies in the Indian Ocean...Today, they are merely SLOCs; tomorrow they will be the Chinese Jugular...a flotilla of (Indian) nuclear submarines and a three carrier air group in the Indian Ocean can economically cripple mainland China.'[19] To be sure, this view is not uncontested, and the tactical and strategic efficacy of such a posture is easier said than done as I alluded to in Chapter 1 of Section III.

Nevertheless, if pushed to the wall or confronting coercion on the Himalayan frontiers, Indian policymakers do have the asymmetric maritime option of targeting China's vulnerability in the IOR. This could be another reason for China to gradually transform the MSR into a collective security framework on its trade routes in order to produce some burden sharing by providing littorals with a 'common stake' in the security of Chinese SLOCs. According to one analyst, the MSR 'could well be a surrogate for a giant Chinese SLOC running all the way from the East African coast, to the Southern coast of China – created, maintained and controlled by Beijing.'[20]

Neoliberal Interdependence

China's lofty discourse that accompanies the MSR ('new opportunities and a new future to China and every country along the road that is seeking to develop', 'economic cooperation area', 'common interests, fate, and responsibilities') actually resembles India's own regional narrative since the mid-2000s where Delhi has also sought to diffuse similar norms towards South Asia.

From the neoliberal interdependence perspective, the MSR resonates as an inevitable trend of globalization and the rise of new economic centres of power in Asia. As one analyst notes, 'The (MSR's) underlying economic logic is based on the observation that no country in modern times has achieved sustained economic development without increasing its share in world trade and investment. And connectivity provides the channel to do so.'[21] This view holds that geoeconomics is what really matters and policymakers should not overplay security considerations in their assessment of the MSR. In the 'complex and interdependent nature of modern geoeconomics and global business', the idea of zero-sum games is passé.[22] Further, since India's own economic and physical connectivity with East Asia is dwarfed by intra-Pacific interdependence between China and her neighbours, the MSR can be a stepping stone to a new Look East policy. It is, therefore, 'unrealistic for India to shy away from connectivity and openness to trade and business with our neighbours... it is important to connect further and deeper into the production and supply chains that stretch across ASEAN right upto China, Japan and Korea.'[23]

Another scholar offers a qualified endorsement: while there is 'no argument per se against the improvement of infrastructure', the first priority should be 'infrastructure within South Asia'. In other words, intra-South Asian 'linkages would have to be hooked with industrial hubs within' India. 'External development opportunity only works if we activate the internal development.'[24] Another qualified endorsement is that the MSR 'can be used to our benefit for greater bilateral and regional cooperation. But we also need to ensure that our presence is also made sufficiently effective along these routes so that we retain the ability to influence any major decisions.'[25] Ultimately, the neoliberal argument rests on 'The hope...that the MSR, which (traditionally) served more for trade and establishing friendly relations would continue to do so in the revived form, rather than create new naval rivalries or power displays.'[26]

For the modern Indian state, it was recognized from the start that India was geopolitically located at the crossroads of several subregions. As Nehru had remarked in 1949:

> India is situated geographically in such a way that we just cannot escape anything that happens in Western Asia, in Central Asia, in Eastern Asia or South-East Asia. Whether it is in terms of war or in terms of peace, we cannot escape it... we just cannot escape the burdens and responsibilities which that position brings to us.[27]

A rejuvenated China has kick-started what will probably be a decades-long process of constructing new lines of communication to these subregions of Eurasia. For China, it is incidental that India lies on the crossroads of Chinese Silk Routes. For India, however, this dynamic holds the potential to reshape its entire periphery and impact India's own role in Southern Asia.

To Indian analysts, the MSR initiative is part of China's attempt to break out of its maritime isolation, constrained by the US-led alliance's domination of the first and second island chains. To many, this is the backdrop to China's pitch for an MSR to ASEAN, and now to countries in South Asia. Further, by investing in states straddling routes along which China's West–East commodity trade flows, China aims to improve its resource security.[28]

As one former NSA remarks, 'I do not see us, or the US, or others who share disquiet being able to stop the very strong Chinese impulse to use her excess industrial and other capacity to bind her periphery and now more distant regions to her economically and strategically.'[29] Nevertheless, there is a sense of losing another important 'match' in the competition. For decades, India has felt that the Indian Ocean is 'our' domain and has tirelessly endeavoured to keep extra-regional powers out of the region. The positive perceptions come from the neoliberal prism of interdependence that views the MSR as an opportunity. But even here there is a recognition that India's capacity constraints to even partially match Chinese investments along the MSR, especially in South Asia itself, could negate potential benefits.

Curiously, an important aspect that has been ignored by the strategic community is to analyse the rationale of engaging China from India's neighbours' perspectives. As India has receded in its traditional role as a regional security provider, India's neighbours have found Beijing more useful as a counterweight and as a hedge against Western pressure and leverage being used against South Asian elites. Therefore, China's rising influence on India's periphery is also a consequence of India's own failure to craft an independent and robust regional role in South Asia.

For a policymaker, the MSR is a classic case of producing security and advancing national goals in a global political economy of interdependence. For the Modi government, the challenge is reconciling the diverse range of interests in the Indian state where development and security goals often produce competing images and policy choices (see Table 1 for the diversity of Indian worldviews). Therefore, how the national interest is 'defined' is often the most crucial element of the policy–strategy equation.

India's former NSA sums up the Indian dilemma:

> What I think is missing in the discussion...is a larger integrated view of how all these various Chinese proposals and actions for connectivity – BCIM, MSR, Land SR, Tibet railway to Nepal/ Yatung, Gwadar corridor, Dawei and other ports, Mekong development, etc. – can be used to serve India's interests...The issue therefore is how to turn these to our advantage, and a piecemeal approach and adhoc responses or delay is really not the answer.[30]

Table 1: Indian perceptions to China's Maritime Silk Road (part of the BRI)

Typology within India's strategic community	**Perception and impact of MSR**	**Degree of receptivity to MSR idea**
Its geopolitics stupid!	US-China great game and India should avoid getting lured into a single political-economic community.	Plug into MSR without closing options to the US-led network
Foreign policy traditionalists/ neorealists	MSR will complicate India's regional role in South Asia and IOR with India's regional ambitions being crowded out by growing Chinese material capabilities and increased bargaining space for littoral states.	Strategic caution

Mahanians	MSR offers India potential leverage over Chinese SLOCs that traverse close to Indian power projection capabilities. But if MSR is accompanied with China's blue water forward deployments in IOR to militarily secure the MSR that poses new strategic challenges for India.	Negative perception
Neoliberal interdependence	An inevitable geoeconomic trend and India must not squander such an opportunity to plug into a dynamic economic space. But India's state capacity constraints pose the main obstacle in drawing potential benefits from the MSR.	High receptivity to MSR

India, China and the Indo-Pacific

The emphasis in recent years on the unity of Asia's vast maritime geography – exemplified by the idea of the Indo-Pacific – might suggest this is a new idea. However, a deeper look at the history of these spaces suggests Asia's key economic centres were connected through the oceans. For over a millennia, the geopolitical norm was interdependence rather than exclusive sway over the seas. This pattern of inter-regional exchanges was disrupted only after the arrival of the European colonialists in Asia who fragmented the Indo-Pacific into spheres of influence. Those ideas have had a long afterlife and Asian powers today must resist reproducing concepts that have historically proven to increase conflict and competition between states.

Historical Unity

In a rare study, K.N. Chaudhuri mapped the Indian Ocean as an area spanning the Red Sea to the South China Sea. The rationale for this definition was the pre-19th-century geoeconomic networks between West Asia, South Asia, Southeast Asia and East Asia. For over a thousand years, transcontinental trade occurred through the Indian Ocean and included connections between many different civilizations and regions. This was, in many ways, a people-centric trading system that had evolved organically more through the initiatives of merchants, traders, sailors and coastal communities than grand political visions or imperial dictates. People 'could sail from one end of the sea to the other until they reached the barrier of the Pacific, which remained practically closed to sailing ships.'[31]

Early Chinese historical works were aware of the eastern and western divisions of the Indian Ocean and the distinctive nature of the contacts between them created by foreign seafarers.[32] Contemporary Arab accounts from the ninth century also reveal that the inter-regional maritime and caravan trade of the Near East [West Asia and the subcontinent], important as it was, existed alongside the highly profitable trans-oceanic trade originating further east [in Southeast Asia and China].[33]

The other factor that historically defined the limits of the Indian Ocean was its navigability dependent on the monsoon winds, which determined the precise sailing patterns from both ends of the ocean. Recent official Indian reflections attest to such a past:

> No other part of the maritime world has its fundamental economic activities so directly derived from cycles of nature. This unity was expressed over the ages primarily through

> maritime trade rhythms, that then carried over into migration, traditions, practices and faith. As a result, this ocean evolved its own special identity that is based on mobility, acceptance and inter-penetration … the overall ethos of the Indian Ocean was one of co-existence and adjustment, where respect for diversity was intrinsic to the promotion of trade.[34]

Instructively, even the European powers had relied on pre-existing networks among the Indian Ocean regions, which they revived or further developed in some cases and obstructed in others. It is also worth recalling that in terms of volume and profit, intra-Asian commerce, until the onset of the Industrial Revolution era, dwarfed what the European powers could generate through Europe–Asia trade. In other words, Europe needed Asia far more than Asian countries needed markets outside the vast Indian Ocean area, and early European geoeconomic activity in Asia was in large measure a continuation rather than a dramatic interruption in older trade links and cultural contacts.

It was only in later phases, especially with the onset of the Industrial Revolution in the 19th century, that Europe gained undisputed military ascendance over Asian civilizations and severed the traditional political economy in the wider Indian Ocean area. The narrower or fragmented definitions of the Indian Ocean were a reflection of imperial policies, particularly of the Portuguese, the Dutch, and the British, who sought to control the freedom of navigation between the subregions of Asia, militarized commercial interactions, and created their own spheres of influence, particularly in the central and Western Indian Ocean. These colonial powers, as one former official notes, 'created artificial firewalls through their administrative jurisdictions that diluted centuries of natural movements and contacts'.[35] The image of the Indian Ocean as a self-contained space or a 'closed sea' from Aden to Malacca was very much a construction of these great powers that sought exclusive economic privileges via their geopolitical control over India and the surrounding west–east sea lanes.

During the postcolonial period, regional powers sought to adapt these imperial ideas for defensive purposes to secure their heartlands. Since both India and China had faced a similar historical experience of maritime intrusion and subsequent subjugation through external power projected via the sea, a memory of maritime weakness and a determination to avoid a repeat of that traumatic past became ingrained in the strategic cultures of both countries. And, when India and China confronted pressure and coercion from the sea during the Cold War, they quickly recognized the value of sea power and the destabilizing role that their maritime peripheries could play to disrupt domestic and regional stability. But, it was largely homeland and territorial concerns that shaped Indian and Chinese maritime thinking. Commerce and connectivity were rarely the driver of state behaviour.

Given that the present era of globalization has not only restored the traditional connectivity between the Indian Ocean's constituent regions, but also significantly enhanced it, the logic to revive an expansive mental map for the Indian Ocean based on open regionalism and social, economic, and cultural interdependence has again become compelling.

A Maritime Commons

At the outset, we must first identify the main interests for India and China in the Indian Ocean today. For China, its outlook and policy priorities depend on which part of this vast ocean we are referring to. The attitude towards the eastern fringes of the Indian Ocean, or where the western Pacific begins, appears to be more geopolitically driven, that is, aimed at the security of China's heartland and eastern seaboard. Chinese interest in the central and western areas of the Indian Ocean appears to be primarily linked to the security of its SLOC for the vast strategic commodities and energy supplies that flow from West Asia and Africa to coastal China. For India, the northern Indian Ocean is a space that has been a part of the subcontinent's evolution through hundreds, if not thousands, of years. In addition to civilizational factors, geopolitics is another variable that shapes how many Indians think about the Indian Ocean. A part of this image, as alluded to earlier, has been influenced by British ideas that promoted a 'closed sea' to exclude rival powers from accessing the subcontinent.

The one factor that both countries recognize as vital for their economic growth and domestic transformation is maintaining open maritime trade routes. So, can India and China envision themselves as joint stakeholders in the maritime commons? After all, one-third of the world's bulk cargo, 50 per cent of the world's container traffic and 70 per cent of crude and oil products pass through Indian Ocean sea lanes. These staggering statistics reflect the Indian Ocean's status as a 'global commons' and an economic highway. About 75 per cent of India's oil imports also use these waterways. For China, too, the share of seaborne energy trade traversing from the western Indian Ocean to the eastern part and into the South China Sea is also high with 80 per cent of its oil imports passing through the Malacca Strait. China is also said to face a Hormuz Dilemma because 40 per cent of its oil imports transit the Strait of Hormuz in the Persian Gulf.[36] More broadly, nearly all of China's trade with Europe, West Asia and Africa travels through the west–east sea lanes just below the South Asian peninsula. This high dependence on Indian Ocean trade routes has reflected in China's maritime strategy where it has gradually developed a presence beyond the Malacca Straits, the historical choke point and transit between the central and eastern Indian Ocean.

In October 2008, a Chinese naval flotilla engaged in its first long-distance operation into the western Indian Ocean. Since that year, China has maintained a small but regular presence in the Gulf of Aden as part of the PLAN's counter-piracy deployments. Between 2009 and 2014, the PLAN also made 49 port calls around the northern, central and western Indian Ocean.[37] Presently, the Chinese deployment in Aden, near one of the world's busiest shipping routes, accounts for four to five warships at any given time.[38]

The Indian government's reactions to these developments generally have been pragmatic. Then Defence Minister A. K. Antony had welcomed cooperation with the PLAN stating that, 'If ever there was a need for consensual and cooperative effort, it is in relation to piracy'.[39] In 2013, India's National Security Advisor Shivshankar Menon remarked that an India-China maritime rivalry 'was not inevitable' as both countries had a 'common interest in keeping sea lanes of communication in the Indian and Western Pacific Oceans open. These lines are vital to India's trade and energy flows. So are they for China'.[40] In 2015, Prime Minister Narendra Modi too acknowledged the global interest in the Indian Ocean: 'We recognize that there are other nations around the world, with strong interests and stakes in the region'.[41] As we can see, Indian policymakers have recognized Chinese interests in the Indian Ocean.

China's strategy to mitigate the vulnerability of its extended Indian Ocean SLOCs is still evolving. Rather than concentrating its maritime attention to a few ports and harbours, China has been dispersing its logistics over a large number of littoral locations: Djibouti, Aden, Oman, the United Arab Emirates, Qatar, Pakistan and Myanmar[42].[43] A parallel dimension of China's strategy has also been to pursue continental lines of communication to the Indian Ocean to bypass the Southeast Asian archipelago altogether. These include the CPEC, BCIM corridor, and China-Myanmar corridor. Of these, only the Myanmar link has so far been operationalized. The Myanmar-China crude oil pipeline originates in Made Island in Rakhine and runs further for 771 kilometres through Myanmar until it reaches Yunnan. This pipeline began operating in May 2017 and has a transmission capacity of 22 million tonnes of crude oil per year. It is expected to reduce China's reliance on the Malacca route by about one-third and cut the transport distance for African and West Asian oil shipments by about 1,200 km.[44] Yet, as a recent US government report notes, these new pipelines will alleviate only slightly China's maritime dependency on either the Strait of Malacca or the Strait of Hormuz. Despite China's efforts, the sheer volume of oil and liquefied natural gas that is imported to China from West Asia and Africa will make strategic SLOCs increasingly important to China.[45]

In short, there seems to be little alternative for China but to focus on a combination of national and multilateral efforts to secure its maritime trade routes.

Motivations and Capabilities

The rapid expansion of China's merchant shipping fleet, the world's third largest today, and investment in South Asian and West Asian ports and harbours is part of a conscious attempt at maintaining economic security. Over the past decade, China's merchant fleet has expanded by 300 per cent, from about 44 million gross tonnes at the end of 2005, to over 130 million gross tonnes at the end of 2015. Since 2010, Chinese and Hong Kong companies have completed or announced deals involving at least 40 port projects worth over $45 billion,[2] the largest five of which are in the Indian Ocean area. China's 2015 white paper on military strategy has obliged the PLAN to protect 'the security of sea lanes of communication and overseas interests'.[46] Interestingly, such a pattern is different from the typical mode of maritime transformations. The Soviet Union, Germany and Japan, for instance, 'built their navies first and then promoted merchant marine development…China's current maritime transformation is led largely by an exceedingly dynamic commercial maritime sector, which in turn is creating synergies for naval development'.[47]

It seems clear that China's presence and involvement in the Indian Ocean is driven largely by China's massive economic footprint on the world trading system. For India, the littoral is seen more as part of an order-building process where the area can be steered towards a common regional identity and purpose. As a former official remarks, India's policy is to 'create the connectivity that promotes a sharper Indian Ocean personality to emerge.' The Mausam project is aimed at constructing and reviving 'the ocean's identity'[48].[49] So, for India, the maritime space around it has a geo-cultural dimension as well as a geopolitical dimension. For the same reason, India appears more interested in intra-regional economic cooperation, where the littoral states can be persuaded to craft subregional or plurilateral cooperation mechanisms, in contrast to China's interest in inter-regional economic connectivity.

Another stark aspect that stands out is the nature of Sino-Indian interactions in the Indian Ocean. In the northern Indian Ocean, India's weight is felt primarily as a naval power rather than a comprehensive and balanced maritime power with the full spectrum of commercial, merchant marine, industrial and technological capabilities. China, on the other hand, has emerged as a more active maritime power with significant investments in ports, infrastructure and pipelines, without posing itself as a major naval power in the central and western Indian Ocean. This makes their bilateral interaction asymmetric and atypical because Indian and Chinese maritime strengths and vulnerabilities exist in different domains of power and consequently, their influence is being projected in different ways and through different instruments.

One trend nevertheless seems clear: the globalization clock cannot be turned back. Both India and China are deepening their economic interdependence with other regions and the maritime spaces around these countries are still the main arteries for those connections. Hence, neither can afford to ignore the other's maritime policies. As China's investment in maritime infrastructure in the central and western Indian Ocean increases, it is likely to get drawn into the neighbourhood's affairs. If Beijing does not handle this process prudently, it could heighten mistrust and fuel a costly competition. Delhi, for its part, needs to candidly reflect on the premodern geoeconomic linkages in the Indian Ocean, which were inclusive and expansive, and China was often an integral part of those inter-regional exchanges. Put plainly, the notion of a closed or privileged Indian space between Aden and Malacca was an imperial aberration rather than the norm in the wider span of Asian history.

Another lesson from pre-modern maritime history is that only when Indian Ocean ports assumed a politically neutral and open status to diverse and competing players did the particular location become a thriving entrepôt for different trading communities and commodities. Both Indian and Chinese policymakers ought to keep this in mind as they scramble for maritime privileges along the Indo-Pacific.

India Stakes a Position Against the BRI

In a previous section, I had highlighted the diversity of worldviews as former Indian officials and analysts began thinking about China's connectivity plans and its implications for India. Since 2017, a security-dominated prism has overtaken more varied perspectives and come to dominate India's official policy.

In a consequential development in 2017, the foreign office decided to stake out a clear position of defiance against the BRI, an ambitious Chinese idea that seeks to reshape the Eurasian geoeconomic space. India's absence in Beijing's high-profile summit with representatives from over 100 countries, including 29 heads of state, evoked surprise and debate. What has been the calculus driving India's policy? Does India risk isolation as Eurasia moves towards a new chapter of connectivity and interdependence?

Delhi's position can be clearly gauged from the May 2017 statement of the Ministry of External Affairs.[50] The China-Pakistan Economic Corridor, a flagship project of the BRI, is seen as a blatant disregard for India's position on Jammu and Kashmir because it passes through PoK. 'No country can accept a project that ignores its core concerns on sovereignty and territorial integrity.'

But Delhi's protest goes beyond the 'core concerns' over sovereignty.

'We are of firm belief that connectivity initiatives must be based on universally recognized international norms, good governance, rule of law, openness, transparency and equality…

Guided by our principled position in the matter, we have been urging China to engage in a meaningful dialogue on its connectivity initiative, "One Belt, One Road" which was later renamed as "Belt and Road Initiative". We are awaiting a positive response from the Chinese side.'[51]

The objection to the BRI is actually more deep-rooted, namely, that China's rise and projection of geoeconomic influence is a direct challenge and threat to India's great power aspirations and traditional position in the subcontinent.

Two Contending Viewpoints

One influential strand of Indian thinking is that unless and until India develops its own regional connectivity plans and economic capacities at home, there can be no serious engagement with Chinese-sponsored projects. Any premature engagement is likely to entrap India and stunt its rise. An alternative view is that India's rise itself needs engagement and connections with the wider Asian and Eurasian economies, especially in the post-2008 crisis world which has reduced the viability of the previous liberalization model of drawing in large quantities of Western capital and basing India's growth on a handful of service sectors linked to the West. In these changed circumstances, the BRI is seen to provide an alternative source of finance capital and manufacturing opportunities to buttress India's economy, if leveraged sensibly.

The first view is based on an image of intense competition and rivalry and leaves little room for constructive collaboration. The second competing view is based on an image of interdependence where the idea of growth and development cannot occur in isolation from the world's second-largest economy. Both worldviews have some merit. The problem really lies in India's inability to imagine security more holistically and reconcile geopolitical interests with wider developmental goals.

If we carefully examine the approaches of other major powers and India's immediate neighbours, we can discern a more sophisticated strategy of dealing with China's connectivity plans. The contrast between the US and Russia is instructive.

American companies have been interested in opportunities that might accrue from BRI projects and hoped to partner Chinese firms as well as hoping to serve as industrial suppliers in specific infrastructure projects. US responses initially 'were benign and even positive at times.' In May 2017, a US-China joint statement had noted that the US 'recognizes the importance of China's One Belt and One Road initiative.' US President Donald Trump sent a senior White House official to China's 2017 BRI conference. Subsequently, however, Trump's trade war with China and structural shifts in US's China policy have replaced this position in favour of more vocal criticism. In October 2017, then US Secretary of Defense James Mattis remarked that, 'in a globalized world, there are many belts and many roads, and no one nation should put itself into a position of dictating "One Belt, One Road".' The 2017 US National Security Strategy stated that 'China's infrastructure investment and trade strategies reinforce its geopolitical aspirations.'[52] In August 2020, China Communications Construction Company (CCCC), a giant flagship enterprise used by Beijing to channel Chinese business with BRI countries, was sanctioned by the US government. Today, the CCCC has 923 active projects in 157 countries and has signed $63 billion worth of contracts in Belt and Road countries since 2013.[53] This escalating competition between the US and China has now been extended to the BRI.

Many in India's strategic community draw solace and policy inspiration from this emerging hardline view on the BRI. Broadly speaking, however, the US as a maritime power has a vested interest in undermining Eurasian connectivity that could over decades diminish the special privileges and leverage that the US has enjoyed by virtue of its control over the maritime commons that circulate international commerce between nations.

As a continental power, Russia's outlook is inherently different. As the original vanguard for Eurasian connectivity with the trans-Siberian railroad conceived in the 19th century, Russia is central to any Chinese trans-Eurasian vision for the most basic reason: geography. Even a cursory glance at a map reveals that any long-range connectivity projects require active cooperation and coordination with Moscow and its Central Asian allies. Three of the six corridors outlined by China as part of the BRI – the China-Mongolia-Russia corridor, the new Eurasian Land Bridge, the China-Central Asia-Western Asia economic corridor – all imply Russian cooperation.

Russia has, therefore, not bought into a zero-sum Indian interpretation of the initiative. This is not to suggest that Russia is unconcerned about its traditional spheres of influence around China's extended periphery. Rather Moscow has chosen a policy of enhancing interdependence along with pursuing its own geostrategies of upholding traditional political-military alliances. Russia is simultaneously developing its own connectivity project called the Eurasian Economic Union, which is actually at a far more advanced stage of institutional development having already established a single market for its members.

Even in the subcontinent we can notice clear trends of a complex approach towards China. India's neighbours such as Nepal, Bangladesh, Sri Lanka and Myanmar are all pursuing economic cooperation with China on a growing scale while also maintaining close connections with India and reassuring Delhi about their foreign policies and geopolitical orientations.

It is instructive that all of India's immediate neighbours, except Bhutan, sent representatives to the 2017 Beijing conference. This triangular setting suggests it would be extremely challenging, if not impossible, for Delhi to persuade South Asia to curtail or cut off ties with China. What India can realistically do is shape the type of relationship that its neighbours pursue with China and uphold certain redlines such as coming down heavily on regimes that invite China's military to establish a foothold in the subcontinent.

Finally, the underlying premise in much of the Indian debate – that Asia, and South Asia, is ripe for Chinese neocolonialism or imperial expansion – can be refuted. Asia's national identities are much too strong for state agency to be brushed aside. Can anyone, for instance, make a credible argument that Vietnam – a country that has resisted China for a millennia – will fall under its neighbour's sway because of an engagement with the BRI? What about Russia, one of the world's strongest military powers with a rich history of geopolitical experience in Eurasia? Will it fall under China's spell because a few billion dollars were invested in its economy or on its Central Asian periphery? Of course not! Even closer home, a tiny island state like Sri Lanka has apparently resisted certain provisions for port usage in the Hambantota project with China on sovereignty grounds. Almost every Asian state has a litany of issues with China's rise but is pursuing a complex strategy of adapting without in any way folding up. There is little evidence of bandwagoning or the proverbial dominoes toppling into a Chinese sphere of influence.

The notion that China can literally purchase 'regional leadership' by financing infrastructure or lending money is ludicrous. Power stems from something much deeper. It requires consent and an ability to provide public goods. China's internationalism has, so far, been more materialistic than ideational, relying largely on the lure of capital and commerce. While a significant source of influence, this cannot be an enduring prerequisite for order-building. It is instructive that the Chinese-sponsored or promoted institutions that have gained the most multilateral traction in the past decade – such as the Asian Infrastructure Investment Bank, the New Development Bank, the Shanghai Cooperation Organisation – are the ones that are perceived to offer public goods and are built around a semblance of democratized norms or rules. India still supports these ventures for precisely this reason.

In short, there is more room to shape the ongoing power transition towards a multipolar world. Schizophrenia and paranoia cannot be substitutes for smart and sober statecraft, which must include dealing directly with China. In the next section, I offer some suggestions for India's policymakers to adapt their regional policies.

Can India Leverage the BRI to Transform the Region?

The second Belt and Road Forum for International Cooperation in April 2019 witnessed a transformed discourse on China's grand connectivity initiative. Evoking an agreeable geoeconomic vision, the joint communique spoke of 'extensive consultation,' 'green,' 'people-centred and sustainable development' as well as 'high quality, sustainable infrastructure' that is 'inclusive and broadly beneficial'.[54] There is little doubt that China viewed the forum as a platform to exude more responsive and multilateral norms, with Xi Jinping himself acknowledging some of the problems with the initiative. Three broader trends might have convinced Beijing that the time was ripe for an adjustment.

To begin with, China has faced a growing tide of criticism against its ambitious connectivity plans since 2017, particularly from India and subsequently from the US. Some of it is not without basis, as the BRI has faced problems ranging from cost overruns to allegations of corruption and lack of transparency in the conception of projects. Nevertheless, US-led propaganda had reached a fever pitch that was complicating the pursuit of the initiative.

Second, contrary to the exaggerated image of Chinese banks sweeping vulnerable states into the orbit of an empire, Beijing has discovered that some of the states where the BRI is finding traction have accumulated massive Western debt over the years and with few avenues to access affordable credit. Such precarious economies view the BRI as a lifeline to recover their macroeconomic stability, often by servicing older Western debt through Chinese loans. Yet, being saddled with a risky portfolio of white elephants along the Silk Road is not the role China envisioned for its flagship initiative. China has now tightened capital controls and keeps a close watch on 'irrational' overseas projects. China's policymakers have become more quality-concious in approving outbound foreign direct investment.[55] Moreover, as economist Yasheng Huang cautions, 'BRI's massive scale, coupled with the lack of profitability of China's state sector, means that projects under the scheme may need substantial support from Chinese banks'.[56] Unsurprisingly, China seeks to hedge its bets by cooperating with established players such as the Asian Development Bank, World Bank, and the International Monetary Fund, as well as private lenders, who some Chinese policymakers believe 'should be the mainstay' for project finance.[57]

Third, stabilizing the global economic landscape and creating a conducive environment for Chinese capital and companies to flourish in non-Western economies is now vital for China's continued growth. Prolonged trade tensions with Washington have convinced Beijing that a successful BRI is more necessary than it was two years ago. Chinese foreign direct investment to the US plummeted by 80 per cent in 2018 and a further 27 per cent in 2019, exemplifying rising walls in the West for Chinese capital. In fact, 2019 witnessed the lowest level of Chinese investment in North America and Europe since 2010.[58]

Since the Donald Trump administration imposed the first round of tariffs in 2018, China's exports to the US have declined by 12 per cent.[59] In contrast, China's annual trade with BRI member countries is now over $1.3 trillion and growing at 16 per cent, a pace faster than China's overall external commerce. American protectionism against mainland China's exports is also increasing the importance of other Asian locales towards whom trade is being diverted (towards the US) and which could host some of China's manufacturing industries. The BRI is one of the ways of creating new global value chains and deepening South–South interdependence.

In short, the BRI remains a vital endeavour for China's continued economic transformation and stability, but it also needs other actors to share the risks of this grand initiative.

RESEARCHERS HAVE BEGUN questioning the simplistic assessment of the BRI as a 'debt-trap' with ominous consequences for its partner states. Not only has little empirical evidence been discovered of Chinese banks 'deliberately over-lending or funding loss-making projects to secure strategic advantages for China',[60] in Latin America and Africa, recent research suggests that Chinese finance has not pushed borrowing countries 'over the debt sustainability thresholds established by the IMF'.[61] Another study found that the 'BRI is unlikely to cause a systemic debt problem in the regions of the initiative's focus.' Assuming a two-decade horizon, 'an $8 trillion investment program for BRI countries would amount to less than 1.5 per cent of

GDP per annum, and about 2.5 per cent excluding China'.[62] Even the infamous case of Hambantota, a Sri Lankan port that slipped into China's hands after its commercial viability never materialised, is now seen as an outlier rather than the trend. Around 90 per cent of Colombo's foreign debt is still held by non-Chinese creditors.[63]

India's main concern has been that the BRI is designed to stamp China's geopolitical dominance. Some argue that such a fear might be misplaced for 'all great infrastructure and connectivity ventures – throughout history – have altered the prevailing geoeconomic matrix, and hence the resulting geopolitical balance. While the geopolitical effects are short-lived, the geoeconomic benefits survive over time'.[64] Or put simply, new trading linkages eventually trump geopolitics. But, it is still worth introspecting as to what extent the BRI has actually eroded India's influence or destabilized South Asia.

If we dispassionately notice the region's rhetoric, what stands out is a similar discourse being espoused by most of the smaller South Asian states. Nearly all of India's neighbours have expressed a preference for: non-alignment or strategic autonomy as a guiding principle in their foreign relations; multi-directional economic engagement with India, China, US, Japan, and other powers; and, sensitivity towards India, including publicly disavowing any move towards offering military facilities or bases to external powers and, thus, reassuring India on its vital interests. As one study recently observed, subcontinental states 'largely still see India as the dominant power in South Asia, suggesting that Chinese economic activity, while welcome, will not necessarily translate into major military or strategic gains'.[65] Obviously, South Asian states have their own agency and are able to juggle foreign policies that are deferential to core Indian interests while engaging China.

Order-building in Subcontinent

It is widely recognized that an under-resourced and incoherent policy setting stifles India's ability to offer quality and time-bound regional infrastructure projects. Yet, overcoming such structural problems has been an elusive exercise because they are linked to a highly distorted political economy that lacks the industrial–technological repertoire and surplus finance capital of East Asian economies. The result is for all to see: merely 5 per cent of South Asian trade is intra-regional and investment flows within the subcontinent constitute less than 1 per cent of total investment in the region. Such a fragmented sub-region with the barest forms of socio-economic interdependence is an unacceptable reality given the transformations that have occurred elsewhere in Asia and Eurasia.

In the meanwhile, dissuading China from altering the economic landscape is a self-defeating policy because a veto – to the limited extent that India can continue to play a spoiler's role – does little to advance India's lofty vision for the subcontinent. Instead, the aim, as underscored in India's own critique of the BRI 1.0, should be to espouse a set of norms that encourage a range of projects. Public diplomacy and Track 2 dialogues that attempt to socialize India's neighbours in more astute project choices and assessments must be part of the policy response. But, India also needs to proactively pursue joint ventures with Chinese companies and establish broader linkages and common standards between otherwise disparate projects in the subcontinent; in other words, prioritizing ambitious order-building over the chimera of a sphere of influence.

An illustration of strategically leveraging the BRI is Russia's proposal, made at the April 2019 BRI forum and subsequently endorsed by Xi Jinping, of linking the Northern Sea Passage to China's 'Polar Silk Road.' This was followed by a Russia-China joint venture to provide year-round liquefied natural gas (LNG) transportation capabilities in the Arctic. For some time now, Russia has been seeking to develop the northern shipping route to connect Europe with North East and Southeast Asia. For its part, China 'is actively looking to both improve supply chains and shipping routes to Europe and reduce the costs in doing so.'[66] Beijing is also looking for reliable access to Russian energy resources. But, most crucially, what China seeks is a shorter geoeconomic connection to western Eurasia that is beyond the reach of the US navy. Just as Russia is drawing the Chinese capital to develop new infrastructure and commercialize its maritime periphery in ways that would also be advantageous to China and to much of East Asia, India too must draw lessons from such types of cooperation.

China's 'Malacca dilemma' is generally recognized as an important motive for the BRI's manifestation in the CPEC and China-Myanmar Economic Corridor that aim to shorten lines of communication between mainland China, and South West Asia and Africa. India as the key regional power in this transit space can enable China to pursue its maritime interests, while drawing Chinese investment in strategically identified port and transport infrastructure sectors in the South Asian littoral. This would allow the subcontinent to recover its historical role as a fulcrum of Eurasia. After all, just like a millenia ago, India's wealth and power will ultimately derive from South Asia's ability to tap into the overland and maritime geoeconomic links between West Asia and Africa on the one hand, and East Asia and mainland China on the other. I briefly highlight this rich history in the final section of this chapter.

India's position on the CPEC, as a former foreign secretary suggests, 'should not exclude working together with China on projects where there is mutual benefit and benefit to a third partner country.' India's plans for the North-South International Corridor through Iran 'can link up most usefully with the Eurasian transport corridor which China is developing.' India's plan to link its North East region with Southeast Asia – the trilateral highway through Myanmar and into Thailand – 'could also be integrated with the north-south rail and road links which are joining southern China to the countries of Indo-China and beyond, with Mandalay as a nodal point'.[67] According to the World Bank, 'BRI transport projects are estimated to increase trade by between 2.8 and 9.7 per cent for corridor economies.'[68] In short, it makes little sense for inter-regional connectivity routes to remain disconnected with each other as they collectively advance economic interdependence.

China's infrastructure projects could also increase South Asia's internal connectivity. Much of the viability of logistical networks and energy projects is linked with India's economy and access to its large market. For example, hydropower projects developed by China with India as the main eventual market could be a form of trilateral cooperation. Another instance is that of projects that increase interdependence between India and its neighbours, such as the Chinese-constructed terminal at the Chittagong port, which buttressed India-Bangladesh coastal shipping cooperation.[69] What has been absent in Indian policy is the conceiving of creative ways of collaboration with the BRI in the immediate and extended neighbourhood to transform the region's economic geography, presumably one of the grand strategic tasks for any Indian leadership.

Although typically associated with transport connectivity, the BRI has forayed into new areas, particularly in the subcontinent. Nearly all the agreements (13 bilateral and 16 multilateral) with Myanmar, Bangladesh, Sri Lanka, Nepal, and

Pakistan at the second 2019 BRI forum related to agriculture, rural development, renewable energy, green development, disaster reduction, and science.[70] What has gone unnoticed is the BRI's contribution to human capital development and technical knowledge in the Global South, formerly an exclusive preserve of the West. Since the BRI's launch in 2013, the Chinese Academy of Sciences (CAS) has invested $270 million on five research and development (R&D) facilities in China and nine in BRI partner countries in South Asia, Southeast Asia, South America, and Africa. The CAS has trained 5,000 students from BRI countries in science and technology courses as well as 200 PhD students each year. In 2017, nearly 40,000 students from BRI countries studied in China on the Silk Road scholarship programme, accounting for two-thirds of all Chinese scholarships.[71]

For one, 'India should look at the possibilities of S&T cooperation with China in areas of interest using the BRI platform'.[72] Delhi could leverage the BRI to establish a regional platform for joint scientific research as a public good and a means to transform the quality of human capital in the neighbourhood. Today, for example, 'mixed Chinese-Pakistani faculty' are undertaking joint research as well as offering advanced degrees in 'artificial intelligence, food technology, mineral resources and railways' in Pakistani universities.[73] Indians and Chinese co-teaching courses for students across the subcontinent would enable India's neighbours to absorb and sustain high-quality investment in a variety of sectors like manufacturing, agriculture, and ecological protection, evaluate environmental risks of large infrastructure projects, and enhance water and disaster management. This would be another intelligent way to embed China into a common developmental agenda for the subcontinent, one being co-authored by India.

There is a quixotic belief in India that a period of sustained economic growth will by itself restore Indian authority in the subcontinent. This is delusional because India's growth is, for the most part, not being accompanied by innovative institutions, scientific and industrial heft, or the socialization strategies that rising powers have historically relied upon to cohere their regions. China's presence is a reality that cannot be wished away or held at bay through India's negative veto power over its neighbours who, albeit in a clear-eyed fashion, are deepening their geoeconomic links with Beijing. Shaping this changing setting would require India to exercise leadership in more imaginative ways, recognize its domestic weaknesses, be attentive to its neighbours' desire for a better life and tap into China's strengths. For the past decade, India's policymakers have not felt confident enough to adopt such a worldview and vision for statecraft. Above all, India's policy debate must shift away from an ideological and overly securitized posture to China's geoeconomic involvement, and towards an order-building approach where regional modernization becomes the heart of India's geostrategy.

At the time of writing, the 2020 Ladakh crisis has brought geopolitics and hard security back to the forefront, making any nuanced conversation on geoeconomics less attractive to the mainstream policy discourse. In such a context of mutual mistrust, and before a new reset in ties, it is unrealistic for both countries to dovetail their connectivity visions and engage in a less prejudiced dialogue where overlapping interests are perceived more objectively.

Yet, the region and structural shifts in globalization will not wait and India will need to juggle its varied interests and priorities in an even more complex China policy framework. Multilateralizing China's future engagement through a subcontinent-wide network of norms is more likely to convert the BRI into an advantageous proposition rather than a purely competitive approach that disappoints India's recipients with her feeble outcomes, and frees China to pursue ad hoc bilateral deals with little concern for the regional political economy. Over time, a sophisticated approach propelled by bilateral and multilateral projects, including partnerships between Indian and Chinese firms, and establishing sub-regional manufacturing zones and industrial parks – all driven by an overarching vision for an open and interdependent subcontinent – will be the shrewdest response to changing the way the BRI is operationalized in the region. It is also the most effective way to re-establish a modicum of Indian leadership in the subcontinent.

MUCH LIKE THE discovery of the Cape of Good Hope in Southern Africa in the 15th century or the construction of the Suez Canal, the trans-Siberian railway across Russia and the trans-continental railway across America in the late 19th century, the BRI is a long-term trend that is likely to alter the geopolitical and geoeconomic landscape and consolidate a fractured Eurasia. In hindsight, all those successful historical projects 'clearly show how imaginatively conceived infrastructure can literally reconfigure geography and, in the course of redrawing the map, that new connectivity can also transform the face of world affairs.'[74] Whether the BRI will prove as consequential as its illustrious predecessors only time will tell. What is clear is the venture's success is predicated on interdependence and the most successful connectivity routes (within the rubric of the BRI) would ultimately depend on the reciprocity and participation of other economic, cultural and geopolitical centres without whose cooperation the emergence of new connections or revival of older networks will be difficult to achieve.

It is crucial for Indians to debate these transformational changes underway and formulate sophisticated policies and strategies to shape some of these connections. It is important to discover ways to benefit from new connectivity. It might also be necessary to resist some projects that lack a rationale or appear ominous. For a strategic discourse that seems to thrive on absolutes, Indians would do well to look back at a longer span of history when multiple connectivity and geoeconomic visions operated in parallel and where competition and collaboration was the natural order of interactions.

5

INDIA'S SEARCH FOR AN EQUILIBRIUM WITH CHINA

Since Narendra Modi's ascent to power in 2014, India's China policy has been changing in multiple ways. Compared to the 2000s, China's rise became more apparent and its footprint in South Asia more visible. Delhi was confronted by the challenge of adjusting to this changing strategic setting as well as formulating a policy framework that could advance India's interests in a stable, secure and interconnected periphery. Has Delhi been successful? The balance sheet is a mixed one. The China relationship has grown acrimonious and competitive during the past five years. The economic and military gap with China has also increased during the past decade. Yet, the strategic task of finding a new and sustainable equilibrium with China remains a priority for India. The alternative – unmitigated competition and conflict – could unravel not only Asia's renaissance but also India's own aspirations for great power status and lasting economic transformation at home.

Structured chronologically, this chapter brings out the most salient aspects of the policy conundrum in recent years and advocates policy options for India in its search for a balance in the different aspects of China policy.

Changing Neighbourhood

The 2014 SAARC summit was a subtle but clear jolt that India had its work cut out in South Asia. If there ever was a gulf between India's regional self-image and capacity, between aspiration and actual power, it is now. China's rise has been testing India's regional role. Pretending that India can catch up quickly or embellish its regional position via rhetoric would be self-deception.

The dragon is already in the house, and Delhi is playing catch up. China's internal re-orientation towards what Xi Jinping calls 'big country diplomacy with Chinese characteristics' and expanding China's political economic influence is impacting its entire periphery. There is nothing unusual about China's new discourse and behaviour. All great powers define their interests beyond their frontiers and seek to shape their primary region and perhaps even beyond. The countries of South Asia, being direct neighbours of China, are naturally poised to feel the impact of these changes.

The Indian dilemma has been to frame the policy challenge sensibly. Since the Modi government is clearly playing catch up, it is easy to get trapped in a defensive narrative that does little to alter ground realities. The instinctive tendency in Indian think tanks is to engage in military-centric conversations dealing with traditional or cross-border threats.

This is, however, not the primary trend in South Asia. Aside from Pakistan's identity-driven conflict with India that has fueled a destructive proxy war over decades, the rest of the region is *relatively* more normal. None of the smaller South Asian states define their identity or foreign policy goals to spurn India. The regional trend can be more accurately characterized as a quest for regime stability, enhanced development, and more foreign policy autonomy and options. China fulfills many of these needs because of its proximity, domestic capacity, and (compared to previous decades) an active neighbourhood diplomacy.

It is not axiomatic that this process is undermining South Asian stability or producing anti-India orientations in South Asia. India's neighbours have two much bigger powers vying for their attention and these smaller states have learnt the art of successfully extracting developmental and security benefits from this game. Can India conceptualize and pursue a role where it isn't necessarily locked in a zero-sum game of influence with China, a game that is ironically becoming positive-sum for other South Asian states?

Geographically, India holds a commanding position in the subcontinent, and, to confront traditional threats India is still geopolitically dominant and will remain so. But beyond that, India's geographic centrality has proven to be inadequate to maintain its position as a regional power. India, however, has enough economic resources, if mobilized prudently, to play its part in South Asia. The more pertinent question is grounding the regional order on a set of shared norms for the smaller nations as they engage with the rest of the world. India can no longer hold a veto on whether its neighbours pursue multivector foreign policies. But India can hold a veto on keeping its neighbours in a non-aligned status. India can also shape the types of partnerships that outside powers pursue with its neighbours. In some cases, trilateral dialogues and bilateral conversations between the Special Representatives can be useful in gauging

China's interests and reducing mistrust. But to do all this the strategic community needs a more sophisticated conversation on regional affairs and statecraft.

For example, China's interests in South Asia are not always directed at or derived from China-India relations. Nepal is important because of its potential to become a base to destabilize Tibet. Sri Lanka and Maldives are becoming useful as part of China's maritime strategy to secure its SLOCs, and, to access transit points along these trade routes to West Asia and Africa. Unless India's neighbours go along with it, China cannot be excluded from pursuing its interests in this region. What India should be doing is finding ways to accommodate some Chinese interests and simultaneously drawing red lines, which become costly for China and India's neighbours to cross. One such red line would obviously be a Chinese military base in South Asia.

This is, arguably, a more strategic and realistic approach to modulating China's South Asia policy than expending resources without a clear sense of what India seeks for itself and from its neighbours.

To influence the trajectory of the region India needs a regional policy. First, India should redefine its role away from defending a narrow notion of state and territorial security towards a wider conception of regional welfare and human security. Second, India should promote norms for the region that emerge from a thoughtful conception of Indian and South Asian interests. For example, India has direct interests in both the makeup of subcontinental regimes, and how these regimes behave internally and externally.

Third, recognize that different regional orders are intersecting geopolitically and geoeconomically. India needs cooperation and interdependence with other regions to transform itself and South Asia. The idea of 'open regionalism' fits in with India's own discourse of connecting to multiple economic centres. Rather than be a 'frog in the well' and engage in a schizophrenic discourse around China's rise, realism demands accepting a prolonged period of interdependence with East Asia and West Asia for South Asia's domestic transformation.

This, of course, implies an inherent tension with the more traditional conception of a region as a privileged sphere managed by a single regional power. China's own rise exemplifies this contradiction where interdependence, and, the impulse for a larger say on regional geopolitics in East Asia is often in tension. India too will perhaps confront a similar dialectic as its relative power increases in the coming decades.

In an ideal world, a South Asia in splendid isolation, and, an India with the economic and institutional capacities might have produced an order for the entire region. But India's internal pre-occupations, a lop-sided growth model with a weak state, and, China's rise has exposed the idea of South Asia as an exclusive sphere of influence. It is no longer a viable venture.

If policymakers do not adapt to changing conditions, India is in danger of losing control over the regional narrative and indeed over the direction of change in the subcontinent.

Modi and Nehru's Ghost

The Modi-Xi rendezvous in September 2014, their first in a series of encounters over the past decade, evoked several images but the one that stood out was the public courting of a Chinese leader by an Indian prime minister since the brief bonhomie of the early 1950s. By spending several hours showing Xi Jinping around under the live gaze of the Indian media, Modi was hoping to endear the Chinese leader to the Indian people. Modi seemed to recognize that the China equation cannot be transformed by stealth, and, without public and elite support it would be difficult for him to re-craft a new relationship. In this case it is even more important because the China factor remains historically trapped in contested images.

It could be argued that Modi was diffusing his worldview on a generally conservative elite that was and still is mostly comfortable with the West. Let us be clear, while Modi is not anti-West, he is not enamored by the Atlantic world either. For Modi, Eurasia and East Asia is where he had been most exposed to during his tenures as Chief Minister of Gujarat, and, this is the part of the world that is poised to become an even more important centre of gravity in the coming decades.

Can Modi change Indian attitudes on China? Yes, but this will be an uphill task because the notion of 'Western-ness' is deeply ingrained in the Indian strategic mind, and, in the past two decades multiple epistemic communities have flourished to endear the Indian elite to a Western conception of world order despite the objective conditions no longer meriting such a predisposition.

Ironically, it was Jawaharlal Nehru, a leader deeply Westernized by habit and experience, who socialized the Indian people to a post-independence identity. Similar to Modi's predicament today, Nehru sought to diffuse ideas to an otherwise conservative and relatively insular elite on what ought to be India's worldview and international role. Nehru and many of his peers instinctively viewed Asia's resurrection from colonialism and imperialism as a wider phenomenon that Indians could identify and empathize with. The Nehruvian image of China – as a fellow Asian state recovering from its century of humiliation as a semi-colonial prize for external predators – seemed similar to India's even more degrading experience as a full colony.

Inheriting the mantles of power at another inflexion point in world politics, it has fallen upon Modi to re-craft India's role for the emerging world order. Similar to Nehru, Modi is ahead of the curve, and, does not appear constrained by any deep ideological preferences other than to secure India's place in the sun. Just as Nehru was quick to recognize the consequences of a bipolar world, Modi has understood that the coming decade is likely to be very different from that faced by his predecessors.

It is, however, the contrast of Modi with Nehru that defines the contemporary phase. As Gandhi once observed, Nehru's 'nationalism' was 'enriched by his fine internationalism'. For Nehru, while bipolarity was a reality, he was more interested in stabilizing the balance of power rather than extracting selfish benefits for India. While Nehru passionately diffused an independent identity for India, he was a reluctant nationalist. Nehru's definition of India's national interest in 1947 set the tone for his foreign policy. He said, 'we propose to look after India's interests in the context of world cooperation and world peace.' Instead of exploiting the bipolar balance, Nehru pursued a different role for India: as a peacemaker and bridge-builder between the two antagonistic blocs. The available archives reveal how actively India intervened in attempting to stabilize East-West ties in the 1950s. Ironically, it was China that ultimately brought Nehru and his ideas down with the confrontation of 1962.

For Modi, the national interest is defined differently. For example, although Modi has invoked the traditional concept of Vasudhaiva Kutumbakam or 'one world', he has no intentions of trying to bridge the two mutually suspicious worlds that we witness today. Modi is not interested in entering any great game between the great powers. Instead, an 'India first' approach animates his worldview.

Modi is a nationalist but also of an era where complex global interdependence has made an element of internationalism a vital part of any foreign policy. Even the recent mantra of

Atmanirbhar Bharat is seen as a dualism of the local and the global. Modi finds no contradiction between nationalism and globalization. Modi views the international system primarily in instrumental terms – how can the disruptions in globalization and great power equations be leveraged to benefit India.

To truly leverage the multi-polar world for national and geopolitical advantage, India needs to possess a normal and stable equation with all the great powers. China is the only major power with which India has struggled to normalize its relationship, despite years of high-level summitry, multilateral coordination and inter-state commerce. The obstacle lies more in the realm of beliefs and choices. Although there is a large measure of continuity in India's foreign policy, Modi is attempting to effect change to make the necessary adjustment to a post-unipolar order. Modi is re-steering India's role to focus on the neighbourhood, which in his words, 'occupies a special place in my national development plans and foreign policy.'

In each of his summits, Modi's body language with Xi Jinping has been one of confidence and equality with his Chinese interlocutor. But Modi has also appeared conscious of Nehru's ghost and the enduring suspicion and mistrust for China in the Indian mind. It will require statesmanship and a clear communication strategy to transcend the deep elite resistance against re-setting India's equation with China. For Modi, changing China policy truly is as much a domestic challenge as getting China to take India more seriously.

Engaging the US to Gain Leverage on China

The 2015 Barack Obama presence during India's Republic Day parade was a turning point in India-US relations. An American president flanked by the Indian commander-in-chief and prime minister celebrating the founding of our Republic would have been inconceivable previously. After a fairy tale like courting of India in the early 2000s, US geostrategy lapsed into its old ways by 2009. The global economic crisis and a pushback from rising power centres like Russia and China meant that Modi inherited a world very different from his predecessors.

The Bush administration's outreach in the early 2000s was based on co-opting India for a potential role in Asia's regional security architecture. The strategy was one of integrating India, eventually into a defacto-allied role with a robust military alignment. The success of the geostrategy relied on an asymmetric convergence of interests, whereby India's outlook and interests on regional geopolitics would become more conforming to US interests and preferences on India's extended periphery.

South Asia was always the area of contradiction for US policies had to contend with maintaining a durable equation with Pakistan while developing a relationship with India. Here the Bush White House forged the nuclear deal – in essence a de facto acknowledgement of India's nuclear weapons programme and status – as an implicit quid pro quo for acquiescence to otherwise persistent US policies in the region.

This single agreement was transformative in that it removed an outdated posture against India's nuclear programme, thereby enabling the two countries to normalize and heighten their engagement. However, the implied wider linkage with India's perceptions and policies across other issue-areas gradually, that is, an expectation that India would jump into the US camp dampened the enthusiasm of US policymakers. India's innate preference for an independent path in its rise could not be easily reconciled with the US framework and attendant vision for India's role in South Asia, Asia and the world. Delhi's inability to re-define and re-negotiate an acceptable framework for Indo-US ties produced a period of apathetic drift until 2013.

It fell upon a new nationalist-oriented dispensation after Narendra Modi's dramatic 2013 victory, in the elections to become the Prime Minister, to restore some conceptual and operational energy to India's foreign policy. Having learnt the lessons of the 2000s where an overly ambitious agenda was imposed on Indo-US relations, Modi has sought to reframe and anchor the relationship in three core areas – economic development, Pakistan-driven terrorism, and, China's rise – where India's self-interest and perceptions guided how these issues were transacted in bilateral interactions.

While Modi's optics and effort to connect the Indian people to the world of diplomacy and high politics is new, it is the substance of statecraft that ultimately matters. There appear to be two competing worldviews related to the China part of the India-US equation.

One view is that India is swinging towards a total alignment in its wider Asia-Pacific policy with the US. For example, the 'Joint Strategic Vision' for the Asia Pacific and Indian Ocean is an endorsement of each other's roles in the Indo-Pacific. Yet, given US maritime predominance over this large area, India is in effect bandwagoning with the US and its allied network.

A second view is that India's overall foreign policy vis-à-vis the major powers has not changed fundamentally. As India's foreign minister recently clarified 'a rejection of non-alignment does not mean a rush to alignment: India will not join an alliance system.'[1] India is seeking to benefit from the global balance of power rather than assume the unpredictable and potentially costly role of a swing power who buttresses the strength of one great power or bloc in its competition with another. This reluctance to aggregate its moral and material strength with one great power against another is apparent from the overall official discourse during the Modi years. To be sure, this does not preclude seeking support from one power in the search for security against another. Nor does it exclude issue-based cooperation that might run contrary to the position of another great power.

From the above two worldviews on Modi's foreign policy it is evident that each interpretation is based on a set of assumptions around India's interests and role, and China's policies.

The first view presumes that Delhi is still uncertain of its China policy and takes a more zero-sum view of China's rise, especially in the security realm. The second view presumes that Asian politics and China's rise is an evolving dynamic and different strategic futures would drive different policy responses. It is the implementation or 'roadmap' of the Joint Strategic Vision that matters and this would evolve based on China's regional and particularly South Asia policies.

The first view presumes the securitization of Asian geopolitics is now irreversible and India has chosen one side. This outlook is shaped by the concept of indivisible security where China's strategies in East Asia will directly impact India. The second view leaves open the possibility of multiple outcomes in India-China interactions – including the possibility of a new modus vivendi and equilibrium – and a subsequent recalibration of India's Asia policy. This is based on an outlook of divisible security where India and China can craft a bilateral modus vivendi even as China engages in strategic competition with the US in East Asia, which has a logic of its own given the global power transition and Beijing's quest to attain a higher status in the international system.

The first view presumes a less sanguine outlook for India's emergence as a regional power centre that requires a dramatic external balancing prop. The second view is more confident of

India's strategic future and ability to craft asymmetric strategies to maintain India's regional role despite the probability of a much stronger China for several decades.

But perhaps most important is that the first view has constructed China's rise as an existential threat while the second view is more complex and nuanced in this assessment. The latter presumes that Chinese intentions and Beijing's India policies can be influenced by Indian statecraft, atleast on certain issues. Indeed, the 'soft balancing' against China's maritime ambitions could accelerate opportunities to alleviate, if not address, the roots of Sino-Indian problems – such as their territorial dispute and competition in South Asia.

China's Counter-Move on Pakistan

Three months after Barack Obama's highly symbolic visit to Delhi in Janaury 2015, Xi Jinping undertook a landmark visit to Pakistan in April 2015. On the eve of his visit, Xi Jinping recited an Urdu couplet in an article: 'My friend's lovely image dwells in the mirror of my heart; I tilt my head slightly, and here it comes into my sight.' For decades, such hyperbole has substituted for a meaningful China-Pakistan relationship. But Xi's visit marked a turning point.

Since 2001, China has played second fiddle to Pakistan's primary benefactor – America. Keeping their head down as Deng Xiaoping had instructed, Chinese policymakers steered clear of assuming any burden in the US-led mission in Afghanistan and its concomitant policy in Pakistan. The inability of the US to stabilise the area and arrest the turmoil in Afghanistan and Pakistan, and, Deng's dictum has given way to a stronger and extroverted China. Xi's China, however, has not evolved into a great power in the classical European sense seeking adventure and expansionism everywhere. The Chinese define their interests carefully and pursue them with resilience but with flexible means and via complex statecraft. Is China changing the way it defines its interests in Pakistan?

The original glue for a China-Pakistan entente – a shared hostility towards India – has not disappeared from Beijing's calculus. Pakistan was the largest recipient of Chinese arms in the past decade with nearly 70 per cent of China's arms exports flowing to three countries: Pakistan, Bangladesh and Myanmar. Yet, China's South Asia and Pakistan policy is evolving into a more sophisticated one. China's interests in Pakistan now transcend the India factor. The goal can be described as an attempt to shape a new regional order based on interdependence with China's still robust political economy and integration into new institutional networks focusing on different facets of regional security and economics. The core of Xi's Pakistan play is about buttressing Pakistan's state and developmental capacity, which is linked to China's energy security, periphery security and counter-terrorism interests.

It is well established that Uighur-based extremism in Xinjiang, a minority border province, traces its roots to Pakistan's tribal areas via the East Turkestan Islamic Movement. A spurt of terror incidents across China in recent years has made Beijing more anxious about neutralizing this threat. Xi explicitly pointed out Pakistan's importance in the 'security and stability of China's Western border areas' during his speech in Pakistan's parliament. A weak state with a dilapidated infrastructure has exacerbated Pakistan's efforts to weed out extremists targeting even its quasi-ally. It is this reality that has persuaded Chinese policymakers to seriously plan about Pakistan's future.

While there is no overt evidence of Beijing seeking to cultivate a new civil-military balance or assist in Pakistan's fragile democratic process, Chinese scholars have expressed a more active interest in Pakistan's internal affairs. In conversations with Chinese scholars since 2013, I have discerned a bolder outlook and a confidence that China's industrial and financial strength can be leveraged to assist in Pakistan's domestic transformation. But it is also evident that China's prism for analysing Pakistan's domestic problems is essentially a materialist one. That is rather than viewing Pakistan's structural contradictions as a national identity problem, it is viewed primarily through a materialist lens – a weak state as the primary cause of instability and radicalism. It is unclear if pumping money into something, which at its roots is ideological, can by itself alter Pakistan's body politic. After all, Pakistan was one of the largest recipients of western development aid during the Cold War and yet was unable to find a stable political system and foreign policy. But this has not perturbed Beijing. As one scholar told me a few years ago, 'China-Pakistan economic cooperation will help make Pakistan become a normal country, which is also good for India.'

At first glance, the intent appears similar to the US discourse during its Afghan intervention phase where Pakistan's long-term prospects were deemed as crucial to stabilize Afghanistan and the region. American actions on the ground, however, never seemed to go beyond mollifying the Generals in Rawalpindi. It has been unclear if China has been thinking any differently. The planned development projects and the envisaged scale of China's investment in Pakistan's infrastructure sectors are of a much higher magnitude. The energy sector is projected to receive the largest share – 75 per cent or $34 billion – of the projected $45 billion of envisaged direct investment and financial loans. Accounting for over 16,000 MW, diverse renewable and conventional power projects would eventually double Pakistan's installed capacity. That Pakistan's energy crisis is a big political issue was probably not far from Chinese policymakers' minds when they designed the overall investment package.

The second big theme for China has been regional connectivity. In 2013, Xi articulated the idea of reviving the old silk routes. When fully developed over the coming decades, these lines of communication will traverse across the Eurasian continent – transiting Russia, Central Asia, Iran, Southern Asia, and, maritime Asia around the Western Pacific and northern Indian Ocean littorals. Pakistan became the first harvest – at least on paper – of this ambitious idea of reconnecting disparate economies with each other but more importantly with China's eastern heartland.

Twenty per cent or $9.5 billion of the projected $45 billion investment will be used in Pakistan's road and rail sectors. The trans-Karakoram highway is envisaged to expand and connect to a robust road and rail network connected to Pakistan's coastal outlet of Gwadar (for which $622 million was earmarked for a variety of infrastructure and human capital development projects). But a functioning and secure corridor that serves as a two-way geoeconomic link between eastern China and West Asia and Africa is conditional on several intermediate pieces of the puzzle coming together. The central assumption, of course, is that Pakistan's rulers possess the vision and resolve to transform their country. Nevertheless, China made a large down payment to assist Pakistan in reaching a modicum of internal stability.

As of March 2020, $19 billion worth of infrastructure projects had been completed under the rubric of CPEC. That China remains serious about the next phase of CPEC – 'industrial cooperation, trade, agriculture and socioeconomic development' – was underscored by its recent selection of a political appointee with experience in economic diplomacy as Beijing's new envoy to Islamabad.[2]

India's Options

The implications for India are profound regardless of how prolonged the operationalization of China's big push will be in Pakistan. For India, it appears that history is one recurring loop of Pakistan's continuing importance for its two major benefactors – US and China. Can India exploit the growing Sino-American rivalry when it comes to this region? It is difficult to foresee American and Chinese policymakers competing actively over Pakistan. Even during their fierce propoganda wars, Beijing and Washington have not really crossed swords in Pakistan. And, for good reason. A largely unchanged Sino-American convergence towards supporting Pakistan as a functioning state and underwriting its territorial integrity will override most secondary geopolitical contradictions. Furthermore, US policymakers have always sought to restore the alliance with Pakistan whenever Islamabad's ties with China became stronger. India has borne the brunt of this recurring geopolitical dynamic. For its part, Pakistan's foreign policy is unlikely to disrupt this historical dynamic by overplaying its hand and losing the strategic privilege of having two formidable benefactors. Pakistan's neutrality during the recent deterioration in US-China ties is instructive.

Within this evolving matrix, what India can do is formulate a more sophisticated regional policy. Instead of a crude strategy of hoping to counteract Beijing's every move in the region, Delhi can craft a framework where competitive and cooperative elements are bound together in a more holistic strategy, and, one that is more consistent with actual Indian capacities. For example, restoring a modicum of civilian legitimacy and state capacity in Pakistan might not necessarily be antithetical to long-term Indian interests. Even if they cannot coordinate policies, both India and China have a common interest in converting

Pakistan from a frontline 'hired gun' into a normal state at peace with itself and the region. But such an alternative vision of the regional picture is predicated on a new India-China relationship. This has not been forthcoming.

Persistence of Mistrust

India-China relations are typically framed in a cooperative-competitive-conflictual framework to describe the operational state of affairs. Each of these images reflects the India-China relationship in some issue area or region. But there is also something of an overarching image and attitude that reflects how a state defines a relationship. In this sense, there has been reticence and mistrust in both Delhi and Beijing. There is a premium for being risk averse and eschewing ambitious policy innovations. This applies on all fronts – the border dispute, economy, regional affairs, and global politics.

In 2014, the Modi government came to office with an initial impulse to implement the accumulated consensus that has been established in recent years – that despite the border dispute, 'common interests' in diverse areas should be tapped. These include the economy both at a bilateral trade and investment level and co-developing or participating in new multilateral institutions of global finance emerging in the non-Western world. The idea that India and China can establish a 'developmental partnership' was the big narrative that Narendra Modi sought to bring to an otherwise conservative bureaucracy.

Yet, the dominant image of mistrust remained unchanged and was reinforced as the frontier witnessed more frequent crises. It is by no means evident that India-China relations can be transformed by focusing only on the economy. Some kind of a wider geopolitical understanding – at its core is the border dispute – seems essential for the bilateral equation to yield positive outcomes in the areas where common interests are generally presumed to prevail. Now, the question that can be asked is why change the framework at all?

The short answer is, despite the decades-long glacial process of diplomatic normalization and incremental expansion in the bilateral menu of engagement, the dominant image of discord remains more resilient than ever. The second factor is the economy. The Modi government had underpinned its domestic and foreign policy themes around industrial modernization, and selective collaboration with China was perceived as an opportunity to redress structural weaknesses in India's economy and overcome some of its capital needs to propel faster growth. The third factor, which has made it imperative for India to re-evaluate its China policy framework, is China's changing interests in the neighbourhood. This change in the regional context has become too apparent to wish away. China is changing its South Asia policy and is going beyond just an India-centric and Tibet-centric security approach. We are still in the initial phase but China is transitioning towards a more active regional policy where its earlier arms-length posture is being displaced by a more strategic and proactive attempt to shape the regional order and link it with China's political economy.

The above three reasons are collectively making it more and more challenging for India to sustain a China policy that is built on tentatively dealing with the parts rather than addressing the whole. If we examine the two big rapprochements between China and other major powers – the 1970s Sino-American normalization, and, the post-1986 and post-Cold War China-Russia normalization – both were driven by a political-level decision and choice to alter the conflict-dominant image. The economic and strategic interdependence of the last three decades between China and the advanced economies of US, UK and other European countries, and those between China and Russia was a *consequence*, not the *cause*, of a grand political détente. In the case of US and China, they reached an understanding on East Asian and global security and stability. Although it was originally built on an anti-Soviet platform, the basic accommodation survived for more than two decades after the end of bipolarity. It has only recently begun to fray with the changing balance of power. In the Russia-China case, it was a mutual recognition that the Sino-Soviet conflict had gone too far and was undermining national interests of both sides. By 2004, China and Russia had solved all their territorial disputes, and by 2008 their 4,200 km border had been demarcated paving the way for a genuine strategic partnership. Importantly, none of these political accommodations with China inhibited the pursuit of national interests.

This is something that India's policymakers and the strategic community need to recognize as we think about different kinds of China policies and strategic pathways in the changing global context that we now face. Attempting to reach a new modus vivendi with China does not mean throwing in the towel. It does not mean India cannot pursue its interests and aspirations. Yet, it also does not mean the end of longstanding differences. What it implies is exploring ways to dovetail parts of India's regional vision and development priorities with the reality of China in the background and foreground.

Modi's quest to emulate a Deng Xiaoping-style modernization strategy requires a China policy that is both realistic and open to fundamentally altering the meta-image of the bilateral relationship by probing for a limited geopolitical understanding with China. The next section lays out a framework and the logic for arresting the escalating competition in India-China relations and forging a new equilibrium.

Logic of a Limited Geopolitical Accommodation

Over the past decade, three historical forces have been shaping India-China relations. Some of these forces have been pushing both countries towards competition and some impelling them towards cooperation and collaboration. The first is a changing world order and the rise of Asia, a phase that is generally traced to the period after the 2008 global economic crisis. The second is the idea that with the West's declining capacity and inclination to responsibly manage international and Asian affairs, India, China and other re-emerging powers are being thrust into new order building roles that would require coordination and cooperation to preserve global stability and co-develop new governance institutions and norms. The third is a changing South Asia with China's 2013 and 2014 policy declarations of deepening ties with its periphery including with subcontinental states, followed soon after with the ambitious BRI and the CPEC in April 2015.

While all three factors have contributed to the complexity of India-China relations during this period, the region became the main arena of interaction, with both sides adopting antagonistic approaches and strategies. Much of this acrimonious build-up can be traced to China's decision to expand linkages with its southwestern periphery and India's perception and reaction to that process. Two major border crises, the 2017 Doklam and 2020 Ladakh standoffs, in the high Himalayas are the culmination of a deeper festering question – how would India and China relate to each other as their footprints and search for greater security grew in their overlapping peripheries?

ANY EVALUATION OF India-China relations should attempt to analyse the operating framework that guides this relationship. The bilateral equation has been in stress for most of the period between 2014 and 2020, with a series of border crisis during this period. The main reason for this flux is that the old framework established in the closing years of the Cold War has been unable to handle the intersection of interests between the two countries at a time of rapid change in various settings – the Asia-Pacific or Indo-Pacific, Eurasia, the subcontinent, and the global economy.

The old framework essentially sought to mute the security dilemma, which was largely, though not entirely, a consequence of a long disputed frontier, while opening the possibility of developing a mutually beneficial relationship in other non-security areas. After the 1979 China visit of then Foreign Minister Atal Bihari Vajpayee, a three-point formula was established. Both sides agreed to pursue a resolution of the boundary dispute; both agreed to maintain peace and tranquility during that process; both agreed that there should be no impediment to the development of bilateral relations in various fields. This basic framework was eventually enshrined in the 1988 Deng Xiaoping–Rajiv Gandhi summit.

In many ways, this was a pragmatic attempt to craft a stable equilibrium without actual or meaningful accommodation of the core or vital interests of either side. In this sense, the late 1980s and the manifestation of a detente in the 1990s in the form of confidence-building agreements, built around peace and tranquility on the frontier, were far less ambitious and more incremental than the grand strategic detente one notices in other normalization processes among the major powers. This is not to diminish the importance of these agreements. The September 1993 agreement, for instance, 'formalized in an international treaty a bilateral commitment by India and China to maintain the status quo on the border...Both countries also formally renounced the use of force to settle the issue.'[3] As alluded to earlier, the US-China rapprochement in the 1970s and the Russia-China rapprochement in the late 1980s stand out as alternative models for a bilateral normalization after a prolonged period of intense conflict, rivalry, and competition. In these two cases, we can notice more elements of transformation in the bilateral relationship.

This did not occur in the India-China case. Rather, the detente framework was in essence a contingent truce with possibilities of incremental change in the India-China relationship. Its main result was that it kept a modicum of peace and tranquility on the Himalayan frontier (until the 2020 Ladakh crisis) while enabling tentative and relatively modest transactions in non-security areas. The old framework was, thus, never intended to produce a transformation or a complete normalization in ties. It was a stopgap arrangement formulated within the political constraints of both sides, neither of whom were able nor willing to 'give-and-take' on core issues. The fragility of this improvised arrangement has been exposed in recent years, as more and more issues in bilateral ties are being perceived and framed in competitive and adversarial terms. Given the absence of an agreed bilateral framework to regulate India-China differences, a real danger that looms ahead is one of an over-reaction from both sides to the perceived and real challenges to each side's ambitions and interests. The 2020 border crisis exemplifies this zero-sum approach to regional security that has been gaining ascendance since 2013.

A Complex Picture

One of the main reasons, arguably, for the challenges and frustration that India's strategic community is confronting in dealing with China is a general reluctance to accept the emergence of a stronger, more capable China across many domains of power. For some reason, almost in utter defiance of a realistic appraisal of the balance of power, we have expanded the image of rivalry into more and more domains. Indian policymakers are struggling to conceive an approach that is realistic, pragmatic, and strategic. But, if we carefully examine the points of intersection between India and China, we might discover a more complex picture, rather than the binaries that animate the popular discourse.

Instead of defining the relationship in broad brushstrokes that tend to fall prey to a noisy media and a fickle public discourse, let us briefly explore five issue areas where Indian and Chinese interests intersect in order to evaluate the potential for conflict, rivalry, competition, and cooperation. I urge the reader to engage in a similar mental exercise, as it would empower each of you to think more independently and creatively about India-China ties. Each issue area could also hold multiple, even contradictory, facets that condition the nature of Sino-Indian interactions (See Table 2 below).

Table 2 reveals that of all the issue areas where Indian and Chinese interests will intersect in the foreseeable future, South Asia is the sub-region most fraught with the possibility of negative scenarios, uncontrolled rivalry and a heightening security dilemma. The areas of tension, mistrust and competition are primarily in the immediate vicinity of the subcontinent. Crafting a sensible policy and ensuring consistency between means and ends in this area is going to be one of India's big foreign policy challenges in the coming decade.

For the remainder of this chapter, I engage with the most contentious issue area – the overlapping periphery – and make the case for a limited geopolitical accommodation whereby India and China can also preserve their vital interests.

The Policy Challenge

In recent years, India and China have been working according to rival geopolitical visions. Although China has been a direct neighbour of South Asia and India since 1950, it is only in the past decade that Chinese policymakers have re-formulated their regional policy to pursue more sustained political and economic relationships with several states in the subcontinent and the Indian Ocean littoral. Following Xi Jinping's foreign policy guidelines of 2013 and 2014, China has adopted a policy aimed at enhancing development options of its neighbours as well as promoting new lines of communication or corridors with its south western periphery. Much of this impetus has been provided by the BRI – a grand connectivity plan that envisions a network of states economically linked to China through a variety of commercial-financial relationships and industrial projects. South Asia is one of five regions or sub-regions that has been identified as an area to expand China's geoeconomic footprint.

Since the 1990s, India too has contemplated ways to re-connect with its South Asian neighbours and inculcate a spirit of integration and interdependence in the subcontinent. While this process has found bipartisan political appeal, the ideas, resources, and institutions to advance meaningful regional integration remain at a fragmentary and inadequate level. Nothing underscores the meagre level of interdependence than the following stark statistics: merely 5 per cent of South Asian trade is intra-regional; intra-regional investments constitute less than 1 per cent of total investment in the subcontinent.

Although India and China are today seen as regional competitors, neither power has succeeded in implementing its vision fully. The main reason has been the inability of both countries to situate their rival visions in a region-wide approach. India has not fully come to terms with the utter lack of intra-regional trading and infrastructure networks; nor has Delhi been able to allocate adequate resources and capacities or adapt or renew institutions to match its aspirational rhetoric. Despite possessing far greater economic strength, China too has been unable to make a meaningful regional impact despite the scale and ambition of the BRI. Recent experience has proven that circumventing India – given its geopolitical centrality and market size – is not a viable path for any sustainable connectivity plan for the subcontinent.

Unbridled competition, however, risks fragmenting the subcontinent in the coming decade, a future that would undermine India's interests far more than China. Transforming South Asia must, therefore, be predicated on tapping India's unique advantages – both the size of its domestic market, that makes any geoeconomic plan's success predicated on India's participation and involvement, and the overt and subtle geopolitical influence that India continues to wield across the neighbourhood – as well as leveraging China's obvious financial and industrial capabilities to construct infrastructure and connectivity capacities in the neighbourhood.

In short, both countries have strengths that are not being fully leveraged to advance an open sub-regional geoeconomic order. What has been missing from Indian conversations is an attempt to explore alternative futures and more constructive frameworks to visualise the changing regional setting in ways that would still secure vital Indian interests, advance stability, deepen regional economic development while also enabling China to pursue its engagement with South Asia.

How Do Indian and Chinese Interests Intersect in the Region?

The first step in such an exercise is to undertake a brief assessment of how Indian and Chinese interests interact in the region. What we can observe about China's involvement in South Asia is that it usually works with whatever regime is in power and avoids interfering in domestic political battles. Beijing's main priority is protecting its economic investments. In some cases, where China has deeper geostrategic interests, particularly in Pakistan and Myanmar, it has cushioned adverse reaction from the US towards these states. Hence, in limited ways, China is already a security provider – certainly at the political and diplomatic level – and this factor shapes how many neighbourhood regimes now perceive China: as a potential insurance card against possible Western pressure and as a hedge against uncertainty about Indian positions in times of domestic crises in these states. There is little doubt that China's engagement has improved the bargaining position of India's neighbours vis-à-vis India and other major external powers.

An observation of India and China's regional policies suggest that there are both overlapping features as well as geopolitical faultlines at play. Both India and China have a common interest in managing non-traditional threats such as terrorism, extremism, separatism, distress migration that impact regime stability of smaller South Asian states; promoting secular and stable regimes; promoting open sea-lanes and ensuring the security of their maritime trade routes; geoeconomically connecting South Asia with East Asia.

At the same time, there are some key differences in India and China's regional approaches. Firstly, China appears to be more interested in inter-regional interdependence and connectivity, while India is mainly interested in sub-regional integration. Put another way, China seeks to connect South Asia with China; India seeks to integrate South Asia internally as well as deepen its connections with Eurasia and Southeast Asia. Secondly, there is a large measure of uncertainty about the geopolitical implications of the BRI in South Asia. India's main concern is that deeper connectivity between India's neighbours and China might re-orient the foreign policies of South Asian states in ways that could eventually undermine Indian interests and challenge its claims to regional authority. More broadly, China's engagement in South Asia might also adversely influence domestic politics in the subcontinent and strengthen anti-India political forces that spillover onto the domestic politics in India's states thereby impacting periphery security and social stability. Thirdly, a major faultline would be the militarizing of China's regional connectivity projects in the form of bases. Such a hypothetical scenario would pose military security challenges to India as well as place China in a position to act as a direct security provider in the subcontinent, an outcome that would have profound consequences for the geopolitics in the region.

ONE OF THE key geopolitical challenges for Asia over the next decade is whether and how a rising India and a rising China learn to be sensitive to each other's core interests while pursuing engagement with each other's neighbours. In their bilateral summits of 2018 and 2019, Narendra Modi and Xi Jinping have sought to arrest the escalating tension and competition in the relationship. While their differences and disputes remain unresolved, both sides recognise the costs and disadvantages of a semi-hostile and contentious relationship. In particular, building trust and 'strategic communication' in the neighbourhood has now been recognised by both leaderships as a shared policy goal. There are three specific areas where India and China can realistically have a constructive regional dialogue.

(1) Capacity building and assisting weak states: Although India and China have a common interest in regime stability, both sides have yet to explore structured cooperation on this front. One form such cooperation could assume is by jointly assisting weak states with coordinated capacity enhancing projects and training programs. Indeed, the April 2018 summit laid a framework for 'India-China plus one', that is, India-China cooperation in third countries in the region.[4] In October 2018, India and China launched a programme to train Afghan diplomats as an initial step in a long-term effort for trilateral cooperation (India-China-Afghanistan).[5] This confidence-building measure, albeit modest, opened a window for precisely the type of coordination between two regional powers that have often been ambivalent of their overlapping interests. Such third party cooperation should be extended to other states confronting domestic challenges such as supporting Bangladesh's secular forces in their struggle against extremism or assisting Myanmar in responsibly managing domestic order.

(2) Coordinating geoeconomic plans: Short of finance capital and industrial resources, India cannot undertake the sole burden of lifting South Asia from underdevelopment and low interdependence given growing domestic claims within India itself. If Indian requirements in the subcontinent are to advance connectivity (both within and between South Asian states) and deepen the developmental process, China's engagement should be nudged and leveraged in directions that also advance India's long-term interests. Building constructive regional partnerships are unavoidable and China is one of the key players that need to be engaged more strategically by India.

Can China's infrastructure projects increase South Asia's internal connectivity and economic interdependence? Much of the viability of logistical networks and energy projects is linked with India's economy and access to its large market. For example, hydropower projects developed by China with India as the main eventual market could be a form of trilateral cooperation. Another instance is China's construction of a new terminal at the Chittagong port in Bangladesh, which complemented India-Bangladesh coastal shipping cooperation.[6] Similarly, projects like the BCIM corridor could dovetail India's vision to deepen connectivity with its smaller neighbours with China's vision to connect its southwestern provinces with South Asia.

More broadly, India-China geoeconomic coordination and cooperation, including through joint bilateral and multilateral projects, is necessary to avoid duplicating large infrastructure projects that could otherwise burden the region with excess supply-side capacities and fiscal burdens. Since India's official position on the BRI (beyond the CPEC that contradicts India's sovereignty over Jammu & Kashmir) is based on legitimate questions around sustainability, viability, transparency, and industrial benefits to the local communities of some of China's economic projects, India-China coordination in third countries could help in addressing these issues by giving India a say in the choice and design of projects as well as making China's economic involvement more in sync with the sub-regional political economy as well as with established international norms. The second BRI forum held in Beijing in April 2019 indicated that Chinese leaders might be responding to the critique from India and other countries. The communiqué called for 'extensive consultation', 'green', 'people-centred and sustainable development' as well as 'high-quality, sustainable infrastructure' that is 'inclusive and broadly beneficial'.[7] But for India to explore whether the BRI's adaptation does genuinely augur for a consultative and sustainable geoeconomic approach by China in the subcontinent, India's own position on the BRI needs to evolve where its legitimate sovereignty concerns do not constrain the formulation of a more sophisticated policy.

(3) Maritime cooperation: In recent years, India has recognized China's 'Malacca dilemma', a reference to the long and insecure lines of communication through the northern Indian Ocean that China relies upon for much of its international trade, and its corresponding interest in improving the security of its Indian Ocean trade routes. China, for its part, too needs to reassure India on its port projects and the military aspects of its involvement in the northern Indian Ocean littoral. Even as they recognize some of China's maritime security concerns, Indian policymakers must be prepared to counteract any attempts at militarization or conversion of Chinese infrastructure investments in South Asia into forward basing facilities for the Chinese military. A failure to do so might impel other great powers to respond to China with their own military bases on the subcontinent's maritime periphery, a process that would pose adverse consequences for regional geopolitics as well as eroding India's influence in the neighbourhood.

Competitive Co-existence in a Common Neighbourhood

India and China's policies are beginning to resemble each other. Just like Beijing's engagement with India's neighbours increases the status and bargaining position of these smaller states vis-à-vis India, Delhi too engages with many Southeast Asian states who seek to hedge their dependence on China by developing more economic and geopolitical options. Yet, neither side is under any delusion that India's neighbours (with the exception of Pakistan) can be rallied against it or that India can rally Southeast Asian states to balance Chinese power. The balance of power simply would not allow such a thing in practice. The defence budget of the entire Southeast Asian region is about $45 billion. China's is five times that figure and with far more modernized and balanced capabilities. Similarly, the asymmetry between India and its neighbours is even higher. In South Asia, other than Pakistan, none of the smaller states are in any position even with outside assistance to present a threat or challenge to India. This proposition should be even truer over the course of the next decade.

If we notice the official rhetoric from the region, what stands out is a similar discourse that is being espoused by most of the smaller South Asian states. Nearly all of India's neighbours have expressed a preference for non-alignment or strategic autonomy as a guiding principle in their foreign relations; multi-directional economic engagement with India, China, EU, US, Japan and other powers; sensitivity towards India including publicly disavowing any move towards offering military facilities or bases to external powers and thus reassuring India on its vital interests. As one recent study observed, smaller South Asian countries 'largely still see India as the dominant power in South Asia, suggesting that Chinese economic activity, while welcome, will not necessarily translate into major military or strategic gains.'[8]

Another discernible trend is that neither India nor China seems to be pressuring or cajoling smaller South Asian states to make hard choices or persuading these states to adopt postures and policies that run contrary to the main interests of their regional competitor. In short, we do not see a Cold War-style competition, which suggests some sort of a tacit Sino-Indian acceptance of a competitive co-existence in their overlapping peripheries. As one Chinese scholar notes, 'China has no intention to replace India as the dominant power of Southern Asia, though it reserves the right to disagree with how India practices its leadership, especially in overlapping physical areas that are important for China's national interest.'[9] So, while India and China are competing they are doing so within a framework of self-restraint. This could gradually pave the way for a conception of a regional order with informal norms on the 'rules of the game' in the subcontinent. Other things being equal, internally resilient and economically vibrant neighbours are likely to be in both India and China's interests. If stability in their overlapping peripheries is a common interest, it should pave the way for more sustained bilateral conversations to mitigate some of the uncertainty-induced geopolitical competition and mistrust, and, proactively exploit the untapped overlapping interests that might be emanating from China's growing involvement in South Asia. None of this would be possible before India reinvents and adapts its regional role to provide more emphasis on human security goals and regional welfare rather than narrowly conceived geopolitical ideas.

Far-sighted and pragmatic voices in the West are advocating for 'stable competition' or 'responsible competition' with a rising China to avoid precipitating a second and costly Cold War. Indian policymakers must take the long view and pursue an approach of peaceful competition in the neighbourhood. India and China need to be engaging in a strategic conversation on the subcontinent and its various parts so that constructive attempts can be made at coordinating some of their regional visions and policies. Absence to pursue such a dialogue and lack of an understanding on an agreed framework for Indian and Chinese policies is a recipe for regional instability and a costly zero-sum rivalry that neither country can afford in a rapidly changing international environment.

An Overview: India-China Interactions Based on Interests and Goals

The nature of India-China interactions across five issue areas highlights that Delhi and Beijing have more overlapping interests than is generally recognized. Such an analytical exercise also reveals that the subcontinent of South Asia is potentially the most contentious arena for the relationship. Yet, a limited Sino-Indian geopolitical accommodation in the immediate neighbourhood is both viable and necessary to arrest the deterioration in the bilateral relationship in recent years and ensure regional stability.

Table 2. India-China interactions based on interests and goals

Issue area	India's defined interests and goals	China's defined interests and goals	Nature of interaction
Border dispute	A stable frontier and LAC prior to a final resolution of dispute. Avoid military conflict or major border crisis Future resolution via an east–west	A stable frontier Stability in Tibet Avoid military conflict or major border crisis. Future resolution via an east–west swapping of claims?	Uncertainty around future geopolitical intentions but shared interest in frontier stability. Potential for conflict/ hostilities if any side attempts to alter territorial status quo

	swapping of claims?		by coercion or force in disputed areas.
Military security	Deterrence Avoid two-front situation of coordinated military pressure by Pakistan and China.	Deter and dissuade India from choosing to destabilize Tibet Provide material and psychological assistance to Pakistan to dissuade Indian coercion against Pakistan Prevent an India-Pakistan crisis from spiraling out of control.	Rivalry Limited military competition. Overlapping interest in sub-regional strategic stability, crisis management.
Asia	Multipolar Asia that does not fall under the sway of any one power or bloc. Provide limited material options to middle and smaller states who seek to hedge China's rise or seek bargaining leverage vis-à-vis China. Avoid getting entrapped in regional disputes	Counteract US alliance system by promoting neutralized/non-aligned zones on China's periphery Compete for influence with US and Japan in several Asian states. Counteract the emergence of a coordinated or tacit anti-China coalition in the Asia Pacific.	Limited competition No direct conflict or dispute. Uncertainty around power transition and its impact on different sub regions and wider Asia Pacific order Overlapping interests in existing/additional institutions to manage Asian security.

	Asian Cold War or a divided Asia undermines wider geoeconomic and geopolitical stability by complicating India's foreign policy and economic development options.	Avoid a direct military clash with the US in Asia. Encourage economic interdependence and maintain a posture of open regionalism.	
South Asia	Stabilize sub-region. Encourage political economy conditions that increase sub-regional interdependence. Promote friendly, cooperative regimes that do not undermine stability on India's peripheral regions. Resist emergence of anti-India regimes or regimes that open strategic space for external powers.	Stabilize China's south-western periphery to secure Tibet and stave off anti-Chinese geopolitical actions on this front. CPEC as a complex balancing strategy to internally stabilise and modernize a strategic partner and neighbour to partially offset India's Act East policy. CPEC allows China to	Rivalry and geopolitical competition as India perceives its traditional 'sphere of influence' being eroded by China's political economy involvement in sub-region. Overlapping interests in expanding sub-regional economic activity. Overlapping interests in managing non-traditional security threats (terrorism, extremism) impacting regime stability of smaller South Asian states.

	Modulate or counteract Chinese political and economic influence in South Asia.	develop positive and negative leverage with the two key states in South Asia. Deepen ties with Nepal, Myanmar to secure Chinese periphery and Tibet. Develop new export, FDI and financing markets in India, Bangladesh, Sri Lanka.	Overlapping interests in emerging multilateral institutions such as SCO to manage Eurasian/ regional security and crisis management period.
Inter-national economic order	Reforming global economic order to increase development options (technology, manufacturing investment and financial flows to emerging economics). Acquiring rule-making status and bargaining leverage on global economic governance.	Preserving globalization processes to ensure China's continued economic transformation and stability. Acquiring rule-making status and bargaining leverage on global economic governance. Developing/ supporting new financial and	Common interests in preserving the advantages of an open economic order. Cooperation in co-developing and legitimizing new democratically-governed financial institutions. Common interest in leveraging each other's economic capacities and market size.

	Supporting/ developing non-Western financial and trading networks and institutions.	trading institutions to both compete with and supplement Bretton Woods arrangements.

A MULTIPOLAR WORLD ORDER: AN EPILOGUE

Dizzying changes in Asia and the world, a Himalayan border crisis with military casualties for the first time in 45 years, globalization under deep stress, an America that is unable to resolve its domestic fissures and craft a new international role, are together changing the context for India-China relations. The conundrum which surrounds China's rise has led to a debate that is long on rhetoric and short on realistic ideas for India's foreign policy. History might provide some lessons and clues since the cycles of competition and acrimony have played out previously when new global powers have emerged and erstwhile ones have declined.

Looking back at the outbreak of the first Cold War in the late 1940s and early 1950s, the world witnessed an even more dramatic change in the balance of power. The post-Second World War order in Asia was one of multiple power transitions: a decolonization process that from the perspective of the West was fairly disruptive and a strategic set back to their centuries long dominance in Asia, China's return to the international mainstream after their century of humiliation in 1949, India's return to the world stage in 1947 after a prolonged period of colonialism. In a sense, we have been dealing with major changes in the vast Indo-Pacific region for a long time. The challenges India faces on the Himalayan frontiers are also not new. The 1950s witnessed a destabilized periphery as China sought to aggressively restore its presence and authority over Tibet after a long period where the British had diminished Beijing's influence in Lhasa and altered the geopolitics of the Himalayan areas in favour of British India.

It is always disconcerting to see India's strategic discourse mystify China. After all, we have been living with the PRC as a neighbour for 70 years and the fact that we are constantly trying to reinvent the wheel is something that needs to be set aside. Policymakers during the Cold War were quick to recognize that dealing with China requires a framework that is tailored to India's circumstances. This means an advantageous realpolitik where India leverages the international environment to augment its power potential and cultivate a network of partners. It also implies a sophisticated understanding of what it means to live with China in a common Asian and South Asian neighbourhood with overlapping peripheries extending to thousands of kilometres. India has struggled to find that equilibrium between shaping not only a balance of power but also a balance of interests. The emerging multipolar world order will call upon Indian leaders to strike that balance.

Reflecting on how India dealt with China during the Cold War might provide some lessons. Delhi had developed fairly positive ties with Washington and Moscow and was able to draw on economic and military assistance because both those superpowers, in their own strategic calculations, sought a balance of power in Asia and did not wish to see Chinese hegemony extend all the way into Southern and Southeastern Asia. Thus, there was a natural convergence between India and the superpowers and how they looked at China's future in the vast region. That basic convergence continues to exist even today. This is despite a Russia-China partnership that seeks to counteract some of the unilateralist impulses of the US and despite a massive $700 billion commercial relationship between the US and China.

It is surprising when observers talk of India's reticence or timidity in developing strategic partnerships. Take, for example, the India-US relationship after 2005 that has seen a sustained evolution towards a similar outlook on shaping Asia's balance of power. It has not been a smooth ride nor has it culminated in (or will ever) total convergence. But there is a basic understanding between the two countries. Similarly, with Russia too we have seen a high level of military assistance, high technology support, and the more recent Indian initiatives to dovetail Russia's eastern pivot with India's 'Act East' policy towards the Arctic and Northeast Asia. Also noteworthy are India's attempts at persuading Moscow to assume a deeper role in the Indian Ocean. With Japan and Vietnam too, India has similar motives of driving cooperation. In sum, India has been consistently seeking to establish common ground with other players on China's periphery who are also looking out to where China is headed in the next 15–20 years, taking into consideration simply the sheer size of its future power.

The problem really arises about the avenues for India to convert that convergence and gain leverage vis-à-vis China in an operational sense whereby Beijing adjusts its policies. For the last decade-and-a-half, India has been pursuing a very similar approach where it is trying to deepen ties with China's other neighbours and the major powers with an aim to unsettle the Chinese into making a deeper outreach to India in terms of both engagement and perhaps even some concessions on certain fronts. But that has not entirely played out as Indian strategists would have hoped and the primary reason is that the asymmetry of comprehensive national power between India and China is far higher – indeed it widened during this phase – than it was during the first Cold War. The aspects that Indian policymakers might believe would serve as a pressure point on China do not appear significant enough for Beijing to make that adjustment or accommodate India's preferred position that it would like to hold in Asia and the subcontinent.

ONE CAN DISCERN a Chinese approach to South Asia, which is remarkable for its conservative consistency and the way Beijing defines its interests in the region. The approach has four pillars – maintain some sort of balance between India and Pakistan; ensure that India does not create trouble in Tibet; develop political and economic ties with all South Asian states including India; prevent South Asia from falling into a US sphere of influence and thereby pose a major regional challenge to China's southwestern periphery. While in practice, India's place and status has increased in this overall framework, especially over the past two decades, the overall Chinese approach is still driven by counteracting any adverse spillover effects on Chinese security interests on its periphery rather than a dynamic and sophisticated strategy of crafting a wider political equation with India.

This is not to say that Chinese policymakers are unmoved by India's rise. Debates in China in the last few years do suggest that India is being looked at more seriously. The Chinese are looking at their southwestern periphery and South Asia from a perspective where India can no longer be ignored. Some also see India as a spoiler and an irritant that can undermine Chinese interests and ambitions. The dominant view is that 'India has to be kept under control.'[1] Other than lofty rhetoric, however, we have not seen a sophisticated approach from China to reach out to India and attempt a new modus vivendi. The Chinese still assume a position of safeguarding their narrow strategic interests and zones of concern and hope to slot India into that geopolitical map, and if unsuccessful then work around it.

Is China being short-sighted in not adjusting to India's rise, even though the power asymmetry might not require it to do so today? There is merit in this argument. After all, with a 5-1 advantage in economic power and perhaps even greater, when measured in a qualitative sense of high technology and available pool of human and scientific capital, there is no historical precedence for an accommodation between a major power (China) and a rising power (India) under such apparent circumstances of an asymmetry. Yet, what if China were to take a position that India is going to be a major player in southern Asia and the northern Indian Ocean and more gradually in the Asian geoeconomic space over the next several decades? If Chinese leaders and thinkers were to adopt such an outlook on India's future, then they should logically consider investing in the anticipation of India's rise and making some adjustments to accommodate Indian concerns and aspirations. Why has China not been able to visualize such a framework? Is it because they are deeply invested in Pakistan? Is it inertia? Is it an unwillingness to accept the risk of getting it wrong?

While the Chinese have kept their cards close to their chest, some of these dilemmas are reflected in their debates. It does appear that they are not able to justify making these geopolitical investments because they feel no matter what they do, in their perception China will never be able to cultivate an India that is going to move away from the West and towards them. As one Chinese scholar put it, 'From the foreign policy of the Indian government it is now very clear that India has decided to stand with the US in the great power competition.'[2] Yan Xuetong, a leading Chinese scholar, recently remarked, 'the view in Chinese eyes is the current government in India has given up non-alignment and has a motivation to become a US ally, using non-alignment as a cover to make policy.'[3] Some Chinese strategists also 'see India enticed, entangled, and potentially enmeshed in institutionalized (US-led) cooperative frameworks that it later cannot reject despite its aspiration for autonomy.'[4]

Whether such assessments reflect reality is less important because perceptions are what ultimately shape high policy and India needs to take it seriously. Then 'there's also a psychology in China…that if China makes a concession to India, because India is now in a better (geopolitical) position, the Chinese concession will not be interpreted as Chinese goodwill. It will only be interpreted as a result of India's improved strengths. (And) by that logic, India is going to make demands for more concessions, and instead of reciprocating to what the Chinese would deliver.'[5] Another scholar, Yun Sun summarizes the key problem obstructing a geopolitical accommodation, 'Key concessions India demands from China on the border settlement are hard commitments that cannot be reversed. By contrast, what China seeks from India, such as its neutrality in the US-Chinese strategic competition, is ephemeral and easily adjustable.'[6] This problem of uncertainty and fluidity in strategic intentions has no apparent solution for the foreseeable future. Neither are the Chinese persuaded that India will defy its own uneven track record and undertake a domestic transformation like conventional great powers in history. This belief, again, reduces China's incentives for an early modus vivendi.

That being said, China does find strategic value in seeing an India that has strategic autonomy and 'does not in any way influence or jeopardize the larger and crucial strategic ongoing struggle with the US.'[7] It is worth recalling that the so-called 2018 Wuhan reset was predicated on an Indian reassurance to China that Delhi would maintain its independence – 'strategic and decisional autonomy' – in a changing global environment.[8] What can be discerned from Chinese public debates is the recognition that the relationship with India can no longer be handled by simply ignoring it.

The debate really is about the means – there is disagreement between Chinese strategists and scholars on how to attain a more manageable periphery and stable relationship with a large neighbour like India. Some advocate an uncompromising policy of pushing back because India's friendship and cooperation can never be obtained; others advocate a more sophisticated approach where China does not lose sight of its primary direction of threat in the Western Pacific emanating from the US, and therefore urge dealing with India in a way that supports its strategic autonomy and does not feed into US grand strategic goals. As one Chinese specialist on South Asia candidly observes, 'If India chose to balance China in the region through a 'soft alliance' with the US, China will likely respond by increasing its influence with other states in the region to hedge India's leadership. But if India proceeds more cautiously regarding American cooperation, mutual learning will be easier.'[9]

China's India policy debate will not be settled any time soon, just as India's debates that weigh the maintenance of an independent foreign policy with the alternative option of a pro-US tilt and participation in a military structure with the US and its allies. So, both Delhi and Beijing are weighing different options to shape the balance of power while simultaneously preventing it from deteriorating. What we have not seen enough of is an approach that provides a framework for a balance of interests. This is something of a puzzle. If there is one common theme in Indian and Chinese debates, it is that both sides recognize the adverse impact of a destabilized overlapping periphery or a broader Cold War-style rivalry in the region. The way out – China needs to adjust to India's rise and sensitivities, while India needs to recognize China's primary direction of threat lies in the east.

DENG XIAOPING ONCE advised the Chinese people, 'The role we play in international affairs is determined by the extent of our economic growth. If our country becomes more developed and prosperous, we will be in a position to play a greater role in international affairs.' India's leaders would do well to remember this dictum. The sinews of power are inextricably linked to a strong and balanced economy. During its domestic transformation – a process likely to last for the next several decades – it is in India's national interest to have a degree of competitive, but peaceful, co-existence with China. The only realistic way to cultivate such a stable relationship with China – and history underscores this – is when both legs of a policy framework operate in tandem. One is having a balance of power policy, that is, stable ties with the major powers including avoiding getting entrapped in their power plays with China and on the other hand, having a very sustained policy of engagement with China. This does not merely mean a flurry of summitry between the leaderships or public diplomacy but developing a complex interdependence – through people-to-people, commercial and cultural connections – a meaningful dialogue on regional security (without, of course, yielding on any core interests), and more creative collaboration in safeguarding and reforming the next chapter of globalization so the interests of large developing economies are secured in a multipolar world. This is not dissimilar to the strategic approach adopted by the US and Russia in their management of China's rise.

In the immediate South Asian region too, India needs to choose how it wants to stabilize the Himalayan neighbourhood sandwiched between India and China, define what kind of space it sees in the subcontinent for China and then mobilize national resources to manage China's footprint. A regional framework for China has not really been conceived in India. Delhi has mostly been reacting to and catching up with what is a recent phenomenon – China's growing geoeconomic footprint in South Asia is barely a decade old. During this brief period, China has established a position – with the cooperation and invitation of regional political and economic elites – that is not easy to dislodge. India's challenge is to shape the future of China-South Asia ties in a constructive direction where Delhi can get the neighbourhood on board to support at least certain core fundamental norms. It is a challenge of strategy but also one of re-defining India's regional role more intelligently.

On the economy, the debate over the extent of cooperation with China has evoked much controversy, partly triggered by the 2020 border crisis but also in the backdrop of India seeking to promote large Indian business houses and domestic industry, many of whom find Chinese competition overbearing. The politics surrounding the US-China trade conflict has also influenced Indian policymakers in attempting something similar for India-China relations. Decoupling, however, should not be pursued until a deeper assessment is undertaken to determine the cost-benefit calculations and impact, across sectors, and for the economy as a whole. Only after this has yielded credible data should policymakers formulate a plan to develop more interdependence with China in select sectors or lessen it in others by import-substitution and sourcing from elsewhere. It must not be a blanket policy, nor motivated by ideological considerations. We first need to articulate a sophisticated industrialization blueprint and identify where Beijing and other major economies bring value or can be a catalyst in the way the US was for China's reform process.

The US-China competition over high technology, particularly in digital sectors, is posing another policy challenge. Here, India's policymakers need to avoid leaping from one digital superpower to another. After all, both Chinese and US companies bring the same baggage to the table – the risk of compromising data sovereignty and privacy, dependence on imported software and hardware, and impact on domestic capabilities. Before handing over the family silver, India needs to support a framework for domestic innovation that promotes a competitive digital ecosystem and one that moves India up the value chain. More broadly, India's policymakers should recognize that China and East Asia's innovation and technological transformations occurred by strategically leveraging interdependence with major economies and not building walls.

As the debate rages on in the bilateral dimension, India's policymakers should keep an eye on India's quest to deepen economic ties with Asia more broadly. If you look at the Indo-Pacific geoeconomic space, the preceding decades have created a political economy of deep trade and investment linkages between China and its neighbours – from Western Europe, the heart of Eurasia to Northeast Asia, Korea, Japan, Australia, ASEAN. This is an extensive economic space that is likely to evolve further as more integration processes and connectivity linkages develop in the coming decade. The question for India should be how it wants to fit into that emerging geoeconomic community. One cannot fit into the Asian economy by completely sealing off China from the Indian economy. This is because China is going to be involved in some way or the other with all major Asian economic centres – China is already the biggest commercial partner for all its neighbours – which include India's strategic partners. A prudent course would be to identify the sectors and technological areas in which India wants to engage with China, because its integration with Asia is at another level linked with that choice and strategy.

Finally, what can we discern through the haze in the post-Covid world? One probable scenario is if the US fails to get its act together at home, China's linkages with other major economies of Asia would deepen. India might find itself with an uphill task upon re-entering that space in a decade from now because of its choice to step back from trading arrangements such as the Regional Comprehensive Economic Partnership (RCEP) ostensibly to industrialize and regenerate – captured in the phrase, 'Atmanirbhar Bharat'– its domestic industry and innovation ecosystem. The Asia of 2030 will look very different from the Asia of today and will most likely be an amplified version of the interdependence that has already been established over decades. For the first time in several centuries, we are facing the prospect of an Asia that can actually flourish on its own economically, and not simply by playing a role as an assembly-hub and export powerhouse to the West. Greater Eurasia has the energy resources and strategic commodities of Russia including its strong scientific base of human capital, as well as the commercial technologies of Japan, China and Korea. It also has the human capital and the demography to maintain a self-sustaining political economy.

In essence, Asia is returning to what it was for 1,800 years of the last two millennia, and, it is that big picture trend that

India needs to pay attention to. While the West will remain important, there is no viable way for India to avoid being part of this dynamic Asia and Greater Eurasia. Eventually, that boils down to having some sort of a stable India-China relationship. It has, thus, fallen upon the present generation of policymakers to steer India towards this complex multipolar world order. Major strategic choices have to be made and one hopes that India's leaders have the long-term view.

The historian Odd Arne Westad recently remarked, 'The more the US and China beat each other up, the more room for manoeuver other powers will have.' One should equally apply that mantra to India and China. Unrestrained competition only benefits other powers. As the 2020 Ladakh crisis bookends a tumultuous decade of India-China relations, both Delhi and Beijing would do well to heed the call of our time. History is obliging both countries to step up and play constructive roles to shape the emerging world order even as it is impelling both sides to learn to co-exist in a common neighbourhood.

NOTES AND REFERENCES

A Complex Relationship: An introduction

1. 'Xi, Modi meet to promote China-India mutual learning for shared prosperity,' *Xinhua*, October 12, 2019.

2. Speech by Liang Qichao (April 1924) in Sisir Kumar Das (ed.), *The English Writings of Rabindranath Tagore: Volume 2* (New Delhi: Sahitya Akademi, 2017), pp. 573, 578.

3. Tansen Sen, *India, China, and the World: A Connected History*, (Delhi: Oxford University Press, 2018), pp. 7, 35.

4. Ibid., pp. 41–55, 125–26.

5. Ibid., pp. 82, 96–97, 100–1

6. *'Agreement between the Government of the Republic of India and the Government of the People's Republic of China on the Political Parameters and Guiding Principles for the Settlement of the India-China Boundary Question,' April 11, 2005.* Accessed at: https://www.mea.gov.in/bilateral-documents.htm?dtl/6534/Agreement+between+the+Government+of+the+ Republic+of+India+and+the+Government+of+the+Peoples+ Republic+of+China+on+the+Political+Parameters+and+Guiding+ Principles+for+the+Settlement+of+the+IndiaChina+Boundary+ Question

7. Shivshankar Menon, *Choices: Inside the Making of Indian Foreign Policy* (Gurgaon: Allen Lane, 2016), pp. 26–27.

I. BORDER DISPUTE

Chapter 1: Himalayan Stalemate: A short history of the India–China dispute

1. Charles Bell, *Tibet: Past and Present* (Oxford University Press, 1924), p. 155.

2. A.G. Noorani, 'Strategic differences', *Frontline*, 25:26, December 20, 2008–January 02, 2009.

3. The archival material for this sub-section is drawn from A.S. Bhasin, *India-China Relations 1947–2000: A Documentary Study, Volume-I* (Delhi: Geetika Publishers, 2018), pp. 1–249.

4. Chad Haines, 'Colonial Routes: Reorienting the Northern Frontier of British India', *Ethnohistory*, 51:3, Summer 2004, pp. 535–65.

5. Malcolm Yapp, *The Legend of the Great Game,* Elie Kedourie Memorial Lecture, School of Oriental and African Studies, May 16, 2000; Malcolm Yapp, *Strategies of British India: Britain, Iran and Afghanistan 1798–1850*, (Oxford: Clarendon Press, 1980).

6. Haines, 'Colonial Routes', *Ethnohistory*, 2004, pp. 535-65.

7. Interestingly, the 1899 Macartney-MacDonald Line corresponds with the Chinese claim line, which in turn generally coincides with the Line of Actual Control (LAC). Interestingly, it has been argued that the 1899 Line, when plotted on a modern map rather than on one relying on survey knowledge, available at the turn of the nineteenth century, would leave the eastern portion of Aksai Chin, including the area covering the Xinjiang-Tibet road to China. See Alastair Lamb, *The Sino-Indian Border in Ladakh* (Canberra: Australian National University Press, 1973), pp. 15–16.

8. Quoted in Amar Jasbir Singh, 'The Tibetan Problem and China's Foreign Relations', in Surjit Mansingh (ed.), *Indian and Chinese Foreign Policies in Comparative Perspective* (Delhi: Radiant Publishers, 1998), pp. 257–8.

9. See, Robert J. McMahon, 'US Policy toward South Asia and Tibet during the Early Cold War', *Journal of Cold War Studies*, 8:3, Summer 2006, pp. 131–44.

10. Sarvepalli Gopal, *Jawaharlal Nehru: A Biography*, (Cambridge, MA: Harvard University Press, 1980), Vol. 2, p. 185. Indeed, even after the debacle with China in 1962, India turned not to Washington, which sought to link military assistance with resolution of the Kashmir dispute, but to the Soviet Union that offered economic and military assistance without prior political commitments by India.

11. This phase and the reasons for India's decisions have been examined in detail in my book *Power and Diplomacy: India's Foreign Policies during the Cold War* (Delhi: Oxford University Press, 2019).

12. Srinath Raghavan, *War and Peace in Modern India: A Strategic History of the Nehru Years* (Delhi: Permanent Black, 2010), p. 242.

13. Zorawar Daulet Singh, *Power and Diplomacy*, p. 177.

14. Raghavan, *War and Peace in Modern India*, pp. 238, 240.

15. For instance, speaking to a visiting delegation from Nepal in 1964, Mao reportedly stated that the major problem between India and China was not the McMahon Line but the Tibet question.

16. Chen Jian, 'The Tibetan Rebellion of 1959 and China's Changing Relations with India and the Soviet Union', *Journal of Cold War Studies*, 8:3, Summer 2006, pp. 54–101; Steven A. Hoffmann, 'Rethinking the Linkage between Tibet and the China-India Border Conflict: A Realist Approach', *Journal of Cold War Studies*, 8:3, Summer 2006, pp. 165–94.

17. Alastair Lamb, *Kashmir: A Disputed Legacy, 1846–1990* (Hertingfordbury: Roxford Books, 1991), p. 72.

18. Chen Jian, 'The Tibetan Rebellion of 1959', *Journal of Cold War Studies*, 2006, pp. 54–101

19. Hoffmann, 'Rethinking the Linkage', *Journal of Cold War Studies*, 2006, pp. 165–94.

The author quotes two studies–Kenneth Conboy and James Morrison, *The CIA's Secret War in Tibet* (Lawrence: University Press of Kansas, 2002), and J. Kenneth Knaus, *Orphans of the Cold War: America and the Tibetan Struggle for Survival* (New York: Public

Affairs/Perseus Books Group, 1999). At a CIA-staffed training base in Colorado, Tibetan resistance fighters learned guerrilla warfare, and the CIA air-dropped those Tibetan men, arms and equipment into Tibet. By 1959, large pockets of central Tibet came under rebel control. But most Tibetans were unwilling or unable to adopt guerrilla tactics, and the CIA, according to Knaus (who retired in 1995), greatly underestimated China's willingness to decimate the Tibetan resistance. Hoffmann, relying on the aforementioned works, notes, '(There are indications) that CIA airplanes flying through Tibetan airspace were allowed to land in India when they ran short of fuel. Landings and takeoffs of CIA flights were made in Pakistan, too, which, as a US ally, did significantly more to cooperate with the CIA's Tibet operations through 1961 or 1962. The stops in India would be treated as emergency landings, although advance preparations would have been made. The Indians did not welcome the arrangement, "fearing" that "its discovery would lead to trouble with China". They "fussed about it constantly".'

20. Ibid., pp. 165–94.

21. John W. Garver, 'China's Decision for War with India in 1962', in Robert S. Ross and Alastair Iain Johnston (eds.), *New Directions in the Study of China's Foreign Policy* (Stanford California: Stanford University Press, 2006), p. 88.

22. Hoffmann, 'Rethinking the Linkage', *Journal of Cold War Studies*, 2006, pp. 165–94.

23. Menon, *Choices*, 2016, p. 15.

24. P.B. Sinha, A.A. Athale, and S.N. Prasad (Chief Editor), *History of The Conflict with China, 1962* (New Delhi: History Division, Ministry of Defence, Government of India, 1992), published online by the *Times of India*, December 2002, www.bharat-rakshak.com.

25. Ibid., see 'Introduction' section of the Report, pp. xix–xxiv.

26. Ibid.

27. Ibid., p. 339.

28. Ibid., p. 314.

29. The famous Soviet TASS statement of September 9, 1959 taking a neutral position on the India China dispute was the first

important indication of the Sino-Soviet split and came after a brief skirmish between China and India on a disputed pocket in the eastern sector.

30. Garver, 'China's Decision for War with India in 1962', 2006, pp. 120–21.

31. Klaus H. Pringsheim, 'China, India, and their Himalayan Border (1961–1963)', *Asian Survey*, 3:10, October 1963, pp. 474–95.

32. Quoted in A.G. Noorani, 'Facts of history', *Frontline*, 20:18, August 30, 2003.

33. The Indian Foreign Secretary in the early 1950s, R.K. Nehru, later wrote that 'in 1953, our experts had advised us that our claim to Aksai Chin was not too strong'. The Prime Minister was 'agreeable' to adjustments in 'Aksai Chin and one or two other places' being made 'as part of a satisfactory overall settlement'. See, Raghavan, *War and Peace in Modern India*, 2010, p. 240.

34. Steven A. Hoffmann, *India and the China Crisis* (New Delhi: Oxford University Press, 1990), p. 81.

35. P.N. Haksar Papers, Nehru Memorial Museum Library, New Delhi.

36. I am indebted to Ambassador (retd.) Ranjit Sethi for sharing information on the period 1977–85. He was a key member of India's diplomatic team during the early phase of the boundary talks.

37. The popular notion being that India sought a piecemeal settlement of the border.

38. As against the durable and persistent misconception that the Indian delegation in fact attempted settlement of the 'Eastern Sector', as part of a 'sector by sector' approach.

39. The Chinese delegation was led by a Vice Minister of Foreign Affairs. The Chinese practice of having a Vice Foreign Minister to lead the talks has not varied, indeed to the present day. India was represented by the Secretary (East Asia) assisted by the Ambassador to China. This practice only changed in 1999, when the National Security Advisor on the Indian side and the Political Counselor from the Chinese side, took over to lead the talks, which were renamed as the talks between the Special Representatives.

40. Inder Malhotra, 'The Colombo "compromise",' *Indian Express*, October 17, 2011.

41. The Colombo Proposals (December 10–12, 1962) was an effort by six Afro-Asian countries led by Sri Lanka to seek a compromise on the border conflict that could bring the two Asian powers on the negotiating table. The essence of the proposal was that 'there must not be any territorial gain on account of military operations'.

42. Keshav Mishra, *Rapprochement Across the Himalayas: Emerging India-China Relations in Post Cold War Period*, 1947–2003, (Delhi: Kalpaz Publications, 2004), p. 60.

43. Jerrold F. Elkin, and Brian Fredericks, 'Sino-Indian Border Talks: The View from New Delhi', *Asian Survey*, 23:10, October 1983, pp. 1128–39.

44. John W. Garver, *Protracted Contest: Sino-Indian Rivalry in the Twentieth Century* (New Delhi: Oxford University Press, 2001), p. 104.

45. Nikhil Chakravarty, 'The Chinese Shift', *Indian Express*, July 27, 1986.

46. Garver, *Protracted Contest*, 2001, p. 106.

47. 'India Objects to Chinese Activities in PoK', *The Times of India*, October 14, 2009.

48. The 1993 Agreement established the concept of 'equal and mutual security'. Translated on the ground, this would imply a mutual understanding on reasonably defined military requirements for the defence of each side's vital interest. In this context, interpretation of geographical principles, such as watersheds and valleys on which each side bases its claim, will need to be informed by military defensibility. The 1996 Agreement included specific provisions to reduce military presence, which included the withdrawal of offensive weapons. Exercises involving more than one division were to be avoided, and all maneuvers with more than 5,000 soldiers needed to be announced in advance and combat aircraft were banned within a distance of 10 kilometres from the LAC except after prior permission.

49. Pallavi Aiyar, 'Another Round of Talks Begins', *The Hindu*, September 24, 2007.

50. Neville Maxwell, *India's China War* (London: Jonathan Cape, 1970), p. 23.

51. Sheela Bhatt and Nikhil Lakshman, 'Interview with India's National Security Advisor', www.rediff.com, January 18, 2007.

52. Atreya, Sarikah, 'No major problems along Indo-China border: Antony', *Hindu Business Line*, December 3, 2007.

53. Menon, *Choices*, p. 33.

54. Ibid., p. 31.

55. Kanti Bajpai, 'Strangely at Odds', *The Telegraph*, November 9, 2009.

56. P. S. Suryanarayana, 'India, China Need New Rationale, New Passion for Ties', *The Hindu*, February 4, 2010.

57. Keynote Address by Shiv Shankar Menon, National Security Advisor at the Seminar on 'India and China: Public Diplomacy, Building Understanding' at ICWA, Sapru House on April 1, 2010. Accessed at http://www.icwa.in/.

58. John W. Garver, 'The China-India-US Triangle: Strategic Relations in the Post-Cold War Era', *NBR Analysis*, 13:5, October 2002. Also see, Riedel, Bruce, 'US-China Relations: Seeking Strategic Convergence in Pakistan', Policy Paper, Number 18, *The Brookings Institution*, January 12, 2010.

59. Ananth Krishnan, 'In Talks, China to Press for US Support on Pakistan Nuclear Deal', *The Hindu*, May 3, 2010.

60. 'India to have "pre-eminent" role in South Asia: US', Press Trust of India, Washington, May 8, 2010.

61. Surjit Mansingh (ed.), *Indian and Chinese Foreign Policies in Comparative Perspective* (New Delhi: Radiant Publishers, 1998), p. 28.

62. From 2009 to early 2010, the Government of India sent the Defence Minister, Home Minister and Finance Minister to visit Tawang signalling India's vital interests in this frontier town. 'PC is 3rd Minister to Visit Tawang after China Claim', *Deccan Chronicle*, April 4, 2010.

Chapter 2: Himalayan Clash: Looking back at 1962

1. This chapter has been developed from the author's remarks at the IIC-Subbu Forum-SPS Round Table on '50 Years after 1962:

Recall and Review' on September 6, 2012 at the India International Centre, New Delhi.

2. Sinha and Athale, *History of the Conflict with China, 1962*, 1992.

3. The report that has been released online by Maxwell is a section of Volume 1 of the *HBR*. There is a Volume 2 containing several annexures, which is still classified. Apparently, this latter volume was not leaked to Neville Maxwell in the 1960s. It includes important correspondence between the Army Commands (Western and Eastern) and Army Headquarters (HQ) Delhi.

4. Chen Jian, 'The Tibetan Rebellion of 1959 and China's Changing Relations with India and the Soviet Union', *Journal of Cold War Studies,* 8:3, Summer 2006, pp. 54–101.

5. Garver, 'China's Decision for War with India in 1962', 2006, pp. 86–130.

6. G. Parthasarathi to Nehru, May 3, 1959, *Selected Works of Jawaharlal Nehru-SS (henceforth SWJN-SS)*, Volume 48, p. 601.

7. *Sardar Patel's Correspondence*; 10, pp. 344–45. Quoted in A.G. Noorani, 'Fateful "Note"', *Frontline*, 29:14, July 14–27, 2012.

8. Zorawar Daulet Singh, *Power and Diplomacy: India's Foreign Policies during the Cold War,* (Delhi: Oxford University Press, 2019).

9. Jawaharlal Nehru to Vijaya Lakshmi Pandit, November 2, 1959, *SWJN-SS*, 54, p. 607.

10. Menon to Nehru, September 13, 1959, *SWJN-SS*, 52, p. 322.

11. Nehru to U Nu, September 29, 1959, *SWJN-SS*, 52, 233–234.

12. Discussion between N.S. Khrushchev and Mao Zedong, October 3, 1959, Cold War International History Project (henceforth CWIHP).

13. Subimal Dutt to G. Parthasarathi, October 10, 1959, *SWJN-SS*, 53, p. 556.

14. Press conference with the Prime Minister, November 5, 1959, *SWJN-SS*, 54, p. 226.

15. Nehru-Nasser talks, March 29–31, 1960, *SWJN-SS*, 59, p. 402.

16. Nehru to Secretary General and Foreign Secretary, October 17, 1959, *SWJN-SS*, 53, p. 507.

17. Nehru to Secretary General and Foreign Secretary, October 14, 1959, *SWJN-SS*, 53, p. 489.

18. The Sino-Indian Dispute: Section 1, Central Intelligence Agency (CIA) Staff Study, (March 2, 1963), Released May 2007. Accessed via: www.foia.cia.gov/CPE/POLO/polo-07.pdf

19. Nehru-Khrushchev conversation, February 12, 1960, *SWJN-SS*, 57, pp. 410–12.

20. Motion on India-China Relations, November 25, 1959, *SWJN-SS*, 54, p. 514.

21. The Sino-Indian Dispute: Section 3, Central Intelligence Agency (CIA) Staff Study, (March 2, 1963), Released May 2007. Accessed via: www.foia.cia.gov/CPE/POLO/polo-09.pdf

22. Sinha and Athale, *History of the Conflict with China, 1962*, p. 65.

23. Nehru to U Nu, September 29, 1959, *SWJN-SS*, 52, p. 234.

24. Interview in the *Guardian* (London), October 23, 1961. Quoted in S. Gopal, *Jawaharlal Nehru: A Biography, Volume 3, 1956–1964*, (Delhi: Oxford University Press, 1984), p. 207.

25. Gopal, *Jawaharlal Nehru: A Biography, Volume 2, 1947–1956*, 1979, p. 229.

26. Gopal, *Jawaharlal Nehru: A Biography, Volume 3, 1956–1964*, 1984, p. 209.

27. HBR Report (Part 1) released online in March 2014.

28. Nehru to Secretary General and Foreign Secretary, 13 September 1959, *SWJN-SS*, 52, pp. 211–13.

29. HBR Report (Part 1).

30. Ibid.

31. Ibid.

32. Garver, 'China's Decision for War with India in 1962', 2006, p. 106.

33. S. Gopal, *Jawaharlal Nehru: A Biography, Volume 3, 1956–1964*, 1984, p. 208.

34. The Sino-Indian Dispute: Section 3, Central Intelligence Agency (CIA) Staff Study, (March 2, 1963), Released May 2007. Accessed via: www.foia.cia.gov/CPE/POLO/polo-09.pdf

35. HBR Report (Part 1).

36. Garver, 'China's Decision for War with India in 1962', 2006, p. 110.

37. HBR Report (Part 1).

38. Kishan Rana, 'India's envoy to China 1961–63: PK Banerjee's China days,' *Economic & Political Weekly*, LV:35, August 29, 2020.

39. Ananth Krishnan, 'A Last Opportunity, Missed,' *The Hindu*, October 26, 2012.

40. HBR Report (Part 1).

41. Ibid.

42. Prasad, *History of the Conflict with China, 1962*, 1992, p. 264.

43. Maxwell, *India's China War*, 1970, pp. 254–55.

44. HBR Report (Part 1).

45. Ibid.

46. Rana, 'India's envoy to China 1961–63', *Economic & Political Weekly*, LV:35, August 29, 2020.

47. Nehru to Menon, November 5, 1959, *SWJN-SS*, 54, p. 488.

48. Quoted in A.G. Noorani, 'Facts of History', *Frontline*, 20:18, 30 August 2003.

49. P.N. Haksar Papers (Installment III), (New Delhi: Nehru Memorial Museum Library).

50. Hoffmann, *India and the China Crisis*, 1990, p. 81.

51. Hong Yuan, 'China Won, but Never Wanted, Sino-Indian War', *Global Times*, June 28, 2012.

52. Garver, 'China's Decision for War with India in 1962', in Alastair Iain Johnston and Robert Ross, 2006, p. 117.

53. The Sino-Indian Dispute: Section 3, Central Intelligence Agency (CIA) Staff Study, (March 2, 1963), Released May 2007. Accessed via: www.foia.cia.gov/CPE/POLO/polo-09.pdf

54. Niu Jun, '1962: The Eve of the Left Turn in China's Foreign Policy', *Cold War International History Project, Working Paper No. 48*, (Washington, D.C.: Woodrow Wilson International Center for Scholars), October 2005.

55. Ibid.

56. 'Mao ordered 1962 War to Regain CPC Control, Reveals Chinese Strategist', *Press Trust of India*, October 18, 2012.

Chapter 3: Changing Geopolitics and Negotiating Postures

1. 'Discussion between N.S. Khrushchev and Mao Zedong' on October 3, 1959, Cold War International History Project – Virtual Archive. Accessed at http://www.wilsoncenter.org/.

2. White Paper 1 (1954 – August 1959). Notes, Memoranda and Letters Exchanged and Agreements Signed between the Governments of India and China.

3. A.S. Bhasin, *India-China Relations 1947–2000: A Documentary Study, Volume 4* (Delhi: Geetika Publishers, 2018), pp. 3278–80.

4. Ibid., pp. 4044–46.

5. Ibid., pp. 4049–51.

6. Ibid., pp. 4050–51.

7. Singh, *Power and Diplomacy*, p. 207.

8. Inder Malhotra, 'The Colombo "Compromise"', *Indian Express*, October 17, 2011.

9. Vajpayee had expressed the Indian position that it should be possible to deal with areas of little or no difference first (the eastern sector) and then move on to areas where there was greater divergence (Aksai Chin).

10. National Archives of India, Box File 2: Folder title: HI/103/7/76.

11. Ronen Sen, *The Telegraph*, January 31, 2012.

12. Menon, *Choices*, 2016, pp. 26–27.

Chapter 4: Instability on the frontier: 2013–2017

1. Saint-Mézard, Isabelle, 'The Border Incident of Spring 2013: Interpreting China-India Relations', *Hérodote*, 2013, 150:3, pp. 132–49.

2. 'Xi Says World Needs Common Development of China, India', *Xinhua*, March 28, 2020.

3. '16th Round of Talks between the Special Representatives of India and China on the Boundary Question', June 29, 2013. Accessed at https://mea.gov.in/press-releases.htm?dtl/21884/16th+Round+of+Talks+between+ the+ Special+Representatives+of+India+and+China+ on+the+ Boundary+Question

4. Author's interview with Ambassador Vinod Khanna (IFS retired), July 28, 2017, New Delhi.

5. Sheela Bhatt and Nikhil Lakshman, 'We have no Confrontation with China', January 18, 2007. Accessed at http://imworld.rediff.com/news/2007/jan/18inter1.htm

6. Prasad, *History of the conflict with China*, 1992.

7. Sudhi Ranjan Sen, 'An Airstrip at 16,000 Feet Becomes Meeting Point Between India and China', August 1, 2015. Accessed at https://www.ndtv.com/india-news/India-China-activate-5th-border-meeting-point-at-16000-feet-1202883

8. Josy Joseph, 'What is the Doklam Issue All About?', *The Hindu*, January 27, 2018.

9. Joel Wuthnow, Satu Limaye, and Nilanthi Samaranayake, 'Doklam, One year Later: China's Long Game in the Himalayas', June 7, 2018. Accessed at https://warontherocks.com/2018/06/doklam-one-year-later-chinas-long-game-in-the-himalayas/

Chapter 5: A 'New Normal': Ladakh 2020 and after

1. Rangoli Agrawal, 'Are Border Development Works Driving India-China Conflict?,' www.livemint.com, August 26, 2020.

2. D.S. Hooda, 'In LAC Talks, from Peace to Conflict Prevention,' *The Hindu*, September 14, 2020.

3. Anita Joshua, 'India-China Standoff: Rajnath Admission on LAC patrol,' *The Telegraph*, September 18, 2020.

4. The CSG is a secretary-level grouping which includes the foreign secretary, home secretary, defence secretary, and the

vice-chiefs of the three services, along with the chiefs of the Intelligence Bureau and R&AW. Since 2003, it has been under the charge of the National Security Advisor. Amrita Nayak Dutta, 'China Study Group, the Elite Indian Govt. Body that Guides Policy on Ties with Beijing'. Accessed at www.theprint.in, July 18, 2020.

5. Sushant Singh, 'Patrolling Points: What do these Markers on the LAC Signify?,' *Indian Express*, July 13, 2020.

6. Dutta, 'China Study Group', www.theprint.in, July 18, 2020.

7. Menon, *Choices*, 2016, p. 33.

8. Hooda, 'In LAC Talks, from Peace to Conflict Prevention', *The Hindu*, September 14, 2020.

9. Aidan Milliff, 'Tension High, Altitude Higher: Logistical and Physiological Constraints on the Indo-Chinese Border'. Accessed at www.warontherocks.com, June 8, 2020.

10. Menon, *Choices*, 2016, pp. 27–28.

11. Hooda, 'In LAC Talks, from Peace to Conflict Prevention', *The Hindu*, September 14, 2020.

12. Joint Press Statement – Meeting of External Affairs Minister and the Foreign Minister of China, September 10, 2020. Accessed at https://mea.gov.in/press-releases.htm?dtl/32962/Joint_Press_Statement__Meeting_of_External_Affairs_Minister_and_the_Foreign_Minister_of_China_September_10_2020

13. Yun Sun, 'China's Strategic Assessment of the Ladakh Clash,' June 19, 2020, https://warontherocks.com/2020/06/chinas-strategic-assessment-of-the-ladakh-clash/

14. Sushant Singh, 'Six Years Ago, How a Standoff in Ladakh Ended after Discussion,' *Indian Express*, June 16, 2020.

15. Sushant Singh, 'Big Surge in Chinese Transgressions, Most of Them in Ladakh,' *Indian Express*, May 22, 2020.

16. Yun Sun, 'China's Strategic Assessment of the Ladakh Clash', June 19, 2020. Accessed at https://warontherocks.com/2020/06/chinas-strategic-assessment-of-the-ladakh-clash/

17. Dinakar Peri, 'LAC standoff: If PLA Comes Close, Indian Troops can Fire: Official', *The Hindu*, September 24, 2020.

II. GEOPOLITICS AND WORLD ORDER

Chapter 1: World Order without Hegemony

1. Previously published in *Economic and Political Weekly*, 53:51, December 29, 2018.

2. Full Text of Chinese President Xi's Speech at APEC CEO Summit, Xinhua, November 17, 2018. Accessed at http://www.xinhuanet.com/english/2018-11/17/c_137613904.htm.

3. 'Prime Minister's Keynote Address at the Shangri La Dialogue, Singapore', Ministry of External Affairs, India, June 1, 2018. Accessed at https://www.mea.gov.in/Speeches-Statements.htm?dtl/29943/Prime+Ministers+Keynote+ Address+at+Shangri+La+ Dialogue+June+01+2018.

4. Graham Allison, 'The Thucydides Trap: Are the US and China Headed for War?' *The Atlantic*, September 24.

5. Robert Gilpin, *War and Change in World Politics* (New York: Cambridge University Press, 1981).

6. Ibid., pp. 185–87.

7. Ibid., p. 206.

8. Mlada Bukovansky, 'The Responsibility to Accommodate: Ideas and Change,' *Accommodating Rising Power: Past, Present, and Future*, T.V. Paul (ed.), (Delhi: Cambridge University Press, 2016), p. 91.

9. Ibid., p. 87.

10. Edward Hallett Carr, *The Twenty Years' Crisis, 1919–1939* (New York: HarperCollins), pp. 222–23.

11. Yan Xuetong, 'The Age of Uneasy Peace: Chinese Power in a Divided World', *Foreign Affairs*, January-February 2019. Accessed at https://www.foreignaffairs.com/articles/china/2018-12-11/age-uneasy-peace.

12. Ibid.

13. 'Speech by Wang Yi at the Opening of Symposium on the International Situation and China's Foreign Relations in 2018,' Ministry of Foreign Affairs of the People's Republic of China,

December 11, 2018. Accessed at https://www.fmprc.gov.cn/mfa_eng/wjdt_665385/zyjh_665391/t1621221.shtml.

14. 'India-China Informal Summit at Wuhan, Press Release', April 28, 2018. Accessed at https://mea.gov.in/press-releases.htm?dtl/29853/IndiaChina_Informal_Summit_at_Wuhan.

15. 'Prime Minister's Keynote Address at the Shangri La Dialogue, Singapore, June 1, 2018. Accessed at https://www.mea.gov.in/Speeches-Statements.htm?dtl/29943/Prime+Ministers+Keynote+Address+at+Shangri+La+Dialogue+June+01+2018.

Chapter 2: End of the Liberal World Order?

1. Previously published in *Economic and Political Weekly,* 53:39, September 29, 2018.

2. Jeff D. Colgan and Robert O. Keohane, 'The Liberal Order Is Rigged: Fix It Now or Watch It Wither,' *Foreign Affairs*, May/June 2017.

3. Nick Danforth, 'What's So Disordered About Your World Order?' June 20, 2018, https://warontherocks.com/2018/06/whats-so-disordered-about-your-world-order/.

4. Quinn Slobodian, *Globalists: The End of Empire and the Birth of Neoliberalism* (Cambridge: Harvard University Press, 2018), pp. 16–17.

5. Danforth, 'What's So Disordered about your World Order?' June 20, 2018.

6. Graham Allison, 'The Myth of the Liberal Order: From Historical Accident to Conventional Wisdom,' *Foreign Affairs*, 97:4, July/August 2018.

7. Patrick Porter, 'A World Imagined: Nostalgia and Liberal Order,' *Policy Analysis* (Washington DC: Cato Institute), 843, June 5, 2018. Accessed at https://www.cato.org/publications/policy-analysis/world-imagined-nostalgia-liberal-order. Daniel Deudney and G. John Ikenberry, 'Liberal World: The Resilient Order', *Foreign Affairs*, 97:4, July/August 2018.

8. Danforth, 'What's So Disordered about your World Order?' June 20, 2018.

9. Paul Staniland, 'Misreading the "Liberal Order": Why We Need New Thinking in American Foreign Policy,' *Lawfare*, July 29, 2018. Accessed at https://www.lawfareblog.com/misreading-liberal-order-why-we-need-new-thinking-american-foreign-policy.

10. Inderjeet Parmar, 'Racial and Imperial Thinking in International Theory and Politics: Truman, Attlee and the Korean War,' *British Journal of Politics and International Relations*, 18:2, 2016, pp. 351–69.

11. Porter, 'A World Imagined: Nostalgia and Liberal Order,' *Policy Analysis*, June 5, 2018

12. Staniland, 'Misreading the "Liberal Order",' *Lawfare*, July 29, 2018.

Chapter 3: US-China: From Chimerica to Cold War 2.0?

1. David M. Lampton's speech 'A Tipping Point in U.S.-China Relations is Upon Us', May 6–7, 2015. Accessed at http://www.uscnpm.com/model_item.html?action=view&table=article&id=15789

2. Wang Jisi, 'Uphold Three Bottom Lines for China-US Relations,' *Global Times*, June 5, 2020.

3. Ryan Hass and Abraham Denmark, 'More Pain than Gain: How the US-China Trade War Hurt America,' August 7, 2020. Accessed at https://www.brookings.edu/blog/order-from-chaos/2020/08/07/more-pain-than-gain-how-the-us-china-trade-war-hurt-america/

4. Ibid.

5. Tom Mitchell, 'US companies Defy Trump's Threats About "Decoupling" from China', *Financial Times*, September 9, 2020.

6. 'The Chinese Communist Party's Ideology and Global Ambitions,' *Remarks delivered by National Security Advisor Robert C. O'Brien on June 24, 2020, in Phoenix, Arizona*, June 26, 2020.

7. Ibid.

8. Ethan Paul, 'The Dangerous Idealism of Competing with China,' June 4, 2020. Accessed at https://responsiblestatecraft.org/2020/06/04/the-dangerous-idealism-of-competing-with-china/

9. John Ikenberry, 'The Future of the Liberal World Order,' *Foreign Affairs*, May 2011.

10. Liu Ming, 'Xi Jinping's Vision of a Community with a Shared Future for Humankind: A Revised International Order?,' *The National Bureau of Asian Research*, Special Report #85, June 2020.

11. Wang Jisi, 'Uphold Three Bottom Lines for China-US relations,' *Global Times,* June 5, 2020.

12. 'Shared Future or America First', *Xinhua*, January 24, 2018. Accessed at http://www.xinhuanet.com/english/2018-01/24/c_136921547.htm

13. 'United States Strategic Approach to the People's Republic of China,' *White House*, May 20, 2020.

14. Michito Tsuruoka, 'China Isn't Losing Europe Yet,' *The Diplomat*, June 6, 2020. Satoshi Sugiyama and Jesse Johnson, 'Japan Threads the Needle as U.S.-China Animosity Hits New Highs,' *The Japan Times*, June 7, 2020.

15. 'Merkel says EU has "Strategic Interest" in Working with China', www.bloomberg.com, May 27, 2020. Accessed at https://www.bloomberg.com/news/articles/2020-05-27/merkel-says-eu-has-strategic-interest-in-working-with-china

16. 'United States Strategic Approach to the People's Republic of China,' *White House*, May 20, 2020.

17. Liu Ming, 'Xi Jinping's Vision of a Community with a Shared Future for Humankind: A Revised International Order?,' *The National Bureau of Asian Research*, Special Report #85, June 2020.

Chapter 4: India and the Great Powers

1. Singh, *Power and Diplomacy*, 2019, pp. 253–54.

2. Ibid.

3. P.S. Raghavan, 'What is in a NAM and India's Alignment,' *The Hindu*, September 9, 2020.

Chapter 5: The Belt and Road Initiative and China's Policy Re-orientation

1. Previously published in *Economic and Political Weekly*, June 24, 2017, 3:2.

2. Kurt M. Campbell, 'Asia Overview: Protecting American Interests in China and Asia,' Testimony before the House Committee on Foreign Affairs Subcommittee on Asia and the Pacific, Washington, DC, March 31, 2011, http://www.state.gov/p/eap/rls/rm/2011/03/159450.htm; Hillary Rodham Clinton, 'America's Pacific Century,' remarks delivered at the East–West Center, Honolulu, November 10, 2011, http://www.state.gov/secretary/rm/2011/11/176999.htm; Tom Donilon, 'America is Back in the Pacific and Will Uphold the Rules,' *Financial Times*, November 27, 2011.

3. E. Leon Panetta, 'Remarks by Secretary Panetta at the Shangn-La Dialogue in Singapore,' Singapore, June 2, 2012.

4. Michael Swaine, 'Chinese Leadership and Elite Responses to the US Pacific Pivot,' *China Leadership Monitor*, 38, August 6, 2012.

5. Ibid., pp. 14–15.

6. Michael D. Swaine and M Taylor Fravel, 'China's Assertive Behavior Part Two: The Maritime Periphery', China Leadership Monitor, No 35, September 21, 2011, p. 15.

7. Wang Jisi, '"Westward" Rebalance of Chinese Geopolitics,' *Global Times*, October 17, 2012.

8. Sun Yun, 'Westward Ho! As America Pivots East, China Marches in the Other Direction,' *Foreign Policy*, February 7, 2013.

9. Wang Jisi, '"Westward" Rebalance of Chinese Geopolitics,' *Global Times*, October 17, 2012.

10. Michael D. Swaine and M Taylor Fravel (2011), 'China's Assertive Behavior Part Two: The Maritime Periphery,' China Leadership Monitor, No 35, 21 September.

11. Michael Swaine, 'Chinese Views and Commentary on Periphery Diplomacy,' *China Leadership Monitor*, 44, July 28, 2014, p. 25.

12. Peter Cai, 'Understanding China's Belt and Road Initiative,' *Lowy Institute Analysis*, March 3, 2017.

13. Michael Swaine, 'Xi Jinping's Address to the Central Conference on Work Relating to Foreign Affairs: Assessing and Advancing Major-Power Diplomacy with Chinese Characteristics', *China Leadership Monitor*, 46, March 19, 2015, p. 4.

14. Ibid., pp. 4–5.

15. Ibid., p. 5.

16. Ibid., p. 5.

17. Nadege Roland, 'China's Eurasian Century? Political and Strategic Implications of the Belt and Road Initiative' (Washington, DC: National Bureau of Asian Research, 2017), pp. 118-19. Igor Denisov, 'China Going West: The Silk Road to Bring Beijing out of the Shadows,' *Russia in Global Affairs*, March 19, 2015.

18. Barry Naughton, 'Supply-Side Structural Reform at Mid-year,' *China Leadership Monitor*, 51, August 30, 2016, p. 2.

19. Simeon Djankov and Sean Miller (eds), 'China's Belt and Road Initiative: Motives, Scope and Challenges,' (Washington D.C.: Peterson Institute for International Economics, March, 2016).

20. Olga Borokh and Alexander Lomanov, 'Supply-Side Reform, Chinese Style,' *Russia in Global Affairs*, June 17, 2016.

21. To be sure, state-owned enterprises (SOEs) dominate infrastructure sectors; 72 per cent of infrastructure investment comes from SOEs.

22. Although domestic Chinese contestations have been a constant feature of the reform and opening-up era, the period leading up to Xi Jinping's ascent to leadership in 2012 witnessed intense power struggles, reflecting the gradual diffusion of state power and authority in the last two decades.

23. SOEs have an advantage over access to the banking system and have received the lion's share of credit expansion in recent years.

24. Nadege Roland, 'China's Eurasian Century?' 2017, p. 109.

25. Wang Yiwei, *The Belt and Road Initiative: What Will China Offer the World in Its Rise* (Beijing: New World Press, 2016), p. 80.

26. Richard Ghiasy and Jiayi Zhou, 'The Silk Road Economic Belt: Considering Security Implications and EU-China Cooperation Prospects' (Sweden: Stockholm International Peace Research Institute, 2017), p. 3.

27. Chen Liubing, 'Private Companies Play Key Role in Belt and Road Initiative,' *China Daily*, March 22, 2017.

Chapter 6: BRICS and a New Development Vision for a Multipolar World

1. South Africa joined the grouping in 2011.

2. Yaroslav Lissovolik, 'BRICS: The Stepping Stones Towards New Global Governance,' February 28, 2020. Accessed at https://valdaiclub.com/a/highlights/brics-the-stepping-stones-towards-new-global/

3. Zorawar Daulet Singh, 'BRICS is What We Make Of It,' *Business Standard*, July 30, 2014.

4. Speech of K. V. Kamath, President, New Development Bank at the fifth annual meeting of the board of governors, April 20, 2020. Accessed at https://www.ndb.int/president_desk/speech-mr-k-v-kamath-president-new-development-bank-fifth-annual-meeting-board-governors/

5. Thomas L. Friedman, *The Lexus and the Olive Tree: Understanding Globalization* (New York: Farrar, Straus and Giroux, 1999), p. 112.

6. Speech of K. V. Kamath, President, New Development Bank at the fifth annual meeting of the board of governors, April 20, 2020. Accessed at https://www.ndb.int/president_desk/speech-mr-k-v-kamath-president-new-development-bank-fifth-annual-meeting-board-governors/. Anuradha Chenoy, 'Bypassing the Dollar: The Rise of Alternate Currency Systems,' May 25, 2020. Accessed at https://thewire.in/trade/dollar-currency-trade

7. 'Russia says BRICS Countries Favor Idea of Common Payment System,' November 15, 2019, *CGTN*, https://news.cgtn.com/news/2019-11-15/Russia-says-BRICS-countries-favor-idea-of-common-payment-system-LDj1tGjDLq/index.html

8. Giovanni Arrighi and Beverly J. Silver, 'Capitalism and World (Dis)order' *Review of International Studies*, 2001, 27, p. 272.

9. Ibid., p. 272.

10. Robert W. Cox, *Approaches to World Order* (Cambridge: Cambridge University Press, 1996), p. 535.

11. When measured in purchasing power parity (PPP).

12. Christian Dorninger et al., 'Global Patterns of Ecologically Unequal Exchange: Implications for Sustainability in the 21st century,' *Ecological Economics*, 179, January 2021.

13. Diana Choyleva, 'Chinese workers' share of GDP reaching US levels,' March 13, 2018. Accessed at https://asia.nikkei.com/Opinion/Chinese-workers-share-of-GDP-reaching-US-levels; Zixuan Huang and Nicholas R. Lardy, 'China's Rebalance Reflected in Rising Wage Share of GDP,' October 13, 2016. Accessed at https://www.piie.com/blogs/china-economic-watch/chinas-rebalance-reflected-rising-wage-share-gdp.

14. Such a crisis, inherent in the functioning of capitalist economy, leads to overproduction and over accumulation of capital whereby aggregate demand and the prevailing markets are unable to absorb the supply. In order to preempt or extricate economies from such crises, it is necessary to make adjustments between the sectors of the system that face the asymmetries and imbalances. Some of the public policy measures of rebalancing entail re-distribution strategies that resuscitate the demand potential of the capital-deficit and income-deficit section of the political economy. This typically means small businesses, organized and informal labour that together constitute the backbone of most economic systems.

15. Sergey Lavrov, 'BRICS Strategic Partnership for Global Stability, Shared Security and Innovative Growth,' *The Hindu*, November 13, 2020.

III. STRATEGY AND POLICY

Chapter 1: India's Geostrategy and China: Mackinder versus Mahan

1. Rahul Singh, 'China's Submarines in Indian Ocean Worry Indian Navy', *Hindustan Times*, April 7, 2013.

2. Rahul Singh, 'China Ends Ladakh Standoff, Troops Pull Back', *Hindustan Times*, May 5, 2013.

3. 'Post-Galwan Clash, Indian Navy Quietly Deployed Warship in South China Sea,' *Times of India*, August 30, 2020.

4. Erica S. Downs, 'Money Talks: China-Russia Energy Relations after Xi Jinping's Visit to Moscow', April 1, 2013, available at http://www.brookings. edu/blogs/up-front/posts/2013/04/01-china-russia-energy-relations-downs, accessed on April 30, 2013; Alexandros Petersen, 'China's Latest Piece of the New Silk Road', *Eurasia Daily Monitor*, 10:4, January 10, 2013, available at http://www.jamestown.org/single/?no_cache=1&tx_ ttnews%5Btt_news%5D=40291&tx_ttnews%5BbackPid%5D=620#. UbolVJVgOlI, accessed on April 30, 2013; Li Yingqing and Guo Anfei, 'Third Land Link to Europe Envisioned', *China Daily*, July 2, 2009, available at http://www.chinadaily.com.cn/china/2009-07/02/content_8345835. htm, accessed on April 30, 2013.

5. Agrawal, 'Are Border Development Works Driving India-China Conflict?,' www.livemint.com, August 26, 2020.

6. Sushant Singh, 'Borders Without Railways: The Missing Strategic Link,' *Indian Express*, July 6, 2016.

7. Aidan Milliff, 'Tension high, altitude higher: Logistical and physiological constraints on the Indo-Chinese border,' www.warontherocks.com, June 8, 2020.

8. Ibid.

9. Iskander Rehman, 'A Himalayan Challenge,' *Naval War College Review*, 70:1, 2017, p. 108.

10. Ibid., p. 108.

11. Monika Chansoria, 'China's Infrastructure Development in Tibet: Evaluating Trendlines', Manekshaw Paper No. 32 (New Delhi: CLAWS, 2011).

12. Sunil Khilnani, Rajiv Kumar, Pratap Bhanu Mehta, Prakash Menon, Nandan Nilekani, Srinath Raghavan, Shyam Saran and Siddharth Varadarajan, *Nonalignment 2.0: A Foreign and Strategic Policy for India in the Twenty First Century* (New Delhi: Centre for Policy Research, 2012), p. 41.

13. Pranab Dhal Samanta, 'Incursion Effect: Strike Corps on China Border Gets Nod', *Indian Express*, May 26, 2013; Ajai Shukla, 'New Strike Corps for China Border', *Business Standard*, August 24, 2011.

14. C. Raja Mohan, 'Beijing at Sea', *Indian Express*, April 26, 2013.

15. David C. Gompert, *Sea Power and American Interests in the Western Pacific* (Santa Monica: RAND Corporation, 2013), p. 186.

16. Ibid., p. xiv.

17. Ibid., p. 113.

18. Phillip Saunders, Christopher Yung, Michael Swaine, and Andrew Nien-Dzu Yang (eds), *The Chinese Navy: Expanding Capabilities, Evolving Roles* (Washington, D.C.: National Defense University Press, 2011), p. xii.

19. Kris Osborn, 'Pentagon Calls China's Test of DF-21D and DF-26 Anti-Ship Missiles "Destabilizing",' *The National Interest*, August 27, 2020.

20. Liu Xuanzun, 'China's Two Aircraft Carriers in Apparent Simultaneous Exercises for 1st Time: Reports', *Global Times*, September 6, 2020.

21. 'Annual Report to Congress: Military and Security Developments Involving the People's Republic of China,' Department of Defense, September 2020, pp. vii–ix.

22. Ibid.

23. Kristin Huang, 'China's Navy Drills in 4 Regions Show Ability to Counter US, Observers Say', *South China Morning Post*, August 24, 2020.

24. Bill Gertz, 'Threat in Asia is Anti-ship Missiles', *Washington Times*, March 23, 2010; Roger Cliff, Mark Burles, Michael S. Chase, Derek Eaton, Kevin L. Pollpeter, *Entering the Dragon's Lair: Chinese Antiaccess Strategies and Their Implications for the United States* (Santa Monica: RAND Corporation, 2007).

Chapter 2: Should India 'Be East' or Be Eurasian?

1. President Barack Obama's address to a joint session of the Indian parliament, New Delhi, November 8, 2010; P.S. Suryanarayana, 'US Move to Mentor India in New East Asia', *The Hindu*, February 22, 2011.

2. According to Sipri, China accounted for 51 per cent of Pakistan's arms imports between 2010–2014 and for 73 per cent for the period 2015–2019.

3. A purely defensive 'attritional' orientation is becoming outdated for two reasons: (1) the technological options available to the Indian armed services; and (2) China's own military and doctrinal innovations and the contemporary priorities of its political elite that no longer place a premium on large scale interventions in enemy territory. China's evolving strategy is based on rapid short-duration limited conflicts that are not aimed at acquiring large swathes of territory but are intended primarily for punitive purposes.

4. In other words, a credible nuclear deterrent in relation to China will ensure that conflict remains confined within a limited threshold and will accord India the opportunity to deter conventional Chinese pressure on the frontier areas via a flexible asymmetric strategy outlined above.

5. Shivshankar Menon, 'Towards a New Asian Order', *Indian Express*, February 22, 2011.

6. Zorawar Daulet Singh, 'India Looks on as the East Integrates', *Asia Times*, May 7, 2009.

7. In fact, ironically, one of the most significant strategic missions for the Indian navy is to support continental operations in the event

of a military conflict in the subcontinent. The navy's role would be to deter extra-regional involvement in subcontinental disputes, thereby isolating the area of political-military operations and preventing any interference in bilateral disputes.

8. As Harold Sprout writes, '(I)t it still axiomatic that sea frontiers can be, and are, defended more securely, with less outlay and effort, than land frontiers'. Harold Sprout, 'Frontiers of Defense', *Military Affairs*, 5:4, 1941, p. 218.

Chapter 3: India's Role in Asia

1. Prime Minister's Keynote Address at Shangri La Dialogue, June 1, 2018. Accessed at https://mea.gov.in/Speeches-Statements.htm?dtl/29943/Prime_Ministers_Keynote_Address_at_Shangri_La_Dialogue_June_01_2018

Chapter 4: India, China and the New Silk Routes

1. Xi Jinping's speech at Nazarbayev University, Astana, Kazakhstan, September 7, 2013, *Xi Jinping: The Governance of China*, (Beijing: Foreign Languages Press, 2014), p. 315.

2. Ibid., pp. 321 23.

3. 'China Drafting Plan for Silk Road Cooperation', *Xinhua*, June 10, 2014; 'China's Fujian Province to be Starting Point for Silk Road', *The Hindu*, July 20, 2014.

4. Email interview with Ambassador Eric Gonsalves (Retd.), Indian Foreign Service (IFS), July 15, 2014.

5. Although the SRs (led by India's National Security Advisor and China's Political Counsellor) are mandated by the Indian and Chinese governments to engage in open-ended negotiations over the Sino-Indian border dispute, other aspects of the bilateral relationship are discussed in this format.

6. Email interview with Ambassador Eric Gonsalves (Retd.), IFS, July 15, 2014.

7. C. Raja Mohan, 'Panchsheel 2014', *The Indian Express*, July 4, 2014, available at http://indianexpress.com/article/opinion/columns/panchsheel-2014/, accessed on July 15, 2014.

8. Email interview with Jabin Jacob, July 19, 2014.

9. Email interview with Ambassador Chetput Ranganathan (Retd.), IFS, July 14, 2014.

10. 'Economic Corridor: Pakistan, China Review Progress on Projects', *The Express Tribune*, July 9, 2014, available at http://tribune.com.pk/story/ 732919/economic-corridor-pakistan-china-review-progress-on-projects/

11. Email interview with Brigadier (Retd.) Arun Sahgal, July 5, 2014.

12. Email interview with Vice Admiral (Retd.) Anup Singh, July 5, 2014.

13. Ibid.

14. 'String of Pearls Highly Hyped and Speculative: Expert', available at http://orfonline.org/, accessed on July 24, 2014.

15. Marc Lanteigne, 'China's Maritime Security and the "Malacca Dilemma"', *Asian Security*, 4:2, 2008, pp. 143–44.

16. 'Annual Report to Congress: Military and Security Developments Involving the People's Republic of China,' Department of Defense, September 2020. You Ji, 'Dealing with the Malacca Dilemma: China's Effort to Protect its Energy Supply', *Strategic Analysis*, 31:3, 2007, pp. 467–89.

17. Ananth, Krishnan, 'New Indian Ocean Exercise Shows Reach of China's Navy', *The Hindu*, February 5, 2014.

18. Email interview with Vice Admiral (Retd.) Anup Singh, July 5, 2014.

19. Raja Menon, 'A Mountain Strike Corps is Not the Only Option', *The Hindu*, July 29, 2013.

20. Abhijit Singh, 'China's Maritime Silk Route: Implications for India', *IDSA Comment*, July 16, 2014, available at http://www.idsa.in/idsacomments/ChinasMaritimeSilkRoute_AbhijitSingh_160714.html

21. Email interview with Ravi Bhoothalingam, July 17, 2014.

22. Ibid.

23. Ravi Bhoothalingam, 'Should India Embrace the BCIM Economic Corridor?', *The SARCist*, June 2014.

24. Email interview with Professor Alka Acharya, July 12, 2014.

25. Email interview with Ambassador Eric Gonsalves (Retd.), IFS, July 15, 2014.

26. Chaturvedy, Rajeev Ranjan, 'Reviving the Maritime Silk Route', *The Hindu*, April 11, 2014.

27. Singh, *Power and Diplomacy: India's foreign policies during the Cold War*, 2019, pp. 52–53.

28. Srikanth Kondapalli, 'China Tosses Maritime Silk Route Bait to India', *India Writes*, February 19, 2014, available at http://www.indiawrites.org/ diplomacy/china-tosses-maritime-silk-route-bait-to-india/, accessed on July 15, 2014.

29. Email interview with former National Security Advisor, Shivshankar Menon, July 11, 2014.

30. Ibid.

31. K.N. Chaudhuri, *Trade and Civilisation in the Indian Ocean* (London: Cambridge University Press, 1985), p. 23.

32. Ibid., p. 21.

33. Ibid., p. 49.

34. 'Foreign Secretary's Address to the Indian Ocean Conference, Colombo,' September 1, 2017, Ministry of External Affairs, Government of India, New Delhi. Accessed at http://mea.gov.in/Speeches-Statements.htm?dtl/28909/.

35. Ibid.

36. David Brewster, 'An Indian Ocean Dilemma: Sino–Indian Rivalry and China's Strategic Vulnerability in the Indian Ocean,' *Journal of the Indian Ocean Region*, 2015, 11:1, p. 49.

37. C.S.L. Koh, 'Sino–Indian Maritime Security Dilemma,' *India's Naval Strategy and Asian Security*, Anit Mukherjee and C. Raja Mohan (eds) (London: Routledge, 2016), p. 151.

38. Rahul Singh, 'Chinese Warships Prowl Indian Ocean Ahead of Naval Drills by India, US and Japan,' *Hindustan Times*, July 5, 2017.

39. Jonathan Holslag, 'The Reluctant Pretender: China's Evolving Presence in the Indian Ocean,' *Journal of the Indian Ocean Region*, 2013, 9:1, pp. 43–45.

40. 'India-China Maritime Rivalry Not Inevitable: NSA,' Press Trust of India, March 4, 2013.

41. Narendra Modi, 'Text of the PM's Remarks on the Commissioning of Coast Ship Barracuda,' March 12, 2015. Accessed at https://www.narendramodi.in/text-of-the-pms-remarks-on-the-commissioning-of-coast-ship-barracuda-2954.

42. Recently, China has agreed to take a 70% stake in the Kyauk Pyu seaport in Western Rakhine, Myanmar. 'China to take 70% stake in Rakhine sea port', *Dhaka Tribune*, October 17, 2017.

43. S. Kamerling and F.P. van der Putten, 'An Overseas Naval Presence without Overseas Bases: China's Counter-piracy Operation in the Gulf of Aden,' *Current Chinese Affairs*, 40:4, pp. 119–46.

44. 'Myanmar Exports 2m Tonnes of Oil via Pipeline over Four Months,' *Myanmar Times*, September 21, 2017. 'China-Myanmar Pipeline to Open in May,' *Financial Times*, January 21, 2013.

45. Christopher Len, 'China's Maritime Silk Road and Energy Geopolitics in the Indian Ocean: Motivations and Implications for the Region,' *NBR special report #68*, November 2017 (Seattle: National Bureau of Asian Research), p. 50.

46. 'Full Text: China's Military Strategy,' Ministry of National Defense, May 26, 2015. Accessed at http://eng.mod.gov.cn/Press/2015-05/26/content_ 4586805.htm.

47. Gabriel Collins and Michael Grubb, 'Strong Foundation: Contemporary Chinese Shipbuilding Prowess,' *China Goes to Sea: Maritime Transformation in Comparative Historical Perspective*, Andrew Erickson, Lyle Goldstein and Carnes Lord (eds) (Annapolis: Naval Institute Press), p. 345.

48. 'Remarks by Indian Foreign Secretary at Indian Ocean Conference,' September 1, 2016, Ministry of External Affairs, Government of India, New Delhi. Accessed at http://www.mea.gov.in/Speeches-Statements.htm?dtl/27356/.

49. India is 'Trying to get friendly island nations of the IOR into a common maritime security grid', P.K. Ghosh, "Evolving Indian Ocean Governance Architecture: An Indian Perspective," *Journal of the Indian Ocean Region*, 2015, 11:2, p. 238.

50. 'Official Spokesperson's response to a query on participation of India in OBOR/BRI Forum,' May 13, 2017. Accessed at https://mea.gov.in/media-briefings.htm?dtl/28463/Official+Spokespersons+response+to+a+query+on+participation+ of+India+in+OBORBRI+Forum

51. Ibid.

52. Joel Wuthnow, 'From Friend to Foe-ish: Washington's Negative Turn on the Belt and Road Initiative,' *Open Forum*, May 21, 2018. Accessed at http://www.theasanforum.org/from-friend-to-foe-ish-washingtons-negative-turn-on-the-belt-and-road-initiative/

53. 'With New Wave of Sanctions, US Targets China's BRI; Rallies Allies, Partners,' accessed at https://www.therahnuma.com/with-new-wave-of-sanctions-us-targets-chinas-bri-rallies-allies-partners/

54. 'Joint Communiqué of the Leaders', Roundtable of the 2nd Belt and Road Forum for International Cooperation', April 27, 2019. Accessed at http://www.beltandroadforum.org/english/n100/2019/0427/c36-1311.html.

55. 'China's 2019 Foreign Direct Investment Grew Most in Two Years, but Outbound Investment Fell 6 per cent,' *Reuters*, January 21, 2020.

56. Yasheng Huang, 'Can the Belt and Road Become a Trap for China?' *Project Syndicate*, May 22, 2019.

57. Chun Han Wong and James T. Areddy, 'Beijing Appeals for Foreign Funds in Belt-and-Road Adjustment,' *Wall Street Journal*, April 26, 2019.

58. 'Chinese Investments in North America, Europe Hit 9-year Low in 2019: Report,' *Xinhua*, January 8, 2020.

59. Source: OECD.

60. Deborah Brautigam, 'Is China the World's Loan Shark?' *New York Times*, April 26, 2019; Deborah. Brautigam, 'Misdiagnosing the Chinese Infrastructure Push,' *American Interest*, April 4, 2019.

61. Rebecca Ray and Kehan Wang, 'China-Latin America Economic Bulletin, 2019 Edition,' Global Development Policy Center, Boston University.

62. John Hurley, Scott Morris and Gailyn Portelance, 'Examining the Debt Implications of the Belt and Road Initiative from a Policy Perspective,' Policy Paper 121, Center for Global Development, March, 2018, p. 5.

63. Dushni Weerakoon and Sisira Jayasuriya, 'Sri Lanka's Debt Problem Isn't Made in China,' February 28, 2019. Accessed at, https://www.eastasiaforum.org/2019/02/28/sri-lankas-debt-problem-isnt-made-in-china/.

64. Ravi Bhoothalingam, 'India and China's Belt and Road Initiative: A Turning Point?' *Wire*, May 10, 2019.

65. Nilanthi Samaranayake, 'China's Engagement with Smaller South Asian Countries,' Special Report No 446, United States Institute of Peace, April 2019, pp. 3–4.

66. Chris Devonshire-Ellis, 'EAEU and China Agree on "Ice Silk Road", May 3, 2019. Accessed at https://www.silkroadbriefing.com/.

67. Shyam Saran, 'China's Emergence as a Scientific Power,' *Business Standard*, May 7, 2019.

68. *Belt and Road Economics: Opportunities and Risks of Transport Corridors,* World Bank, 2019.

69. Samaranayake, 'China's Engagement with Smaller South Asian Countries,' April 2019, p. 13.

70. B.R. Deepak, 'It's Time for India to Rethink its Position on BRI,' *China-India Review*, 2019, 31:4, pp. 31–39. Belt and Road Forum, 'List of Deliverables of the Second Belt and Road Forum for International Cooperation,' April 27, 2019. Accessed at http://www.beltandroadforum.org/english/n100/2019/0427/c36-1312.html.

71. Office of the Leading Group for Promoting the BRI, 'The Belt and Road Initiative: Progress, Contributions and Prospects' Belt and Road Portal, April 22, 2019, https://eng.yidaiyilu.gov.cn/zchj/

qwfb/86739.htm. 'Chinese Sciences Academy Provides 268 Million Dollars for BRI Projects,' Chinese Academy of Sciences, Beijing, April 19, 2019, http://english.cas.cn/newsroom/news/201904/t20190419_208623.shtml.

72. Shyam Saran, 'China's Emergence as a Scientific Power,' *Business Standard*, May 7, 2019.

73. Masood, Ehsan, 'South Asia's Pivot Towards China,' *Nature*, 2019, 569:7754, pp. 24–27.

74. Kent E. Calder, *Super Continent: The Logic of Eurasian Integration*, (Stanford: Stanford University Press, 2019), p. xvi.

Chapter 5: India's Search for an Equilibrium with China

1. P.S. Raghavan, 'What is in a NAM and India's Alignment,' *The Hindu*, September 9, 2020.

2. Dipanjan Roy Chaudhury, 'China Appoints Trade Specialist as New Ambassador to Pakistan,' *Economic Times*, September 14, 2020.

3. Menon, *Choices*, 2016, pp. 26–27.

4. After the Wuhan meetings, Chinese Vice Foreign Minister Kong Xuanyou had briefed the media on such trilateral cooperation: 'The two sides will enhance policy coordination in their neighbourhood to discuss cooperation in the form of China India plus one or China India plus X'. 'Modi-Xi Summit: India, China to Step Up Policy Coordination,' *Press Trust of India*, April 29, 2018.

5. 'India, China Launch Joint Training for Afghanistan, Plan More Projects', *Reuters*, October 15, 2018. Accessed at https://www.reuters.com/article/us-India-China-afghanistan/India-China-launch-joint-training-for-afghanistan-plan-more-projects-idUSKCN1MP1KO

6. Samaranayake, 'China's Engagement with Smaller South Asian Countries', April 2019, p. 13.

7. Joint Communique of the Leaders' Roundtable of the 2nd Belt and Road Forum for International Cooperation, April 27, 2019. Accessed at https://eng.yidaiyilu.gov.cn/qwyw/rdxw/88230.htm

8. Samaranayake, 'China's Engagement with Smaller South Asian Countries,' April 2019, pp. 3–4.

9. Yang Xiaoping, 'When India's Strategic Backyard meets China's Strategic Periphery: The View from Beijing,' April 20, 2018. Accessed at https://warontherocks.com/2018/04/when-indias-strategic-backyard-meets-chinas-strategic-periphery-the-view-from-beijing/

A Multipolar World Order

1. 'LAC face-off | Doklam Was a Game-changer for Chinese Thought on India', JNU Professor Hemant Adlakha, Interview with Suhasini Haidar, *The Hindu*, July 4, 2020.

2. Antara Ghosal Singh, 'What Strategic Experts from the Other Side Think About Ladakh standoff,' *India Today*, September 4, 2020.

3. Institute of Chinese Studies webinar with Prof. Yan Xuetong, September 18, 2020. Accessible here, https://www.icsin.org/activity/show/implications-of-china-us-competition-in-the-digital-age.

4. Yun Sun, 'China's Strategic Assessment of India,' March 25, 2020, https://warontherocks.com/2020/03/chinas-strategic-assessment-of-india/

5. Yun Sun interview with Praveen Swami, September 15, 2020, www.moneycontrol.com

6. Yun Sun, 'China's Strategic Assessment of India,' March 25, 2020.

7. 'LAC face-off', JNU Professor Hemant Adlakha, Interview with Suhasini Haidar, *The Hindu*, July 4, 2020.

8. 'India-China Informal Summit at Wuhan', April 28, 2018. Accessed at https://mea.gov.in/press-releases.htm?dtl/29853/IndiaChina_Informal_Summit_at_Wuhan

9. Yang Xiaoping, 'When India's strategic backyard meets China's strategic periphery: The view from Beijing,' April 20, 2018.

INDEX